Test Prep Series

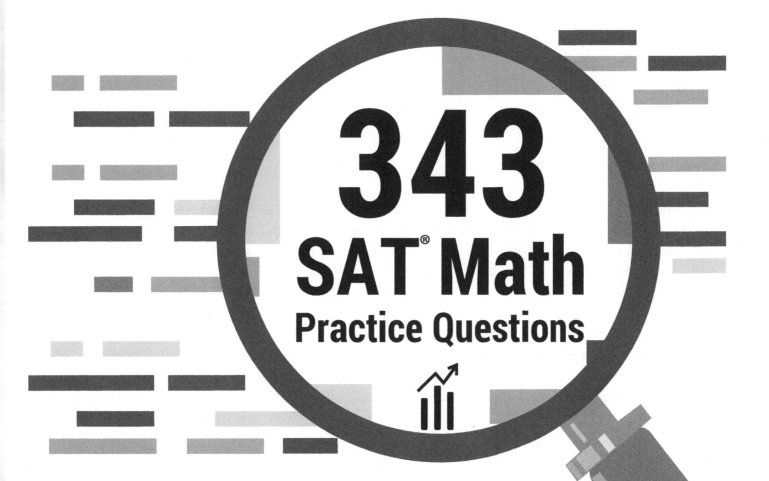

343
SAT® Math
Practice Questions

343	Practice questions for SAT Math
Elaborate	answer explanation for every question
One	full length timed Math test
Extensive	range of questions to give you ample practice

VIBRANT
PUBLISHERS

343 SAT® Math
Practice Questions

ISBN-10: 1-946383-92-9
ISBN-13: 978-1-946383-92-1
Library of Congress Control Number: 2018903571

This publication is designed to provide accurate and authoritative information in regard to the subject matter covered. The Author has made every effort in the preparation of this book to ensure the accuracy of the information. However, information in this book is sold without warranty either expressed or implied. The Author or the Publisher will not be liable for any damages caused or alleged to be caused either directly or indirectly by this book.

Vibrant Publishers books are available at special quantity discount for sales promotions, or for use in corporate training programs. For more information please write to **bulkorders@vibrantpublishers.com**

Please email feedback / corrections (technical, grammatical or spelling) to **spellerrors@vibrantpublishers.com**

For general inquires please write to **reachus@vibrantpublishers.com**

To access the complete catalogue of Vibrant Publishers, visit **www.vibrantpublishers.com**

Table of Contents

This page is intentionally left blank.

Dear Student,

Thank you for purchasing **343 SAT Math Practice Questions.** We are committed to publishing books that are content-rich, concise and approachable enabling more students to read and make the fullest use of them. We hope this book provides the most enriching learning experience as you prepare for your **SAT** exam.

Should you have any questions or suggestions, feel free to email us at **reachus@vibrantpublishers.com**

Thanks again for your purchase. Good luck for your SAT!

- Vibrant Publishers Team

This page is intentionally left blank.

Chapter **1**

SAT Overview

So, you've decided to take the SAT. At this point in your life you probably have a lot of important decisions looming in front of you. What college would I like to attend? What do I need to get in? What classes should I be taking? What's a good GPA? Of course, you are also wondering about the SAT. This chapter provides an overview of the SAT as one of the data points considered for college entrance standards. It also provides the outline of the test, grading overview and some helpful hints to get you started. The most important first step is to know what to expect, so you can make the best-informed choices as you look forward to your exciting future. Congratulations on taking that first step.

What is the SAT

The SAT (Standardized Aptitude Test) is one of the two primary tests which colleges use to gauge whether or not you might be ready for college. It is a test that reflects the things you should have learned in high school and relies on strategic questioning to actively represent those skills and knowledge that are essential as you enter the world of college. But what is it really? The SAT is a measure of how well you can take what you learned and apply it to a timed testing environment. It shows how well you take tests and how well you do in a stressful situation. It does not however, measure your intelligence. In fact, once you learn the tips and tricks of the test, one might argue it measures your testing ability more than what you know.

If that's what it is, why do colleges use it for a standard for admission? Colleges use this as a *predictive analytic tool* to try to figure out if you have the basic abilities required of a college freshman. They want to make sure you can comprehend reading at a level that is expected in your classes. Same with math: do you have a basic understanding of mathematical concepts so you can succeed not just in math class but in other required classes such as economics. Many colleges also want to see if you can write in a way that is conducive to the college classroom. Again, they are not testing whether or not you CAN write but whether or not you can follow instructions and apply what you read to create an essay that would be appropriate for the college classroom. Finally, they are assessing your ability to take lengthy, timed tests. This testing situation mirrors what you might encounter in your college classes. They want to make sure, when they check that box for YES, they will be admitting someone with the tools to succeed. Colleges and universities must report their success rates with students and if all their students drop out, because they are not prepared to succeed, then the college itself cannot succeed. That is one reason why the admission process is so rigorous.

Preparing for the SAT

Knowing all that, it is essential to understand the tips and tricks of this assessment. The SAT is a great vehicle to show what you know. It has recently been realigned with the current high school college readiness curriculum, so it does reflect what you have seen in your classroom. But like any other test, it requires preparation and planning to do your best. It is important to note that you can take the test more than once. It won't count against you to try again, and in the end, you can choose the test you would like to send. Some schools *superscore,* which means you can combine the best sections into one final score. (You can read more about that in the "Words to Know" section). All these options are handy, especially if test taking isn't one of your strengths, but the real goal should be to go into your first testing situation with a plan to succeed.

Here are some tips to prepare for that first testing day:

- Learn strategies, tips and tools

- Practice, practice, practice. The more questions you see; the better you will do

- Learn math and reading formulas

- Practice the essay

- Create a study group and learn from your friends

You also need to:

- Understand the purpose of the test

- Outline the standards and requirements of each section

- Learn strategies and practices that will help you do your best on the test

- And above all, know what to expect and develop a plan to succeed

On the day of the test here are some things to remember:

- Get a good night's sleep and relax. Remember it is not the end of the world if you don't have your best testing day. You can always take the test again.

- Gather your testing supplies. Take several sharpened number 2 pencils, pencil you feel comfortable writing with, if you are taking the essay section, and your calculator (make sure it follows the guidelines set forth by the College Board).

- It is always smart to take a snack with you for your breaks. This will help energize you and keep you going.

- Don't forget your picture ID and your testing ticket. Make sure to double check all the requirements on the College Board site. They will give you a detailed account of all the documents you need to bring.

Words to Know

College Board: The College Board is the manager of the SAT. This organization provides great resources to better understand the application process, the meaning of your score, and the components of the test.

Standardized: Standardized means the same for all. Everyone taking the SAT will be tested on standardized material. There is no truth in the old myth that a red cover is a harder version, or if you take the test in June, it's easier than if you take it in January. Whenever you take it, regardless of the color of your test, the content is the same.

ACT: This is a test similar to the SAT. When the SAT was redesigned, it became more aligned with the content of the ACT. Now the two tests are pretty similar. Both tests are equally important, and you should consult your colleges of choice to see which they prefer.

Data Point: You might hear the SAT mentioned as a data point. This means it is just one measure, one point of data that is used to predict whether or not you will be a good fit for the college or university. Remember, they are using a predicative analysis formula to find the best fit for their programs and campus mission. You'll notice that every institution rates data points differently so that those skills they value most will be the biggest data points to consider.

Old SAT vs. New SAT: In 2016, the SAT made some major changes to its format, grading formula and essay. For the first year that these changes were in place, students could choose which format they would like to take. However, now there is just one SAT. When you sit for the exam, you can be assured that everyone else sitting for the exam that day is receiving a similar version of the test.

Superscore: A Superscore is when after taking the SAT multiple times, you combine the best scores for each section to create the Superscore that you send to your school. For example, if you rocked the first math test but just bombed the reading, if you chose to take it again, and did great on the reading, your score could be composed of the math from the first test and the reading from the second. This sounds great, right? However, this is not a College Board thing. This is a school to school decision. You need to check with the schools you intend to apply to and see if they Superscore. If they do not, then you will use the total scores from each individual test. This is an important distinction.

Who takes the SAT

The typical test taker is a student planning to enter an undergraduate program in the United States or Canada. The SAT may be a requirement for admission, but it is important to check with your colleges of choice to see if they prefer the SAT or ACT. It is also essential to see if they require the essay. Typically, this test is taken in the 11th and 12th grade.

Who gives the SAT

On the day of the test, your exam will be administered by trained proctors. They are employees of the College Board and they specialize in test security. They are not able to answer questions about the test but can answer your logistical questions such as where to take a break and when the test starts. They read their instructions from a script so the College Board can ensure that every test taker is receiving the same information. They are also responsible for watching for testing anomalies or misadministration issues.

The SAT is administered by the College Board. The College Board is an organization which writes, evaluates and manages the registration for the exam. They are your one stop shop for anything you need to know about actually taking the test. You can register through their site as well as receive your final score. Once you register and choose your schools, the College Board will also send your scores directly to your schools of choice. They also provide a thorough explanation of your scores, so you can see your highs and lows and make plans for improvements, if you are considering retaking the test.

Remember, even though you may take the test at your high school, it is not your school that is responsible for the test. The College Board creates, grades and secures all tests, so they can ensure test security. In other words, they can guarantee that you took the correct test with the correct results.

What is tested?

The SAT is divided into four sections:

- Essay

- Reading

- Writing and language

- Math

Essay

Let's start with the essay. The essay is an optional section on the test. However, it is recommended that unless you know for sure that your school doesn't consider the essay, you should take it. Remember, if you have to go back to take the test, you can't just take the essay section. You have to take the whole thing again!

The essay section begins with a passage. You read the passage and then create a response that discusses the argumentative elements in the passage and how successful the author was in delivering the main idea of the piece. You should also be able to discuss that main idea and the supporting details found throughout the essay. Word choice, sentence structure and general comprehension are all important components of this section.

Remember, this doesn't measure you as a writer. It measures your understanding and ability to comprehend the task, the passage and put it together into a well packaged piece.

You have 50 minutes to complete this task and it is graded on reading, analysis and writing. Each one of these grading points receives a score from 2-8, which gives you an overall score between 6 and 24. Keep in mind that this is a written assignment so make sure to bring pencils or pens you feel comfortable using.

Reading

The Reading test consists of 52 multiple choice questions and you have 65 minutes to complete it. You'll encounter passages or pairs of passages that are considered literature, historical documents, social sciences and natural sciences. The biggest advantage you have in this test is to choose the order you attack the passages. The best strategy is to practice. Your strategy will improve as you begin to understand your strengths and opportunities. That understanding comes with practice. For example, if you are a wiz at the historical document, you might want to do that one first and get it out of the way, so you can focus on the natural science passage that you know is a passage that will require more of your time.

You can also learn about question types and develop strategies for each one. The question types you will see include;

- Main idea/big picture questions

- Detail questions

- Inference questions

- Author's purpose and technique questions

- Vocabulary questions

- Analogy questions

- Data reasoning

- Use of evidence support

Each question type carries with it its own strategies and tips. The first step is to be able to decide which question type you are encountering. After you know what type of the question it is, you can decide first what kind of answer you are looking for and next how to use the passage to find the answer. However, as you are deciding these strategies, the clock is ticking, which is why practicing is essential.

Here are some quick tips to get you started:

- Know what to expect: format, time, expectations.

- Choose the order of passages.

- Read the passages in a way that makes sense to answer the questions. You don't have to necessarily read every word to answer these questions.

- Remember this is a passage-based assessment. They are not looking for what you think or what you know. Focus on what the passage says. That's all that matters.

- Save main idea questions for the last. By that time, you will have lived with the passage long enough to get the gist of what it is saying.

Writing and Language

You will have 35 minutes for the 44 multiple choice questions in this section. Questions cover grammar, vocabulary and editing. You will start with four passages and work through the questions in context. What this means is that every question offers you a chance to practice real skills such as editing, choosing the best word and re-ordering sentences. You will be also asked several reading comprehension questions mostly relating to topic sentences and details. Don't get too caught up in reading the passages but make sure as you are working through the questions, you have a general idea of what is going on in the passage. That makes it much easier to answer those tricky reading comprehension questions. You also may need to interpret graphics so make sure you understand their role in the overall passage.

Math

The math section is divided into two parts with a total of 58 questions. Note that in the first section, you cannot use your calculator for the 20 questions. This section takes 25 minutes. The second section has 38 questions and lasts for 55 minutes. In this part, you can use your calculator.

The match section covers four main topics.

- Heart of Algebra

- Problem Solving and Data Analysis

- Passport to Advanced Math

- Additional Topics in Math

The most important thing in this section is to know what the question is asking. Make sure you have worked through all the steps to reach the answer the test really wants. Often times, not completing that last step or not converting inches to feet or pounds to ounces is the difference between a correct and incorrect answer. Also read the word problems carefully. Use your reading strategies to find keywords and again, make sure you understand what they want to see. Finally make sure you are able to use and apply the basic math formulas required for this test. The College Board website provides a comprehensive list of those formulas. Knowing what formula goes with what problem is a big first step towards math success.

Scoring

The SAT has two main scores: Evidence-based Reading and Writing and Math.

For each section you can score between 200 and 800 points. A perfect final score is 1600. Here are some terms to better understand your score. Your total score is the sum of the Reading and Writing and Math sections. This can range between 400 and 1600. A section score is the score you receive on each of the separate sections: Reading and Writing and Math. Remember Reading and Writing are scored as one section. This can be helpful to students who have strengths in one of the sections but struggle in the other. They will eventually balance each other. A percentile is the comparison between you and the rest of the students who took the SAT in the year of your test. This is a test that 11th and 12th graders can take, so you will be compared with all students, not just those students in your grade. A cross-test score shows how you performed on select questions that represent knowledge in science and history. Finally, a subscore is reported as a number between 1-15 and it shows how you perform on basic knowledge questions that specifically relate to what you learned in high school. Topics include: a) Command of Evidence, b) Words in Context, c) Expression of Ideas and d) Standard English Conventions for Reading and Writing and Language tests and a) Heart of Algebra, b) Problem Solving and Data Analysis and c) Passport to Advanced Math for Math test.

The calculation of your overall score is a bit tricky. First there is a raw score. A raw score is found through how many questions you got right. You are not penalized for skipping or guessing questions, but you should always attack each question with your best strategies. Then your score is "equated." What this means is basically your score is curved. The way the curve is determined is far more complicated than you need to understand to figure out your score, but here is the gist. The College Board takes all the tests and determines a high and low scoring range. Based on those highs and lows they set their scale. This scale tries to smooth out all the different testing situations, so everyone's curve is pretty much the same. The bottom line is that the curve never really makes that much difference in your final score. If you have a high raw score, you will have a high SAT score. So, the best strategy is to get as many right answers as you can.

Remember the essay is scored separately. If you take it, you will get a score between 6 and 24. This section is scored by real graders who are highly trained in reading and assessing this writing. Just like with the test, the best strategy is to practice and hit as many required points as possible. The graders work with a rubric and this will help you land a higher score.

Now that you know the basics you are ready to get started. The key is to practice and know what to expect. Good luck and get practicing.

Directions to mark answer responses

For Multiple choice questions

Solve each problem, choose the best answer from the choices provided, and fill in the corresponding circle as shown.

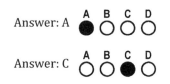

Answer: A

Answer: B

Answer: C

Answer: D

For student-produced response questions

Solve the problem and enter your answer in the grid, as shown.

1. Although not required, it is suggested that you write your answer in the boxes at the top of the columns to help you fill in the circles accurately. You will receive credit only if the circles are filled in correctly.
2. Mark no more than one circle in any column.
3. No question has a negative answer.
4. Some problems may have more than one correct answer. In such cases, grid only one answer.
5. **Mixed numbers** such as $3\frac{1}{2}$ must be gridded as 3.5 or 7/2. (If ⟨3|1|/|2⟩ is entered into the grid, it will be interpreted as $\frac{31}{2}$ not $3\frac{1}{2}$
6. **Decimal answers:** If you obtain a decimal answer with more digits than the grid can accommodate, it may be either rounded or truncated, but it must fill the entire grid.

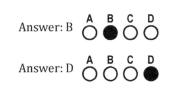

Answer: $\frac{7}{12}$ Answer: 2.5

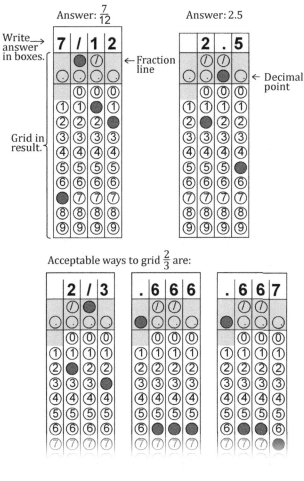

Write answer in boxes.

← Fraction line

Grid in result.

← Decimal point

Acceptable ways to grid $\frac{2}{3}$ are:

Answer: 201 – either position is correct

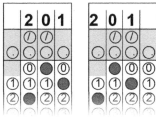

NOTE: You may start your answers in any column, space permitting. Columns you don't need to use should be left blank.

This page is intentionally left blank

Chapter **2**

Problem Solving and Data Analysis

1 The use of calculator is **not permitted**.

The Boulevard Hotel has a peculiar way of numbering its rooms. The first room on each floor is numbered as the product of all floor numbers below it starting from floor number one (the ground floor is not counted). For example, the first room on the fourth floor would be numbered as $1 \times 2 \times 3 = 6$. All successive room numbers would be numbered three more than the previous room number. Thus, on the fourth floor, rooms are numbered as $6, 6 + 3 = 9, 6 + 2 \times 3 = 12, 6 + 3 \times 3 = 15$, etc. If it is known that there are six rooms on each floor, how many room numbers on the fifteenth floor are prime numbers?

(A) 0
(B) 2
(C) 4
(D) 5

$x + 3$
$x + 6$
$x + 9$

A   B   C   D
○   ○   ○   ○

2 The use of calculator is **permitted.**

David, a sweet shop owner, buys some Hershey's chocolates at 5 for \$10 and the same number of Twix chocolates at 8 for \$10. He then mixes them and sells all the chocolates at a uniform price of 12 for \$30. What is the overall percentage profit made by David in the process?

53.8

/	○	○	
. ○	○	○	○
0 ○	○	○	○
1 ○	○	○	○
2 ○	○	○	○
3 ○	○	○	○
4 ○	○	○	○
5 ○	○	○	○
6 ○	○	○	○
7 ○	○	○	○
8 ○	○	○	○
9 ○	○	○	○

3 The use of calculator is **permitted.**

If a, b, c, d are distinct numbers such that: $a + c = 2d$ and $b + d = 2c$, which of the following statements must be true?

I. a cannot be the average of a, b, c, d.

II. b can be the average of a, b, c, d.

III. d can be the average of a, b, c, d.

(A) Only statement (I)

(B) Only statement (II)

(C) Only statement (III)

(D) Both statements (I) and (II)

A	B	C	D
○	○	○	○

4 The use of calculator is **permitted.**

Mc-n-Roe, a popular garment store in New York, purchased some pieces of garments each at the same cost price. The store then sold each garment at 20% profit. Had the store charged \$10 more for each garment, it would have made 25% profit on its cost. What was the cost of each piece of garment that the store procured?

(A) \$200

(B) \$240

(C) \$250

(D) \$300

A	B	C	D
○	○	○	○

5 The use of calculator is **permitted**.

Consider the set of integers P = {1, 2, 3, 4 ..... 51}. Let us define A as the average of the odd integers in P and B as the average of the even integers in P. What is the value of A – B?

(A) − 1

(B) 0

(C) 1

(D) 2

A	B	C	D
○	○	○	○

6 The use of calculator is **permitted**.

A man travels at a speed of 12 miles/hr. How long, in minutes, to the nearest integer, would he take, to cover a distance of 3750 yards? (1 *mile* = 5280 *yards*)

(handwritten annotations: 0.71 mile, 12mmph, 0.71 =0.059=3.55, 0.71/12, 4 min)

7 The use of calculator is **permitted**.

John participated in a game where each participant was asked to pick up six cards from a box without looking at the cards. The participant with the highest total would be declared the winner. Each card had a numerical value from one to a hundred written on it. John's average in the first four cards came out to be 83. What is the lowest he can get in the sixth draw so that he still has a chance of taking his overall average to at least 88?

(A) 100

(B) 98

(C) 96

(D) 92

A	B	C	D
○	○	○	○

8 The use of calculator is **permitted.**

What is the number of ways a four-member debate team be selected from six boys and five girls so that at least one girl is always present in the team?

9 The use of calculator is **not permitted**.

Andrew was asked by his friend to count all the numbers from 1 to 90 that are divisible by two and three but not by five. Andrew made a mistake in the process and counted the result as 10. What is the difference between the actual result and the result that Andrew got?

(A) 2

(B) 4

(C) 6

(D) 10

A B C D

○ ○ ○ ○

10 The use of calculator is **permitted.**

Dominick collected eight different samples of mango juice from different brands. He noted the concentration of each sample and tabulated the results as follows:

Brand Name	Kern's	Nestle	Fusion	Welch's	Splash	Ceres	Snapple	Trop5
Sample name	A	B	C	D	E	F	G	H
Concentration (%)	69	68	64	66	62	60	47	42

A 'shot' refers to a mixture formed using 2 distinct samples in some proportion. How many such combinations of samples may Dominick use to prepare 'shots' with exactly 60% average concentration?

(A) 5

(B) 6

(C) 10

(D) 12

A B C D

○ ○ ○ ○

11 The use of calculator is **permitted.**

A tea connoisseur wants to mix two varieties of tea in order to make a special variant. He wants to use Green Tip priced at $100/lb and Cinnamon Dew priced at $135/lb respectively. In what ratio should he mix them so that the average price of the mixture comes to $150/lb if he wants to make a 25% profit by selling it?

(A) 2 : 7

(B) 3 : 8

(C) 2 : 5

(D) 5 : 2

A   B   C   D
O   O   O   O

12 The use of calculator is **permitted.**

A bartender mixes 30 ml of Port Wine having 10% alcohol concentration and 50 ml of Merlot wine having 21% alcohol concentration. The bartender needs to make a cocktail having 18% alcohol concentration. What volume of Chardonnay wine having 23% concentration must he use so that the final mixture has 18% concentration?

(A) 18 ml

(B) 20 ml

(C) 33 ml

(D) 45 ml

A   B   C   D
O   O   O   O

13 The use of calculator is **not permitted.**

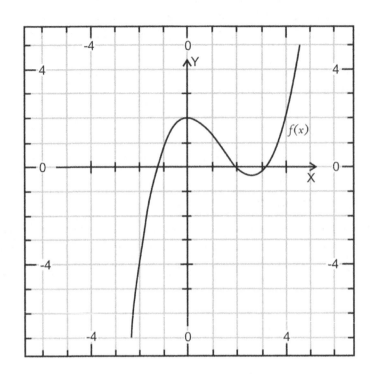

What is the number of possible integer values of k $(5 > k > 0)$ such that $g(x) = f(x) - k$ has exactly one root?

14 The use of calculator is **permitted.**

John decided to treat his friends with some chocolates. On visiting a Hershey's outlet, he found that chocolates were sold in boxes. The boxes had different number of chocolates and the prices of the boxes were also different. The prices are shown in the table below.

Number of chocolates per box	Price per box
5	$2
10	$3.6
15	$5

How much less does John spend if he buys 90 chocolates in boxes of 15 chocolates than if he buys the same in boxes of 10 chocolates?

(A) $1.40

(B) $2.40

(C) $3.60

(D) $6.00

A   B   C   D
O   O   O   O

15 The use of calculator is **permitted**.

If the HCF of two numbers is 18 and their LCM is 360, all of the following cannot be the difference between the two numbers EXCEPT

(A) 8

(B) 12

(C) 18

(D) 54

A   B   C   D
O   O   O   O

16   The use of calculator is **not permitted.**

The Farm-Fresh fruit store in California stocks Apples, Bananas, Peaches and Lychees. While ordering fruits for its store, the owner wanted the fruits in particular ratios as depicted in the table below:

Fruits	Required Ratio
Apples : Bananas	3 : 5
Apples : Peaches	4 : 9
Lychees : Bananas	3 : 8

What is the ratio of Peaches to Lychees?

(A) $\dfrac{5}{18}$

(B) $\dfrac{81}{160}$

(C) $\dfrac{32}{45}$

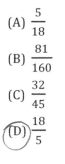 (D) $\dfrac{18}{5}$

A   B   C   D
○   ○   ○   ○

17   The use of calculator is **permitted.**

The Farm-Fresh fruit store in California stocks Apples, Bananas, Peaches and Lychees. While ordering fruits for its store, the owner wanted the fruits in particular ratios as depicted in the table below:

Fruits	Required Ratio
Apples : Bananas	6 : 5
Apples : Peaches	4 : 3
Lychees : Bananas	3 : 2

What fraction of the total fruits are Apples?

(A) $\dfrac{9}{46}$

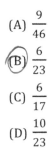 (B) $\dfrac{6}{23}$

(C) $\dfrac{6}{17}$

(D) $\dfrac{10}{23}$

A   B   C   D
○   ○   ○   ○

18 The use of calculator is **not permitted.**

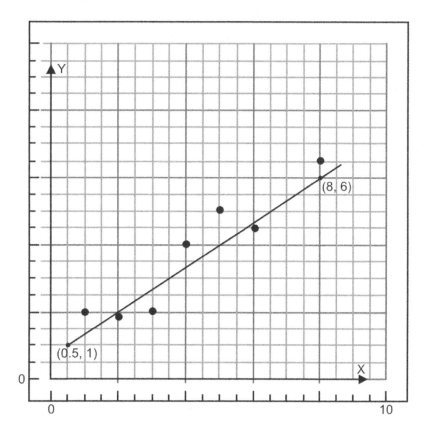

In the graph above, a number of points are shown, and the line of best fit is also shown. What is the sum of the expected values of the Y coordinates of the points having X values 7 and 9?

19 The use of calculator is **not permitted.**

In a three-digit number ABC, where A, B and C represent digits from 0 to 9, the value of the digit A equals the cube of the digit C. How many such three-digit numbers ABC exist?

(A) 5

(B) 10

(C) 20

(D) 30

A   B   C   D
○   ○   ○   ○

20 The use of calculator is **permitted.**

Joe was asked to fill up the missing digits A and B in the number 25A7B subject to the condition that the resulting number has to be divisible by 36. What is the value of (A + B) if A and B are distinct digits?

(A) 4

(B) 8

(C) 9

(D) 13

A   B   C   D
○   ○   ○   ○

21 The use of calculator is **permitted.**

$P = \{1, 2, 3, 4, 5 \dots 25\}$. How many sets of integers can you pick from the set P so that they start with 1, end with 25 and consecutive numbers in the set have a constant gap between them?

For example, one way of selecting such a set of numbers is {1, 7, 13, 19, 25} (since the set starts with 1, ends in 25 and consecutive numbers are at a constant gap of 6).

(A) 4

(B) 5

(C) 8

(D) 10

A   B   C   D
○   ○   ○   ○

22 The use of calculator is **permitted.**

The odds in favor of Ann clearing a driving test is 1 : 4. The odds against Brad clearing the same driving test is 5 : 4. What is the probability that at least one of them would clear the test?

23 The use of calculator is **not permitted.**

The mean of five positive integers is 5. The numbers have a single mode equal to 8. What is the maximum possible value of the lowest term?

(A) 1

(B) 2

(C) 3

(D) 4

A	B	C	D
O	O	O	O

24 The use of calculator is **not permitted.**

Out of 35 students in section A of the 7th grade of Manhattan Public School, 10 students like baseball, 20 students like basketball and 10 students like rugby. 3 students like baseball and basketball, 2 students like only basketball and rugby, 4 students like only baseball and rugby. If only 2 students like all three games, how many students do not like any of the above three games?

(A) 5

(B) 6

(C) 8

(D) 9

A	B	C	D
O	O	O	O

25 The use of calculator is **permitted.**

The Bellinger store charges $30 for each computer-game DVD. The store charges this price keeping a profit margin of 20%. During Christmas, to increase sales, the store offers a discount of 10% on the cost of the DVD. By what amount is the price of a DVD during Christmas less than the normal price offered by the store?

(A) $5.00

(B) $6.00

(C) $7.50

(D) $8.40

A	B	C	D
O	O	O	O

26 The use of calculator is **permitted.**

In a party on New Year's Eve, if the men shook hands among themselves, there would be 21 handshakes in all. However, if the men shook hands with the women, there would be 35 handshakes. How many handshakes would have happened if the women shook hands among themselves?

(A) 5

(B) 7

(C) 10

(D) 12

A	B	C	D
O	O	O	O

27 The use of calculator is **not permitted.**

Let P be a set of 21 integers from -10 to 10, i.e. $P = \{-10, -9, -8, -7 \ldots 7, 8, 9, 10\}$. In how many ways can one select 19 integers from the above set such that their sum comes to one?

28 The use of calculator is **permitted.**

At the Orient Store clearance sale, articles are sold at a price resulting in 10% loss for the store owner. The store owner decides to double the existing selling price of each article. What is his current percentage profit if it is known that all articles have the same price?

(A) 100

(B) 90

(C) 85

(D) 80

A   B   C   D

○   ○   ○   ○

29 The use of calculator is **permitted**.

What is the probability that '4' will appear exactly thrice on rolling a normal dice four times?

(A) $\dfrac{1}{324}$

(B) $\dfrac{5}{1296}$

(C) $\dfrac{1}{216}$

(D) $\dfrac{5}{324}$

A   B   C   D

○   ○   ○   ○

30 The use of calculator is **permitted.**

Martin visited a juice shop and found that there were three varieties of mango juices available Rich, Sweet and Tangy. The details for these varieties is as in the table:

Name	Price (per 60 ml)	Concentration of mango syrup
Rich	$45	80%
Sweet	$20	70%
Tangy	$15	60%

Martin wanted to mix exactly two of these varieties to make a juice having 70% concentration. What would be the price (in dollars per 60 ml) of such a mixture?

31 The use of calculator is **permitted**.

Wal-Mart offers the following discounts on consumables on the list price based on the quantity of goods purchased (all goods have the same list price of $60):

Quantity purchased	Percentage discount offered
Up to 10 lbs	10%
More than 10 lbs. but less than 20 lbs.	20%
More than 20 lbs.	25%

Two friends, John and Jack separately purchase 8 lbs and 15 lbs of goods respectively. How much would they have been able to save if they purchased the goods together instead of purchasing separately?

(A) $115

(B) $117

(C) $180

(D) $345

A   B   C   D

32 The use of calculator is **permitted**.

If a, b, c, d are four distinct numbers such that: $a + c = 2d$ and $b + d = 2c$, which of the following is the correct expression for the average of the four numbers?

(A) $c + d$

(B) $\dfrac{3a+c}{4}$

(C) $\dfrac{a+2c}{2}$

(D) $\dfrac{b+3d}{4}$

| A | B | C | D |
| O | O | O | O |

33 The use of calculator is **not permitted**.

Two positive integers a and b have their HCF as h ($h \neq 1$). How many such integers exist if $(a + b + h) = 15$?

(A) 1

(B) 2

(C) 3

(D) 4

| A | B | C | D |
| O | O | O | O |

34 The use of calculator is **permitted**.

n and p are two positive integers. If it is known that $3n$ is a perfect square and $12n^2p$ is a perfect cube, what is the smallest possible value of np?

35   The use of calculator is **permitted**.

The Washington Post has a daily quota of 60 advertisements. The percentage of advertisements on each page and the corresponding cost of putting an advertisement is as given:

Position of advertisement	Percentage of number of advertisements	Price of each advertisement
Page one	25%	$1000
Page three	60%	$200
Back page	15%	$400

Approximately, what percentage of total revenue from advertisements is generated from the advertisements on the back page?

(A) 14%

(B) 15%

(C) 20%

(D) 30%

A   B   C   D
○   ○   ○   ○

36   The use of calculator is **permitted**.

The price of coffee rose by 20% following shortage in availability in the market. As a result, Carlos decided to mitigate increasing expenses by reducing his coffee intake. By what percentage should Carlos reduce his intake so that there is no effect on the expenditure on coffee?

(A) 5%

(B) 16.67%

(C) 20%

(D) 25%

A   B   C   D
○   ○   ○   ○

37   The use of calculator is **not permitted**.

R is the sum of squares of 50 consecutive even integers starting with 2, and S is the sum of squares of 50 consecutive integers starting with 1. S is what percentage less than R?

(A) 25%

(B) 33%

(C) 50%

(D) 75%

A   B   C   D
○   ○   ○   ○

38 The use of calculator is **not permitted**.

A sequence is shown below:

$1, 4, -2, 1 \ldots$

The first term is 1. The second term is obtained by multiplying the first term with 4, the third term is obtained by dividing the second term by (-2), and the fourth term is obtained by adding 3 to the third term. The same above cycle then repeats for the 5th, 6th and 7th terms and so on. What is the sum of the first 22 terms of the above sequence?

(A) 8

(B) 21

(C) 22

(D) 32

A   B   C   D
○   ○   ○   ○

Questions 39 to 42 are based on the following graph

The graph below gives the production and consumption of crude oil in certain countries of the world. Answer the following questions based on the graph below:

Figures below the names of the countries indicate crude reserves in million tonnes.

Shortfall / (excess) between production and consumption is met by imports / (exports).

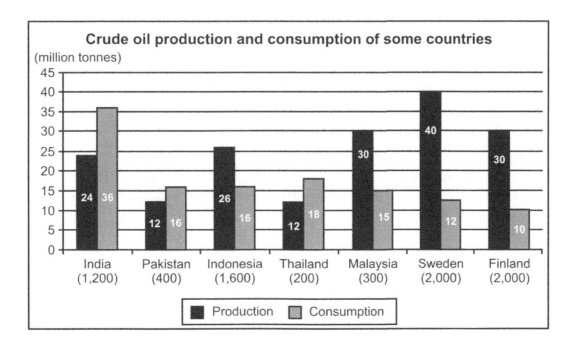

39   The use of calculator is **permitted**.

If Sweden produces 5% of world crude oil produce, then what is the percentage share of India in the world crude oil production?

(A) 1.5%

(B) 3.0%

(C) 3.5%

(D) 4.0%

A   B   C   D
○   ○   ○   ○

40   The use of calculator is **permitted**.

If India's entire import of crude oil is from Finland, what percentages of Finland's exports are not to India?

(A) 40%

(B) 50%

(C) 60%

(D) 75%

A   B   C   D
○   ○   ○   ○

41   The use of calculator is **permitted**.

Which country has the maximum percentage difference between its production and consumption?

(A) Malaysia

(B) Sweden

(C) Finland

(D) Indonesia

A   B   C   D
○   ○   ○   ○

42   The use of calculator is **permitted**.

How long would the reserves last for the given countries together if we assume that there is no production of crude oil in the given countries and the given countries have the same consumption level in the future?

(A) 45 years

(B) 53 years

(C) 62 years

(D) 70 years

A   B   C   D
○   ○   ○   ○

43 The use of calculator is **permitted**.

The Strand Book Store in New York recently purchased 60 copies of *Fahrenheit 451* at an average price of $250 per book. The store sold 75% of the books at $300 each and sold the remaining books to a book dealer for a lump sum of $2000. What was the net profit or loss of the store?

(A) $500 profit

(B) $450 profit

(C) Neither profit nor loss

(D) $500 loss

A   B   C   D
○   ○   ○   ○

44 The use of calculator is **not permitted**.

Mark and Brad, two employees of Intel Corporation have a discussion regarding their incomes and expenditures over a dinner. It was found that their incomes are in the ratio 3 : 4 and their expenditures are in the ratio 2 : 1 respectively. It was also found that Mark saves two-third of his income. What fraction of his income does Brad save?

(A) $\dfrac{2}{7}$

(B) $\dfrac{3}{4}$

(C) $\dfrac{7}{8}$

(D) $\dfrac{9}{10}$

A   B   C   D
○   ○   ○   ○

Questions 45 to 48 are based on the following graph.

The graph shows the **percentage** of population owning TV sets in various countries.

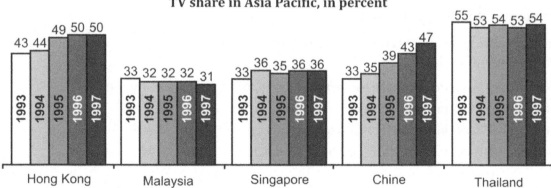

45 The use of calculator is **permitted**.

Which country has shown a nearly constant TV share for the 5 years?

(A) Hong Kong

(B) Malaysia

(C) Singapore

(D) China

	A	B	C	D
	O	O	O	O

46 The use of calculator is **permitted**.

By what "percentage points" has the share of TV sets in Hong Kong grown from 1993 to 1997?

(A) 7

(B) 15

(C) 16

(D) 21

	A	B	C	D
	O	O	O	O

47 The use of calculator is **permitted**.

Which of the following countries has shown the highest percent decline in the percent share of TV sets from 1993 to 1997?

(A) Hong Kong

(B) Thailand

(C) Singapore

(D) Malaysia

	A	B	C	D
	O	O	O	O

48 The use of calculator is **permitted**.

Assuming that the population of all the countries is the same and remains constant for the given years, which of the following options is INCORRECT?

(A) Number of TV sets in Hong Kong has increased by approximately 16.3% from 1993 to 1997.

(B) Number of TV sets in Singapore and China is the same for 1993.

(C) Number of TV sets increased by 12.5% for Singapore from 1993 to 1997.

(D) Number of TV sets for China increased by approximately 42.4% from 1993 to 1997.

	A	B	C	D
	O	O	O	O

49 The use of calculator is **not permitted**.

If the positive integer N leaves a remainder of 3 when divided by 7, which of the following statements would be true?

I. $4N + 2$ is divisible by 14

II. $N^2 - 2$ is divisible by 7

III. $(N + 3)(N + 4)$ is divisible by 7

(A) Only I

(B) Only II

(C) Only III

(D) I, II and III

A	B	C	D
○	○	○	○

50 The use of calculator is **not permitted**.

If x and y are positive integers and $(2x + y)$ is even, which of the following must be even?

(A) $x^3 + 2xy^2$

(B) $3x^2 + 2y$

(C) $4x^2 + x + y^2$

(D) $5x^2 + x + y^3$

A	B	C	D
○	○	○	○

51 The use of calculator is **not permitted**.

Which of the following can be a possible value of the average of 8 consecutive odd natural numbers?

(A) 21

(B) 27

(C) 32

(D) 37

A	B	C	D
○	○	○	○

52 The use of calculator is **not permitted**.

In the final examinations for 9th grade students of New York Public School, 4 students failed in Mathematics, Science and History; 16 students failed in at least two of the above-mentioned subjects and 25 students failed in at least one of the above subjects. How many students failed in exactly one of the mentioned subjects?

(A) 5

(B) 7

(C) 9

(D) 13

A	B	C	D
○	○	○	○

53 The use of calculator is **permitted.**

Kohl's offers a special discount of 10% on the selling price on all products if paid in cash. However, at the same time, the store charges 2% extra (on the selling price) on all products if paid using a credit card. How much does a customer save on a Samsung TV listed at $3000 having a discount of 20% as a promotional offer from Samsung if he pays in cash than if he pays with a credit card?

(A) $180

(B) $240

(C) $288

(D) $360

A B C D
○ ○ ○ ○

54 The use of calculator is not **permitted.**

P = {1,2,3,4 ... 20}. How many integers n can be selected from the set P such that $(n^2 + n^3)$ is a perfect square?

(A) 2

(B) 3

(C) 4

(D) 5

A B C D
○ ○ ○ ○

55 The use of calculator is **not permitted**.

A crate contains green and red apples in the ratio 7 : 11. When ten green apples and ten red apples are removed from the crate, the ratio becomes 9 : 17. How many red apples were originally in the bag?

56 The use of calculator is **not permitted.**

The average of seven distinct positive integers is 8. What is the greatest possible value of one of the integers?

(A) 9

(B) 11

(C) 35

(D) 45

A   B   C   D

○   ○   ○   ○

57 The use of calculator is **permitted.**

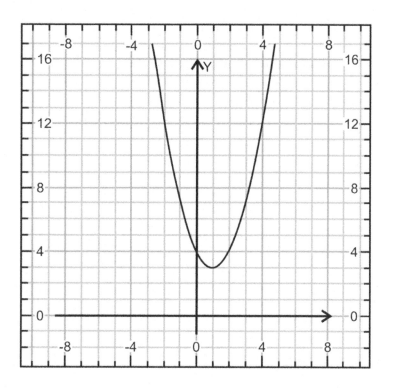

Which of the following forms of the equation below directly gives the coordinates of the vertex of the graph of the quadratic expression shown above without having to do any additional steps?

(A) $y = (x - 1)(x - 4)$

(B) $y = x^2 + 4$

(C) $y = (x - 1)^2 + 3$

(D) $y = 2(x - 1)^2 + 3$

A   B   C   D

○   ○   ○   ○

58 The use of calculator is not **permitted.**

AB denotes a two-digit number with digits as A and B. If $(AB)^2 = ACC$, where ACC denotes a three-digit number having digits A, C and C. What is the value of $A + B + C$ if A, B, C are all distinct digits?

(A) 5

(B) 6

(C) 7

(D) 9

A B C D
○ ○ ○ ○

59 The use of calculator is **permitted.**

A chemist has 20% and 30% concentration of nitric acid with him. In an experiment, he mixed x ml of 20% concentration and 9 ml of 30% concentration in one container and in another container, he mixed 4 ml of the 20% concentration with x ml of the 30% concentration. Surprisingly, the concentration of acid in both containers came out to be same. What is the value of x (in ml)?

60 The use of calculator is **permitted.**

Napster offers discounts on purchase of three garment pieces at a time. On purchase of every garment at the listed price, there is a 10% discount on offer on the remaining two garments. All garments are priced the same. If the garments are listed at 25% above the cost price of \$120, what is the profit made by the store if a customer purchases three pieces of garments?

(A) \$30

(B) \$45

(C) \$60

(D) \$90

A B C D
○ ○ ○ ○

61 The use of calculator is not **permitted.**

A survey was made on the breed of dogs kept by pets in different families in a city and the results were tabulated as shown below:

Breed of dogs	Number of families
Rottweiler	125
Labrador	213
German shepherd	97
Spitz	163
Doberman	n

If the median number of dogs was 163, what is the minimum possible value of n?

62 The use of calculator is **not permitted.**

During the Inter-School Debate championship, students of the 9th grade of Illinois Public School had to be divided in groups. It was found that if they were divided into groups of four, one student was left out. If they were divided into groups of six, then too, one student was left out. What was the minimum number of students in the grade such that they can be perfectly divided in groups of five?

(A) 15

(B) 20

(C) 25

(D) 30

63 The use of calculator is **not permitted**.

In the 10th grade of Brooklyn Public School, the ratio of the number of boys to the number of girls was 3 : 5. Among the students, some had taken up literature as a specialization while the rest had taken up science. The ratio of the number of literature students to science students was 5 : 7. If it is known that one-third the number of boys had taken up science as a specialization, what fraction of the girls had literature as their specialization?

(A) $\dfrac{4}{15}$

(B) $\dfrac{2}{5}$

(C) $\dfrac{3}{5}$

(D) $\dfrac{2}{3}$

A   B   C   D
○   ○   ○   ○

64 The use of calculator is **not permitted**.

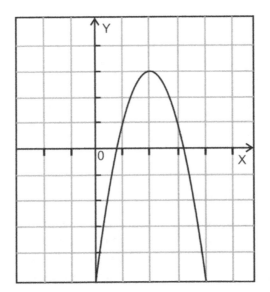

Which of the following can be the correct expression for the graph of the quadratic shown above?

(A) $y = x^2 - 6x + 8$

(B) $y = -x^2 - 6x - 8$

(C) $y = -x^2 + 6x - 8$

(D) $y = -x^2 + 6x + 8$

A   B   C   D
○   ○   ○   ○

65   The use of calculator is **not permitted.**

AB and CA are two-digit numbers which satisfy the multiplication:

$$
\begin{array}{ccc}
 & A & B \\
\times \quad C & A \\
\hline
1 \quad B \quad C & A \\
\hline
\end{array}
$$

If A, B, C are distinct integers from 2 to 5, what is the value of $A + B + C$?

(A) 2

(B) 3

(C) 5

(D) 10

A   B   C   D
○   ○   ○   ○

66   The use of calculator is **permitted.**

Tamarak Street has 30 families, each family owns dogs amongst three different breeds – Alsatian, Spitz and Golden-retriever. A family can have dogs of multiple breeds but at most one dog of any breed. There are 11 families having an Alsatian and 14 families having a Spitz. There are 10 families who own dogs of exactly two different breeds and 2 families own dogs of all three breeds. What is the total number of dogs on Tamarak Street?

(A) 30

(B) 35

(C) 36

(D) 44

A   B   C   D
○   ○   ○   ○

67   The use of calculator is **permitted.**

John has a large collection of coins with him. The coins are split between of one-dollar coins, quarters, and dimes (one quarter is equivalent to one-fourth of a dollar and one dime is equivalent to one-tenth of a dollar). If the ratio of the number of one dollar coins to quarters to dimes is 3 : 8 : 10 and they are exactly $210, how many quarters does John have?

(A) 35

(B) 80

(C) 105

(D) 280

A   B   C   D
○   ○   ○   ○

68 The use of calculator is not **permitted.**

On Children's day celebrations, gifts were distributed among the children of the locality. There was a total of 96 pens and 72 pencils to be given away as gifts. What could be the total number of pens and pencils given to each child if maximum number of children received the gifts and all gifts were identical?

(A) 3

(B) 4

(C) 7

(D) 12

A B C D
O O O O

69 The use of calculator is **permitted.**

In the recently conducted TAS examination, 15% of the candidates got selected from the total number of candidates who wrote the exam. In another exam, the TCA, half the number of TAS candidates appeared and 20% of the candidates got selected. If the number of candidates selected in these two exams combined were 18000, how many candidates actually appeared for the TAS (in thousands)?

70 The use of calculator is **permitted.**

If $2w = \dfrac{3}{2}x = y = \dfrac{5}{3}z$ for four positive integers w, x, y and z, which of the following expressions can represent an integer?

(A) $\dfrac{wx}{yz}$

(B) $\dfrac{x}{w}$

(C) $\dfrac{4x}{y}$

(D) $\dfrac{x^2}{y}$

A B C D
O O O O

71 The use of calculator **is permitted**.

A group of people were surveyed to choose one of the two TV shows they preferred more: Sherlock Holmes and Friends. Of the total 30 people who put forward their choice, 18 chose Sherlock Holmes and 20 chose Friends. Each person had to choose one of the two shows mentioned above. Choose the correct statement(s):

I.   8 people liked both shows.

II. 22 people preferred one show over the other.

III. 12 people liked only one of the two shows.

(A) Only I

(B) Only II

(C) Only III

(D) Both I and II

A   B   C   D
○ ○ ○ ○

72 The use of calculator is **not permitted**.

A sequence is shown below:

1, 4, – 4 ...

The first term is 1. Each even numbered term is 3 more than the previous term and each odd numbered term after the first is (– 1) times the previous term. What is the sum of the first 32 terms of the above sequence?

(A) − 1

(B) 0

(C) 1

(D) 3

A   B   C   D
○ ○ ○ ○

73 The use of calculator is **not permitted**.

In the International Oxford School, all students play at least one of the two games rugby and baseball. 40% of all students play both rugby and baseball. If 20% of the students who play baseball do not play rugby, then what is the percentage of all students who play baseball?

74 The use of calculator is **not permitted.**

If $\dfrac{a}{7} = \dfrac{2b}{5} = \dfrac{3a-4b}{k}$, the value of k is __.

(A) 2

(B) 5

(C) 11

(D) 12

A   B   C   D
○   ○   ○   ○

Questions 75 To 78 are based on the following chart.

The following table gives the number of households in USA during 2000 – 2014.

Year	No. of households (Millions)	Year	No. of households (Millions)
2000	120	2008	132
2002	123	2010	135
2004	126	2012	140
2006	130	2014	145

The following charts give the distribution of households based on the number of children for the years 2000 and 2014.

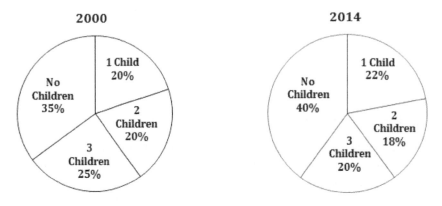

75 The use of calculator is **permitted.**

In 2000, 20% of the households belonging to the category "no children" decided to have children. If those households had 1, 2, and 3 children in the ratio of 4 : 2 : 1, respectively, what would be the share of households having 2 children?

(A) 21.0%

(B) 22.0%

(C) 24.0%

(D) 26.4%

A   B   C   D
○   ○   ○   ○

76 The use of calculator is **permitted.**

In the above problem, how many additional children were born in that year?

(A) 8.4 million

(B) 13.2 million

(C) 15.0 million

(D) 17.6 million

A   B   C   D
○   ○   ○   ○

77 The use of calculator is **permitted**.

What was the approximate average annual percent increase in the number of households from 2000 to 2014?

(A) 1.5%

(B) 1.4%

(C) 1.2%

(D) 1.1%

A   B   C   D
○   ○   ○   ○

78 The use of calculator is **permitted.**

What is the total number of children in 2014?

(A) 57.0 million

(B) 129.5 million

(C) 171.1 million

(D) 201.4 million

A   B   C   D
○   ○   ○   ○

79 The use of calculator is **not permitted.**

A positive integer P, when multiplied by 9 gives a result which consists of 5 followed by some number of 7's. What is the number of 7's in the product thus obtained, if P is the least such number possible?

(A) 16

(B) 11

(C) 9

(D) 7

A   B   C   D
○   ○   ○   ○

80 The use of calculator is **permitted.**

If the relation between A and B is known to be of the form: $B = k \times n^A$, what is the value of $(k + n)$?

The following data was observed between the variables A and B:

A	B
3	24
4	48
5	96

Answers and Explanations

1. **Level Of Difficulty:** Difficult

    The correct answer is (A).

    From the given information, we can say that the first room on the fifteenth floor would be: $1 \times 2 \times 3 \times 4 \times 5 \times ... \times 14 = N$ (say).

    Thus, successive room numbers would be: $N, (N + 3), (N + 6), (N + 9), (N + 12)$ and $(N + 15)$.

    We can see that N is a multiple of all integers from 1 to 14. Thus, N is a multiple of $3, 6, 9$ and 12.

    Again, since N is a multiple of both 3 and 5, it is also a multiple of 15.

    Thus, $(N + 3)$ is not prime since it is divisible by 3.

    Similarly, $(N + 6)$ is not prime since it is divisible by 6.

    $(N + 9)$ is not prime since it is divisible by 9.

    $(N + 12)$ is not prime since it is divisible by 12.

    Finally, $(N + 15)$ is not prime since it is divisible by 15.

    Thus, none of the numbers are primes.

2. **Level of Difficulty:** Difficult

    Topic: Percents

    The correct answer is 53.8.

    Let us assume that David buys 120 chocolates at 5 for $10 and again 120 chocolates at 8 for $10 (since this is a percentage question, the choice of the initial value does not affect the final answer. We choose 120, since 120 is divisible by 5, 8 and 12).

    Thus, cost of chocolates bought at 5 for $10 $= \$\dfrac{120 \times 10}{5} = \$240$.

    Also, cost of chocolates bought at 8 for $10 $= \$\dfrac{120 \times 10}{8} = \$150$.

    Thus, total cost for David $= \$(240 + 150) = \$390$.

    David now sells $120 + 120 = 240$ chocolates at 12 for $30.

    Thus, his sales proceeds $= \$\dfrac{240}{12} \times 30 = \$600$.

    Hence, profit made by David $= \$(600 - 390) = \$210$.

    Hence, percentage profit $= \dfrac{210}{390} \times 100 = 53.85\% \sim 53.8\%$.

    Hence, the answer is 53.8.

3. **Level of Difficulty:** Difficult

    Topic: Data inferences

    The correct answer is (A).

    Since $a + c = 2d$, we can say that d is the average of a and c.

    Thus, if a, c, d are arranged in order, the order would be either a, d, c or c, d, a.

    Similarly, since $b + d = 2c$, we can say that c is the average of b and d.

    Thus, if b, d, c are arranged in order, the order would be either b, c, d or d, c, b.

    Thus, combining the above two results, we can have the following two orders:

a, d, c, b or b, c, d, a.

Thus, we see that a and b either the smallest or the largest of the four numbers. Hence, neither a nor b can be the average of the four numbers.

Again, since d is the mean of a and c, it implies that d is equidistant from a and c.

Similarly, c is equidistant from b and d.

Thus, when arranged in order, the gap between any two consecutive numbers must be the same.

Since the four numbers are distinct, we can thus say that the average of the four numbers would be some number between c and d. Hence, the average of the four numbers cannot be c or d.

Thus, only statement (I) is correct.

Hence, the answer is (A).

4. **Level of Difficulty:** Medium

    Topic: Percents

    The correct answer is (A).

    Let's say that the increase of $10 resulted in the percentage profit increasing by $(25 - 20)\% = 5\%$.

    We know that the percentage profit is always calculated on the cost of an article.

    Hence, we can conclude that 5% of the cost of a garment = $10.

    Thus, the cost price of a garment $= \$10 \times \dfrac{100}{5} = \$200$.

    Hence, the answer is (A).

5. **Level of Difficulty:** Easy

    Topic: Center, spread and shape of distributions

    The correct answer is (B).

    A is the average of 1, 3, 5, 7 ... 51.

    Since the numbers are consecutive odd integers, the average can be simply obtained as

    $$= \frac{\text{first term} + \text{last term}}{2} = \frac{1+51}{2} = 26.$$

    Hence, A $= 26$.

    B is the average of 2, 4, 6 ... 50.

    Since the numbers are consecutive even integers, the average can be simply obtained as

    $$= \frac{\text{first term} + \text{last term}}{2} = \frac{2+50}{2} = 26.$$

    Hence, B $= 26$.

    Thus, A $-$ B $= 0$.

    Hence, the answer is (B).

6. **Level of Difficulty:** Medium

    Topic: Units

    The correct answer is 4.

    $$\text{Distance} = 3750 \text{ yards} = \frac{3750}{5280} = 0.71 \text{ miles}$$

Thus, time $= \dfrac{0.71}{12} = 0.059$ hours $= 0.059 \times 60 = 3.55$ minutes, i.e. 4 minutes (to the nearest integer).

7. **Level of Difficulty:** Difficult

   Topic: Data inferences

   The correct answer is (C).

   In order that John gets the lowest possible number in his sixth draw, he needs to maximize his total in the fifth test. The maximum he can get in the fifth draw is 100.

   Since John needs to get at least 88 as the overall average, in his first four draws, John is $(88 - 83) \times 4 = 20$ behind.

   If he gets 100 in the fifth draw, he makes up $(100 - 88) = 12$.

   So, he is still $20 - 12 = 8$ behind.

   Thus, John needs to draw a number which is at least 8 more than 88 or $88 + 8 = 96$ in the sixth draw so that he can be sure to get an average of 88 overall.

   Hence, the answer is (C).

8. **Level of Difficulty:** Medium

   The correct answer is 315.

   Total number of ways in which four members can be selected from $6 + 5 = 11$ members $= C_4^{11} = \dfrac{11!}{4!7!} = 330$.

   This includes the cases where no girls are present in the team. We need to remove these cases.

   Total number of ways of selecting four members from only boys $= C_4^6 = \dfrac{6!}{4!2!} = 15$.

   Thus, the number of ways in which at least one girl will be present in the team $= 330 - 15 = 315$.

   Hence, the correct answer is 315.

9. **Level of Difficulty:** Medium

   The correct answer is (A).

   We have to find the numbers from 1 to 90 divisible by 2 and 3 but not by 5.

   We know that 90 is a multiple of the LCM of $2, 3, 5$ i.e. 30.

   All integers from 1 to 90 can be categorized according to multiples of $2, 3, 5$, as shown in the tree diagram below:

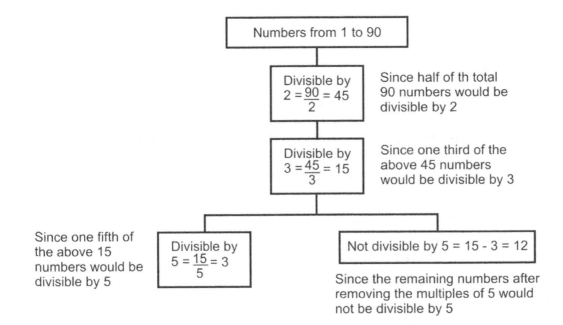

Hence, there are 12 numbers from 1 to 90 which are divisible by 2 and 3 but not divisible by 5.

Thus, the difference between the actual result and the result that Andrew had obtained $= 12 - 10 = 2$.

Hence, the answer is (A).

10. **Level of Difficulty:** Difficult

    Topic: Table data

    The correct answer is (C).

    We know that in order to make a 60% concentration 'shot' from two mixtures, we need one with more than 60% and the other with less than 60% concentrations.

    Thus, sample F cannot be used at all since it already has exactly 60% concentration.

    Possible cases are: G with any of A/B/C/D/E or H with any of A/B/C/D/E.

    Thus, there are $5 + 5 = 10$ combinations possible.

    Hence, the answer is (C).

11. **Level of Difficulty:** Medium

    Topic: Ratios, rates, and proportions

    The correct answer is (C).

    The connoisseur wants to sell the mix at $150/lb making 20% profit in the process.

    Let the effective (average) cost of the mix $= \$x$/lb.

    Thus, we have: $x + \dfrac{20x}{100} = 150 => x = \dfrac{150}{1.2} = 125$.

    Thus, the average cost of the mix $= \$125$/lb.

    Now, we can use the method of allegation very effectively to get the ratio of the quantities of the two varieties of tea:

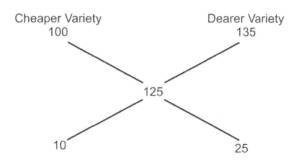

Hence, the ratio of the quantities of the two varieties of tea $= 10 : 25 = 2 : 5$.

Alternative: Let us assume the quantities of the two varieties be m lbs and n lbs.

Thus, the average price of the mixture $= \$\dfrac{(100m+135n)}{m+n}$.

Thus: $\dfrac{(100m+135n)}{m+n} = 125 \Rightarrow 100m + 135n = 125m + 125n \Rightarrow 25m = 10n \Rightarrow \dfrac{m}{n} = \dfrac{10}{25} = \dfrac{2}{5}$.

Hence, the required ratio is $2 : 5$.

Hence, the answer is (C).

12. **Level of Difficulty:** Medium

    Topic: Percents

    The correct answer is (A).

    Let the bartender use x ml of the Chardonnay.

    Comparing deviation about the mean:

    30 ml of 15% concentration: net deviation $= 30 \times (10 - 18) = -240$.

    50 ml of 20% concentration: net deviation $= 50 \times (21 - 18) = 150$.

    x ml of 30% concentration: net deviation $= x \times (23 - 18) = 5x$.

    The deviation about the average should be zero.

    Thus: $-240 + 150 + 5x = 0 \Rightarrow 5x = 90 \Rightarrow x = 18$.

    Thus, the bartender needs to use 18 ml of Chardonnay.

    Hence, the answer is (A).

13. **Level of Difficulty:** Medium

    Topic: Key features of graphs

    The correct answer is 2.

    We know that $f(x) - k$ (where $k > 0$) shifts the graph k units down.

    In order to have a single root, the graph must intersect the X axis at only one point.

    Thus, the graph must shift down by more than 2 units.

    Thus, the possible values of k are 3 and 4. Thus, there are 2 possible values.

    The correct answer is 2.

14. **Level of Difficulty:** Difficult

    Topic: Table data

    The correct answer is (B).

    If John wants to buy the boxes containing 15 chocolates, he will require $\dfrac{90}{15} = 6$ boxes.

    Cost of each such box = $5.

    Hence, his total cost = $5 × 6 = $30.

    However, if John wants to buy the boxes containing 10 chocolates, he will require $\dfrac{90}{10} = 9$ boxes.

    Cost of each such box = $3.6.

    Hence, his total cost = $3.6 × 9 = $32.40.

    Hence, John saves $32.40 − $30 = $2.40.

    Hence, the answer is (B).

15. **Level of Difficulty:** Medium

    The correct answer is (C).

    We know that if a set of numbers have some HCF, each number must be a multiple of the HCF.

    Let the two numbers be a and b.

    Since the HCF here is 18, we have: $a = 18k$ and $b = 18l$, where k and l are some positive integers.

    Thus, we have the LCM of $18k$ and $18l$ as 360.

    Now, we know that k and l must have <u>no common factors</u> except one since all common factors are included in the HCF.

    Thus, the LCM of $18k$ and $18l = 18kl$.

    Hence, $18kl = 360 => kl = 20$.

    Thus, possible values of k and l are tabulated below:

k	l	$a = 18k$	$b = 18l$	Difference between a and b
1	20	18	360	$360 - 18 = 342$
4	5	72	90	$90 - 72 = 18$

    Thus, the difference between a and b can either be 342 or 18.

    Hence, the answer is (C).

16. **Level of Difficulty:** Medium

    Topic: Ratios, rates, and proportions

    The correct answer is (D).

    We have the following information:

    $\dfrac{\text{Apples}}{\text{Bananas}} = \dfrac{3}{5} \ ... \ (i)$

    $\dfrac{\text{Apples}}{\text{Peaches}} = \dfrac{4}{9} \ ... \ (ii)$

    $\dfrac{\text{Lychees}}{\text{Bananas}} = \dfrac{3}{8} \ ... \ (iii)$

Now, we rearrange the ratios so that all common terms cancel out leaving Peaches and Lychees.

Hence, we have:

From (ii): $\dfrac{\text{Peaches}}{\text{Apples}} = \dfrac{9}{4}$ ... (iv)

From (iii): $\dfrac{\text{Bananas}}{\text{Lychees}} = \dfrac{8}{3}$ ... (v)

We now multiply the ratios obtained from (iv), (i) and (v):

$$\dfrac{\text{Peaches}}{\text{Apples}} \times \dfrac{\text{Apples}}{\text{Bananas}} \times \dfrac{\text{Bananas}}{\text{Lychees}} = \dfrac{9}{4} \times \dfrac{3}{5} \times \dfrac{8}{3} => \dfrac{\text{Peaches}}{\text{Lychees}} = \dfrac{18}{5}.$$

Hence, the answer is (D).

17. **Level of Difficulty:** Difficult

   Topic: Ratios, rates, and proportions

   The correct answer is (B).

   Here, we need to find the combined ratio of all fruits and use that ratio to find Apples form what fraction of the total number of fruits. It is best to work with some numbers which would make our calculation easier.

   We have the following information:

   Apples : Bananas = 6 : 5, Apples : Peaches = 4 : 3, Lychees :Bananas = 3 : 2.

   We can see that Apples are common to the first two ratios having numbers 6 and 4 respectively. So, we assume the number of apples as the LCM of 6 and 4 i.e. 12.

   Thus, to maintain the ratio of Apples and Bananas, the number of Bananas = 5 × 2 = 10.

   Again, to maintain the ratio of Apples to Peaches, the number of Peaches = 3 × 3 = 9.

   Finally, we look at the ratio of Lychees to Bananas which is 3 : 2.

   Since we have Bananas as 10, to maintain the ratio, number of Lychees$= 3 \times \dfrac{10}{2} = 15$.

   Thus, the final ratio of Apples : Peaches : Bananas : Lychees = 12 : 9 : 10 : 15.

   Thus, Apples as a fraction of total fruits $= \dfrac{12}{12+9+10+15} = \dfrac{12}{46} = \dfrac{6}{23}.$

   Hence, the answer is (B).

18. **Level of Difficulty:** Easy

   Topic: Scatter plots

   The correct answer is 12.

   From the graph, we can clearly observe that:

   The line passes through the points (0.5, 1), and (8, 6).

   Thus, the equation of the line of best fit is:

   $$\dfrac{y-6}{x-8} = \dfrac{6-1}{8-0.5}$$

   $$\dfrac{y-6}{x-8} = \dfrac{2}{3}$$

   Thus, we have:

   $x = 7: \dfrac{y-6}{7-8} = \dfrac{2}{3} => y = 5.33$

$$x = 9: \frac{y-6}{9-8} = \frac{2}{3} => y = 6.67$$

Thus, the required sum $= 12$

The correct answer is 12.

19. **Level of Difficulty:** Easy

    Topic: Data inferences

    The correct answer is (C).

    We know that $A = C^3$.

    Possible values of (A, C) which would satisfy the relation above are $(1,1)$ and $(8,2)$ (Here, $A \neq 0$ since we need a three-digit number. Also, since the value of A has to be a single digit, $C \neq 3$ or higher values).

    For both the cases above, B can assume any value from 0 to 9, i.e. there are 10 possibilities.

    Thus, we can have the following numbers:

    $101, 111, 121, \dots 191$ i.e. 10 possibilities, and $802, 812, 822, \dots 892$ i.e. 10 possibilities i.e. $10 + 10 = 20$ possibilities.

    Hence, the answer is (C).

20. **Level of Difficulty:** Difficult

    The correct answer is (D).

    To check the divisibility by 36, we need to check the divisibility by 4 and 9.

    For 4, the last two digits of the number i.e. 7B should be divisible by 4.

    We know that multiples of 4 starting with 7 are either 72 or 76.

    Thus, $B = 2$ or 6.

    For 9, sum of all digits of the number i.e. $2 + 5 + A + 7 + B = (14 + A + B)$ should be divisible by 9.

    If $B = 2$, the sum becomes $14 + A + 2 = (16 + A)$.

    In order that $(16 + A)$ is divisible by 9, we must have $A = 2$ (since $16 + 2 = 18$ is divisible by 9).

    Since A and B need to be distinct, we cannot include this as a solution.

    If $B = 6$, the sum becomes $14 + A + 6 = (20 + A)$.

    In order that $(20 + A)$ is divisible by 9, we must have $A = 7$ (since $20 + 7 = 27$ is divisible by 9).

    Thus, $A + B = 7 + 6 = 13$.

    Hence, the answer is (D).

21. **Level of Difficulty:** Difficult

    The correct answer is (C).

    The minimum number on the set P is 1 and the maximum number is 25.

    Thus, the gap between them $= 25 - 1 = 24$.

    In order to pick integers from P so that they start with 1, end with 25 and consecutive numbers in the set have a constant gap between them, we need to pick numbers whose gap is a factor of 24.

    Thus, possible gaps are 1, 2, 3, 4, 6, 8, 12 and 24.

    The set of integers are:

    (i)   Gap is 1: the numbers are all the integers in the set P i.e. 1, 2, 3, 4 … 23, 24, and 25.

    (ii)   Gap is 2: the numbers are the following integers: 1, 3, 5, 7, 9, 11, 13, 15, 17, 19, 21, 23, and 25.

(iii)   Gap is 3: the numbers are the following integers: 1, 4, 7, 10, 13, 16, 19, 22, and 25.

(iv)   Gap is 4: the numbers are the following integers: 1, 5, 9, 13, 17, 21, and 25.

(v)   Gap is 6: the numbers are the following integers: 1, 7, 13, 19, and 25.

(vi)   Gap is 8: the numbers are the following integers: 1, 9, 17, and 25.

(vii)   Gap is 12: the numbers are the following integers: 1, 13, and 25.

(viii)   Gap is 24: the numbers are the following integers: 1 and 25.

Thus, there are 8 possible sets of integers that can be selected from P satisfying all the conditions.

Hence, the correct answer is (C).

22. **Level of Difficulty:** Easy

    Topic: Data inferences

    The correct answer is $\frac{5}{9} = 0.55$.

    Probability that Ann clears the driving test $= \frac{1}{1+4} = \frac{1}{5}$.

    Thus, probability that Ann does not clear the driving test $= 1 - \frac{1}{5} = \frac{4}{5}$.

    Probability that Brad clears the driving test $= \frac{4}{4+5} = \frac{4}{9}$.

    Thus, probability that Brad does not clear the driving test $= 1 - \frac{4}{9} = \frac{5}{9}$.

    Thus, probability that neither of them clears the driving test $= \frac{4}{5} \times \frac{5}{9} = \frac{4}{9}$.

    Thus, probability that at least one of them clears the driving test $= 1 - \frac{4}{9} = \frac{5}{9}$.

    Hence, the correct answer is $\frac{5}{9} = 0.55$.

23. **Level of Difficulty:** Medium

    Topic: Center, spread and shape of distributions

    The correct answer is (B).

    Since the mean of 5 integers is 5, the sum of the integers $= 5 \times 5 = 25$.

    There is a single mode of 8.

    Thus, 8 must be present more than once.

    Now, 8 cannot be present more than thrice as four times 8 becomes 32 which exceeds the total of the five positive integers.

    If 8 is present thrice, then we have the sum as $3 \times 8 = 24$.

    Thus, the other two positive integers would add up to $25 - 24 = 1$; which is not possible.

    Thus, 8 must be present exactly twice, and they add up to $2 \times 8 = 16$.

    Thus, the other three integers add up to 9.

    These three integers cannot be 3 each as then the mode would no longer be 8 and would become 3 instead.

    Thus, the sum of those three integers can be made 9 in the following ways (we cannot repeat the same number even twice; else the set of integers will no longer have a single mode):

    (i)   2, 3, 4: Here, the minimum term is 2.

    (ii)   1, 3, 5: Here, the minimum term is 1.

(iii) 1, 2, 6: Here, the minimum term is 1.

Since we need the maximum possible value of the lowest term, we take it as 2 (since $2 > 1$).

Hence, the correct answer is (B).

24. **Level of Difficulty:** Medium

    Topic: Data inferences

    The correct answer is (B).

    The different regions are shown in the Venn diagram below:

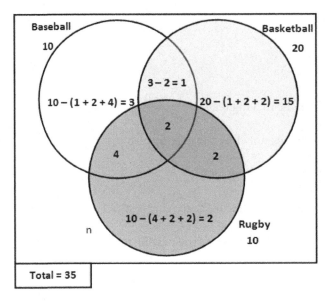

Thus, the number of students who do not like any of the three games is:

$n = 35 - (3 + 1 + 15 + 4 + 2 + 2 + 2) = 35 - 29 = 6$.

Hence, the correct answer is (B).

25. **Level of Difficulty:** Difficult

    Topic: Percents

    The correct answer is (C).

    The selling price of each DVD = $30.

    Percentage profit made on each DVD = 20%.

    Let the cost price be x.

    Thus, we have: $30 = x + \left(\frac{20}{100} \times x\right) => 30 = x + \frac{x}{5} => \frac{6x}{5} = 30 => x = 25$.

    Thus, the cost of each DVD = $25.

    During Christmas, discount offered = 10%.

    Thus, selling price during Christmas = $(25 - 10\% \text{ of } 25) = \$22.50$.

    Thus, the required difference in price = $(30 - 22.50) = \$7.50$.

    Hence, the answer is (C).

26. **Level of Difficulty:** Medium

The correct answer is (C).

Let there be m men and w women.

Since we need two men for a handshake, the number of handshakes among only the men:

$$= C_2^m = \frac{m(m-1)}{2} = 21 => m(m-1) = 42 => m = 7.$$

Since we need one man and one woman for a handshake, the number of handshakes among the men and women $= C_1^m \times C_1^w = 35 => mw = 35 => w = \frac{35}{7} = 5.$

Thus, the number of handshakes between women $= C_2^w = C_2^5 = \frac{5(5-1)}{2} = 10.$

Hence, the correct answer is (C).

27. **Level of Difficulty:** Difficult

Topic: Data inferences

The correct answer is 10.

We can observe that the numbers in the set are consecutive integers and the sum of all the numbers in the set is zero.

Also, the set has 21 numbers and we need to select 19 numbers that add up to 1.

Thus, we need to leave out two numbers from the set P.

So, we need to leave out two numbers that add up to -1 (if we leave out two numbers which add up to -1, then the sum of the remaining numbers would be $0 - (-1) = 1$).

The possible ways of selecting two numbers which add up to -1 are:
$(-10,9); (-9,8); (-8,7); (-7,6); (-6,5); (-5,4); (-4,3); (-3,2); (-2,1)$ and $(-1,0)$.

Thus, there are 10 possible cases.

Hence, the answer is 10.

28. **Level of Difficulty:** Easy

Topic: Percents

The correct answer is (D).

Let the cost price of each article be $100 (since this is a percentage-based question, the choice of the initial value has no effect on the final answer).

Thus, the initial selling price of each article $= \$(100 - 10\%$ of $100) = \$90.$

Thus, new selling price $= \$90 \times 2 = \$180.$

Hence, profit $= \$(180 - 100) = \$80.$

Thus, percentage profit $= \dfrac{\text{Profit}}{\text{Cost price}} \times 100 = \dfrac{80}{100} \times 100 = 80\%.$

Hence, the answer is (D).

29. **Level of Difficulty:** Medium

Topic: Data inferences

The correct answer is (D).

The number '4' has to appear thrice.

The fourth number should be a number other than four.

Thus, the fourth number can be selected in $C_1^5 = 5$ ways.

These four numbers can appear in any order. The number of such ways $= \dfrac{4!}{3!} = 4$.

Thus, number of favorable cases $= 5 \times 4 = 20$.

Number of total cases when a dice is rolled four times $= 6 \times 6 \times 6 \times 6 = 1296$.

Hence, required probability $= \dfrac{20}{1296} = \dfrac{5}{324}$.

Hence, the correct answer is (D).

30. **Level of Difficulty:** Difficult

   Topic: Table data

   The correct answer is 30.

   Since Martin wants to mix two varieties of juices to create a juice with 70% concentration, he cannot use the Sweet variety since it itself has 70% and mixing it with any other variety would change its concentration from 70%.

   Thus, Martin needs to mix the Rich and the Tangy varieties.

   We can observe that the Rich variety has 80% concentration and the Tangy variety has 60% concentration.

   The required concentration i.e. 70% is the simple average of 60% and 80% since $\dfrac{60+80}{2} = 70\%$.

   Thus, it is definite that he must mix the Rich and Tangy varieties in equal proportion.

   Hence, the price of the resulting mixture would have a price $= \$\dfrac{45+15}{2} = \$30$ per 60 ml.

   Hence, the answer is 30.

31. **Level of Difficulty:** Difficult

   Topic: Percents

   The correct answer is (B).

   John would get 10% discount on his total list price since he purchases 8 lbs.

   Total list price for John $= \$(60 \times 8) = \$480$.

   So, the price John finally pays $= \$(480 - 10\% \text{ of } 480) = \$432$.

   Jack would get 20% discount on his total list price since he purchases 15 lbs.

   Total list price for Jack $= \$(60 \times 15) = \$900$.

   So, the price Jack finally pays $= \$(900 - 20\% \text{ of } 900) = \$720$.

   So, total price paid by John and Jack together $= \$(432 + 720) = \$1152$.

   If they purchased together, they would have purchased $8 + 15 = 23$ lbs.

   Thus, they would have got 25% discount.

   Total list price for 23 lbs $= \$(60 \times 23) = \$1380$.

   So, the net price they would have to pay after discount $= \$(1380 - 25\% \text{ of } 1380) = \$1035$.

   So, total savings $= \$(1152 - 1035) = \$117$.

   Alternative:

   If John and Jack purchase together, they would both fall in the 25% discount category.

   Thus, John would get an additional $25 - 10 = 15\%$ discount on his goods worth $= \$(60 \times 8) = \$480$.

Thus, additional savings for John = $(15% of 480) = $72.

Also, Jack would get an additional $25 - 20 = 5\%$ discount on his goods worth = $(60 \times 15) = $900.

Thus, additional savings for John = $(5% of 900) = $45.

Thus, net combined savings = $(72 + 45) = $117.

Hence, the answer is (B).

32. **Level of Difficulty:** Medium

    Topic: Data inferences

    The correct answer is (D).

    We have: $a + c = 2d$ and $b + d = 2c$.

    The average of the four numbers $= \frac{a+b+c+d}{4}$.

    Thus, going by options:

    1) $a + b + c + d = (a + c) + (b + d) = 2d + 2c$

    i.e. $\frac{a+b+c+d}{4} = \frac{2d+2c}{4} = \frac{c+d}{2}$.

    Hence, (A) is incorrect.

    2) $a + b + c + d = a + c + (b + d) = a + c + 2c = a + 3c$

    i.e. $\frac{a+b+c+d}{4} = \frac{a+3c}{4}$.

    Hence, (B) and (C) are incorrect.

    3) $a + b + c + d = (a + c) + b + d = 2d + b + d = b + 3d$

    i.e. $\frac{a+b+c+d}{4} = \frac{b+3d}{4}$.

    Hence, (D) is correct.

    Therefore, the correct answer is (D).

33. **Level of Difficulty:** Medium

    The correct answer is (B).

    We know that if a set of numbers have some HCF, each number must be a multiple of the HCF.

    Since the HCF here is h, we have:

    $a = kh$ and $b = mh$, where k and m are some positive integers (it should be noted that k and m should not have any common factors among themselves as the common factor has been taken out in the HCF i.e. h).

    Thus, we have: $a + b + h = 15 => kh + mh + h = 15 => h(k + m + 1) = 15$.

    Thus, we can conclude that the values of h and $(k + m + 1)$ will be the factors of 15. Thus, the values of h can only be 3, 5 or 15 (it cannot be 1 since it is given that $h \neq 1$). We can tabulate the result as shown below:

h	$k + m + 1$	$k + m$	k	m	$kh = a$	$mh = b$	Pair of numbers a and b
3	5	4	1	3	3	9	3, 9
5	3	2	1	1	5	5	5, 5
15	1	0	Not a possible situation since a, b are positive integers

Thus, there are only two pairs possible (the question does not ask for ordered pairs): 3, 9; and 5, 5.

Hence, the answer is (B).

34. **Level of Difficulty:** Difficult

The correct answer is 6.

Since $3n$ is a perfect square and 3 is not a perfect square in itself, we can conclude that n must be 3 times a perfect square.

Thus, n can be numbers like $3, 3 \times 4 = 12, 3 \times 9 = 27$ etc.

Again, since $12n^2p$ is a perfect cube ($12 = 2^2 \times 3$, is not a perfect cube), we can conclude that n^2p must be ($2 \times 3^2 = 18$) or 18 times some other perfect cube.

Thus, n^2p can be numbers like $18, 18 \times 8 = 144, 18 \times 27 = 486$ etc.

Now, we need to find the minimum possible value of np.

We see that we can take $n = 3$ and in that case, if $n^2p = 18$, we have $p = 2$.

These are the minimum possible values of n and p.

Thus, minimum possible value of $np = 3 \times 2 = 6$.

Hence, the answer is 6.

35. **Level of Difficulty:** Difficult

Topic: Table data

The correct answer is (A).

Let us assume that the total number of advertisements be 100 (since this is a percentage question, the choice of the initial value does not have any effect on the final answer).

So, the breakup of the advertisements can be formed as shown below:

Position	Number of advertisements	Price of each advertisement	Revenue
Page one	25	$1000	$1000 × 25 = $25000
Page three	60	$200	$200 × 60 = $12000
Back page	15	$400	$400 × 15 = $6000
Total Revenue			$43000

Thus, percentage of total revenue generated from advertisements on the back page

$= \dfrac{6000}{43000} \times 100 = 13.95\% \sim 14\%$.

Hence, the answer is (A).

36. **Level of Difficulty:** Medium

Topic: Percents

The correct answer is (B).

We have: (Price of coffee per unit consumed) × (Total units consumed) = (Total expenditure on coffee)

Thus, if price changes by $x\%$ and consumption changes by $y\%$, we can conclude that the expenditure will change by $\left(x + y + \frac{xy}{100}\right)$ %.

Here, $x = 20$ and $x + y + \frac{xy}{100} = 0$ (since there is no change in expenditure).

Thus, we have: $20 + y + \frac{20y}{100} = 0 => y + \frac{y}{5} = -20 => \frac{6y}{5} = -20 => y = -20 \times \frac{5}{6} = -16.67$

Thus, Carlos should reduce his intake by 16.67%.

Hence, the answer is (B).

37. **Level of Difficulty:** Difficult

   Topic: Data inferences

   The correct answer is (D).

   Let us write the terms of the series R: $R = 2^2 + 4^2 + 6^2 + \cdots 100^2$ (since we are looking at 50 consecutive even numbers, it would start with 2 and end in 100).

   So, $R = 2^2(1^2 + 2^2 + 3^2 + \cdots 50^2) = 4k$, where $k = 1^2 + 2^2 + 3^2 + \cdots 50^2$.

   Let us also write the terms of the series S: $S = 1^2 + 2^2 + 3^2 + \cdots 50^2$ (since we are looking at 50 consecutive numbers, it would start with 1 and end in 50).

   So, $S = k$, where $k = 1^2 + 2^2 + 3^2 + \cdots 50^2$.

   Thus, we see that $R = 4k$ and $S = k$.

   Hence, the required percentage $= \frac{4k - k}{4k} \times 100 = \frac{3}{4} \times 100 = 75\%$.

   Hence, the answer is (D).

38. **Level of Difficulty:** Easy

   The correct answer is (C).

   The above sequence starts with 1 and the fourth term also becomes 1.

   Thus, the same three terms 1, 4 and −2 would repeat.

   The sum of the above three terms $= 1 + 4 + (-2) = 3$.

   Thus, each set of the above three terms adds up to 3.

   In the first 22 terms, the above set of three terms would be repeated 7 times (since the quotient of the division of 22 by 3 is 7).

   Each of the above 7 groups would add up to 3.

   Hence, the sum of the terms of the above 7 groups $= 3 \times 7 = 21$.

   The 22nd term is equivalent to the first term of the 8th group i.e. the first term of the sequence = 1.

   Hence, the sum of the first 22 terms $= 21 + 1 = 22$.

   Hence, the correct answer is (C).

39. **Level of Difficulty:** Medium

   Topic: Data collection and conclusions

   The correct answer is (B).

   Production of crude oil in Sweden = 40 million tones

   Production of crude oil in India = 24 million

   Thus, we have:

40 million tones = 5% of world crude oil produce

8 million tones = 1% of world crude oil produce

24 million = 3% of world crude oil produce

40. **Level of Difficulty:** Difficult

    Topic: Data collection and conclusions

    The correct answer is (A).

    Amount of oil imported by India = $(36 - 24)$ million = 12 million tonnes

    Total exports by Finland = $(30 - 10)$ million = 20 million tonnes

    Since India's entire import of crude oil is from Finland, we have:

    Export of oil other than India = 8 million tones

    Thus, the required percent

    $= \dfrac{8}{20} \times 100\%$

    $= 40\%$

41. **Level of Difficulty:** Easy

    Topic: Data collection and conclusions

    The correct answer is (B).

    Malaysia $= \dfrac{30-15}{15} \times 100 = 100\%$

    Sweden $= \dfrac{40-12}{12} \times 100 = 233.3\%$

    Finland $= \dfrac{30-10}{10} \times 100 = 200\%$

    Indonesia $= \dfrac{26-16}{16} \times 100 = 62.5\%$

42. **Level of Difficulty:** Medium

    Topic: Data collection and conclusions

    The correct answer is (C).

    Total consumption of oil

    $= (36 + 16 + 16 + 18 + 15 + 12 + 10)$

    $= 123$ million tons

    Total Reserve $= 1200 + 400 + 1600 + 200 + 300 + 2000 + 2000$

    $= 7700$ million tones

    Time $= \dfrac{7700}{123} = 62.6$ years.

    Thus, the time for which the reserves would last should be 62 years (not 63 years).

43. **Level of Difficulty:** Medium

    Topic: Percents

    The correct answer is (A).

Total cost incurred by the store = \$250 × 60 = \$15000.

Sales proceeds generated by selling 75% or $\dfrac{75}{100}$ × 60 i.e. 45 books = \$300 × 45 = \$13500.

Sales proceeds generated by selling the remaining books = \$2000.

Hence, total sales proceeds = \$(13500 + 2000) = \$15500.

Hence, net profit = (Net sales proceeds – Net cost incurred) = \$(15500 − 15000) = \$500.

Hence, the answer is (A).

44. **Level of Difficulty:** Difficult

   Topic: Ratios, rates, and proportions

   The correct answer is (C).

   Ratio of incomes of Mark and Brad = 3 : 4.

   Thus, let the incomes of Mark and Brad be $3k$ and $4k$ respectively, where k is some constant.

   Now, Mark saves two-third of his income. So, Mark's savings $= \dfrac{2}{3} \times 3k = 2k$.

   So, Mark's expenditure $= 3k - 2k = k$.

   Since ratio of expenditures of Mark and Brad = 2 : 1, Brad's expenditure $= \dfrac{k}{2}$.

   Thus, Brad's savings = Brad's income − Brad's expenditure $= 4k - \dfrac{k}{2} = \dfrac{7k}{2}$.

   Hence, Brad's savings as a fraction of his income $= \dfrac{\frac{7k}{2}}{4k} = \dfrac{7}{8}$.

   Hence, the answer is (C).

45. **Level of Difficulty:** Easy

   Topic: Data collection and conclusions

   The correct answer is (B).

   We can observe from the graph that Malaysia has more or less a constant TV share for 5 years. In three of its years, the share is constant at 32% (1994 − 1996).

   In all the other countries, there have been fluctuations in the TV share percent values.

   In Thailand too, the percent share values have not fluctuated by much. However, on comparing Malaysia and Thailand, it is clear that the share values of Malaysia have been more 'constant'.

46. **Level of Difficulty:** Easy

   Topic: Data collection and conclusions

   The correct answer is (A).

   The "percent points" simply refer to the difference between percent values.

   Thus, from 1993 to 1997, the percent share has increased from 43% to 50%, i.e. an increase of 7 percent points.

   (Note: We do not know the change in population for Hong Kong from 1993 to 1997. Hence, the actual percent change cannot be determined.)

47. **Level of Difficulty:** Medium

    Topic: Data collection and conclusions

    The correct answer is (D).

    The percent share has declined only for Malaysia and Thailand from 1993 to 1997.

    Malaysia: Percent decline in the percent share of TV sets $= \dfrac{33-31}{33} \times 100 = 6.06\%$

    Thailand: Percent decline in the percent share of TV sets $= \dfrac{55-54}{55} \times 100 = 1.82\%$

    Thus, Malaysia has the highest percent decline in the percent share of TV sets from 1993 to 1997.

48. **Level of Difficulty:** Difficult

    Topic: Data collection and conclusions

    The correct answer is (C).

    Since the population is the same for each country and also remains constant, the percent values in the graph are equivalent to the actual number of people owning TV sets in each country.

    Working with each option, we have:

    A. Percent change in number of TV sets in Hong Kong $= \dfrac{7}{43} \times 100 = 16.3\%$ – Correct

    B. Number of TV sets in Singapore and China in 1993 is 33 – Correct

    C. Percent change in number of TV sets in Singapore $= \dfrac{36-33}{33} \times 100 = 9.09\%$ – Incorrect

    D. Percent change in number of TV sets for China $= \dfrac{47-33}{33} \times 100 = 42.42\%$ – Correct

    Answer C.

49. **Level of Difficulty:** Difficult

    The correct answer is (D).

    From the given information, we can write: $N = 7k + 3$, where k is some non-negative integer.

    Substituting the above value of N in each statement, we get:

    I. $4N + 2 = 4(7k + 3) + 2 = (28k + 12) + 2 = 28k + 14 = 14(2k + 1)$.

    Hence, we can see that the resulting number is a multiple of 14. Hence, the statement is true.

    II. $N^2 - 2 = (7k + 3)^2 - 2 = 49k^2 + 42k + 9 - 2 = 49k^2 + 42k + 7 = 7(7k^2 + 6k + 1)$.

    Hence, we can see that the resulting number is a multiple of 7. Hence, the statement is true.

    III. $(N + 3)(N + 4) = (7k + 3 + 3)(7k + 3 + 4) = (7k + 6)(7k + 7) = 7(7k + 6)(k + 1)$.

    Hence, we can see that the resulting number is a multiple of 7. Hence, the statement is true.

    Hence, all three statements are true.

    Hence, the answer is (D).

50. **Level of Difficulty:** Difficult

    The correct answer is (D).

    We know $(2x + y)$ is even, but $2x$ is always even; hence, y must be even as well.

    However, we cannot comment on whether x is even or odd.

    Going by options:

(A): In $x^3 + 2xy^2$, we can say that the term $2xy^2$ is even. However, since x may be odd or even, we cannot comment whether x^3 is even or odd.

Hence, $x^3 + 2xy^2$ may be either even or odd.

(B): In $3x^2 + 2y$, we can say that the term $2y$ is even. However, since x may be odd or even, we cannot comment whether $3x^2$ is even or odd.

Hence, $3x^2 + 2y$ may be either even or odd.

(C): In $4x^2 + x + y$, we can say that the terms $4x^2$ and y are even. However, x may be odd or even.

Hence, $4x^2 + x + y$ may be either even or odd.

(D): In $5x^2 + x + y^3$, we can say that the term y^3 is even. However, since x may be odd or even, we cannot comment whether $5x^2$ and x are individually even or odd.

However, we can determine the nature of the sum $5x^2 + x$.

Let us assume x is even. Then definitely, $5x^2 + x$ is even.

Again, if we assume x to be odd, both $5x^2$ and x are odd. Hence, the sum $5x^2 + x$ is the sum of two odd numbers and hence, is even.

Thus, $5x^2 + x$ is always even.

Hence, $5x^2 + x + y^3$ is always even.

Hence, the answer is (D).

51. **Level of Difficulty:** Medium

   Topic: Center, spread and shape of distributions

   The correct answer is (C).

   The mean of 8 consecutive odd integers (i.e. integers having a constant gap between each other) must be the average of the middle two terms i.e. the 4th and 5th terms. Since the 4th and 5th terms are both consecutive odd integers, their average must be an even number.

   Hence, the only option possible is 32 (In that case, the numbers are 25, 27, 29, 31, 33, 35, 37, and 39).

   Hence, the correct answer is (C).

52. **Level of Difficulty:** Medium

   Topic: Data inferences

   The correct answer is (C).

   The different regions are shown in the Venn diagram below:

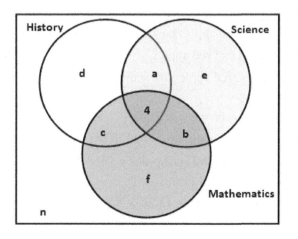

The students who failed in exactly one subject $= (d + e + f)$.

The students who failed in exactly two subjects $= (a + b + c)$.

Thus, we have: $a + b + c + 4 = 16 \Rightarrow a + b + c = 12$ ... (i)

Also: $(d + e + f) + (a + b + c) + 4 = 25 \Rightarrow d + e + f + 12 + 4 = 25 \Rightarrow d + e + f = 9$ ... (ii)

Thus, the number of students who failed in exactly one subject $= 9$.

Hence, the correct answer is (C).

53. **Level of Difficulty:** Difficult

   Topic: Percents

   The correct answer is (C).

   Listed price of the television $= \$3000$.

   Discount based on the promotional offer $= \$(20\% \text{ of } 3000) = \$600$.

   Hence the selling price $= \$(3000 - 600) = \$2400$.

   If a customer pays in cash, he gets an additional discount of $\$(10\% \text{ of } 2400) = \$240$.

   However, if a customer pays using a credit card, he needs to pay an extra of $\$(2\% \text{ of } 2400) = \$48$.

   Hence, by choosing to pay in cash over a credit card, the customer saves $\$(48 - (-240)) = \$288$.

   Hence, the answer is (C).

54. **Level of Difficulty:** Easy

   The correct answer is (B).

   We have: $n^2 + n^3 = n^2(n + 1)$.

   Thus, in order that $(n^2 + n^3)$ be a perfect square, $(n + 1)$ must be a perfect square as well (since n^2 is already a perfect square).

   Thus, from the set P $= \{1,2,3,4 \dots 20\}$, we need to select those values of n such that $(n + 1)$ becomes a perfect square. This is possible only for $n = 3, 8$, and 15 (since $3 + 1 = 4$, $8 + 1 = 9$, and $15 + 1 = 16$, which are all perfect squares).

   Hence, we can select 3 such integers.

   Hence, the answer is (B).

55. **Level of Difficulty:** Easy

   Topic: Ratios, rates, and proportions

   The correct answer is 28.

   Let the initial number of green and red apples be $7k$ and $11k$ respectively.

   Again, let the final number of green and red apples be $9l$ and $17l$ respectively.

   Since an equal number of green and red apples are removed, the difference between the number of green and red apples should remain the same.

   Thus: $11k - 7k = 17l - 9l \Rightarrow 4k = 8l \Rightarrow k = 2l$.

   Thus, the initial number of green and red apples are $7k = 14l$ and $11k = 22l$ respectively.

   Thus, reduction in the number of green and red apples $= 14l - 9l = 5l$ and $22l - 17l = 5l$ respectively.

   Hence, we have $5l = 10 \Rightarrow l = 2$.

   Thus, the initial number of red apples $= 14l = 14 \times 2 = 28$.

Hence, the correct answer is 28.

56. **Level of Difficulty:** Easy

    Topic: Center, spread and shape of distributions

    The correct answer is (C).

    Since the average of seven integers is 8, their sum $= 7 \times 8 = 56$.

    Since we need to maximize one of the integers, we need to minimize the other six integers.

    The minimum possible value of a positive integer is 1.

    Since the integers are distinct and minimum in value, we choose the six integers to be 1, 2, 3, 4, 5 and 6.

    The sum of the above six integers $= 21$.

    Hence, the last number $= 56 - 21 = 35$.

    Thus, the greatest possible value of one of the seven integers is 35.

    Hence, the correct answer is (C).

57. **Level of Difficulty:** Medium

    Topic: Key features of graphs

    The correct answer is (C).

    We know that the equation of a quadratic when expressed in the form $y = a(x - k)^2 + l$, gives the coordinates of the vertex as (k, l).

    Thus, the possible answers are options B, C and D.

    From the graph, we can see that at $x = 0, y = 4$ and at $x = 1, y = 3$.

    Only option C satisfies the same.

    The correct answer is option C.

58. **Level of Difficulty:** Easy

    The correct answer is (C).

    Here, we have the square of a two-digit number as a three digit number such that the left-most digit remains unchanged.

    We know that this is possible only if the left-most digit is 1 (since square of any two-digit number starting with 2 will begin with 4: for example, $20^2 = 400, 21^2 = 441$, etc).

    Among the two-digit numbers starting with 1, we can rule out 11 since we know that A, B are distinct.

    Thus, possibilities of AB are $12, 13, 14$. We cannot use 15 since we know that $15^2 = 225$, i.e. the starting digit is not the same.

    We have: $12^2 = 144, 13^2 = 169, 14^2 = 196$.

    Thus, only $12^2 = 144$ satisfies the fact that the resulting square number should be of the form ACC i.e. last two digits should be same.

    Thus, $A = 1, B = 2, C = 4$.

    Thus, $A + B + C = 1 + 2 + 4 = 7$.

    Hence, the answer is (C).

59. **Level of Difficulty:** Difficult

    Topic: Ratios, rates, and proportions

The correct answer is 6.

Let us name the 20% concentration of nitric acid as A and the 30% concentration of nitric acid as B.

The idea is that in both cases the researcher had obtained the same concentration of acid.

This is only possible if he had mixed the two chemicals A and B in the same ratio in either container.

In the first container, the ratio of A and B = $x : 9$.

In the second container, the ratio of A and B = $4 : x$.

Thus, we have: $\frac{x}{9} = \frac{4}{x} => x^2 = 36 => x = 6$.

Hence, the answer is 6.

60. **Level of Difficulty:** Difficult

Topic: Percents

The correct answer is (C).

The cost of each garment = $120.

Hence, the list price of each garment = $(120 + 25\% \text{ of } 120) = \$150$.

Profit made by the store when it sells a garment at $150 is $(150 − 120) = \$30$.

Thus, discount offered on a garment = 10% of 150 = $15.

Thus, price after discount = $(150 − 15) = \$135$.

Profit made by the store when it sells a garment at $135 is $(135 − 120) = \$15$.

Thus, when a customer purchases three pieces of garments he pays $150 for the first and $135 for each of the remaining two pieces.

Hence, the profit made by the store = $(30 + 2 × 15) = \$60$.

Hence, the answer is (C).

61. **Level of Difficulty:** Easy

Topic: Center, spread and shape of distributions

The correct answer is 163.

Since 163 is the median value, there must be equal number of terms less than or more than 163.

We already have 97 and 125 less than 163. So, n must be more than or equal to 163.

Hence, the minimum value of n is 163.

Hence, the correct answer is 163.

62. **Level of Difficulty:** Medium

The correct answer is (C).

Let the number of students in the 9th grade be x.

Since when divided in groups of four or six, one student was left over, we can say that the number of students must be one more than a multiple of the LCM of 4 and 6 i.e. 12.

Thus, $x = 12k + 1$, where k is some positive integer.

Now, we know that x is divisible by 5.

Thus, the smallest value of x comes when we put $k = 2$ (by hit and trial, we can see that $k = 1$ does not satisfy, so we check with $k = 2$).

Thus, $x = 12 × 2 + 1 = 25$.

Hence, the minimum number of students in that grade was 25.

Hence, the answer is (C).

63. **Level of Difficulty:** Difficult

   Topic: Ratios, rates, and proportions

   The correct answer is (A).

   We can see that the total students in the 10th grade are classified in two ways:

   First, we have Boys : Girls = 3 : 5.

   Second, we have Literature : Science = 5 : 7.

   According to the first classification, the total comes to $3 + 5 = 8$ while according to the second, the total comes to $5 + 7 = 12$.

   Since the total in both cases should be the same, we assume the total to be the LCM of 8 and 12 i.e. 24 for our convenience.

   Thus, if the total number of students in the 10th grade is 24:

   Number of boys $= \dfrac{3}{3+5} \times 24 = 9$ and number of girls $= \dfrac{5}{3+5} \times 24 = 15$.

   Again, number of literature students $= \dfrac{5}{5+7} \times 24 = 10$ and number of science students $= \dfrac{7}{5+7} \times 24 = 14$.

   We also know that one-third the number of boys i.e. $\dfrac{1}{3} \times 9 = 3$ boys have taken up science.

   Thus, the remaining science students i.e. $14 - 3 = 11$ students must have been girls.

   Thus, the remaining girls i.e. $15 - 11 = 4$ girls must have taken up literature.

   Thus, the fraction of girls who had literature as their specialization $= \dfrac{4}{15}$.

   Hence, the answer is (A).

64. **Level of Difficulty:** Difficult

   Topic: Key features of graphs

   The correct answer is (C).

   The graph of the equation $y = ax^2 + bx + c$, is an upside-down parabola if $a < 0$

   Also, the Y intercept in the graph (the point where $x = 0$) is negative $=> c < 0$

   Since both roots are positive, the sum of the roots is also positive $=> -\dfrac{b}{a} > 0$

   $\dfrac{b}{a} < 0$

   Since $a < 0$, we have: $b > 0$

   The correct answer is option C.

65. **Level of Difficulty:** Difficult

   The correct answer is (D).

   The right most digit of a multiplication comes from the product of the right-most digits of the numbers being multiplied. Here, we see that $B \times A$ gives back A. This can happen in the following cases:

   (i) B is 1 and A is any digit

   (ii) A is 0 and B is any digit

(iii) B is 6 and A is any even number like 2, 4, 6, or 8

(iv) A is 5 and B is any odd number like 1, 3, 5, 7, or 9

However, we know that the digits are distinct, and their values are from 2 to 5.

Thus, the only possibility is $A = 5, B = 3$. Hence, C can only be either 2 or 4 (since all digits are distinct).

The right-most digit of a multiplication comes from the product of the right-most digits of the numbers being multiplied along with the carry, if any, from the previous steps.

Here, the right-most digit of AB is $A = 5$ and the right-most digit of CA is $C = 2$ or 4.

Since $A \times C$ (along with any carry) results in the number $1C$ i.e. a number in the tens, C must be 2 (if C were 4, then $A \times C = 5 \times 4 = 20$, i.e. we would have got a number in the twenties).

Thus, we have $A = 5, B = 3$, and $C = 2$.

Let us verify the multiplication:

$$
\begin{array}{r}
5\ 3 \\
\times\ 2\ 5 \\
\hline
1\ 3\ 2\ 5 \\
\hline
\end{array}
$$

Thus, the multiplication is correct. Thus, $A + B + C = 5 + 3 + 2 = 10$.

Hence, the answer is (D).

66. **Level of Difficulty:** Difficult

Topic: Data inferences

The correct answer is (D).

PS: When counting the number of dogs, it has to be kept in mind that the families keeping dogs of two different breeds would have two dogs each and the families keeping dogs of three different breeds would have three dogs each.

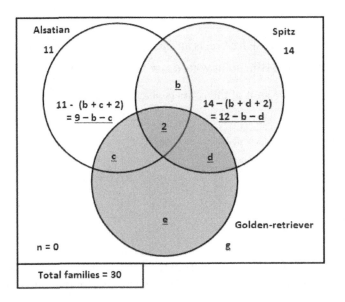

We have: $b + c + d = 10$

Also, the union of the three sets is 30. Thus, the sum of the values in all the regions adds up to 30:

$(9 - b - c) + (12 - b - d) + (e) + b + c + d + 2 = 30$

$11 + (12 - b - d) + d + e = 30 => e = b + 7$

Again: $g = c + d + e + 2 = c + d + (b + 7) + 2 = b + c + d + 7 + 2 = 10 + 9 = 19$.

Thus, the number of dogs = $\{9 - b - c\} + \{12 - b - d\} + e + 2[b + c + d] + 3 \times 2$

$= 27 + e + 2b + 2c + 2d - 2b - c - d = 27 + c + d + e = 27 + c + d + (b + 7) = 34 + b + c + d$

$= 34 + 10 = 44$.

Alternatively, the number of dogs can simply be calculated by just adding the values of the number of families having Alsatian, Spitz and Golden-retriever = $11 + 14 + g = 11 + 14 + 19 = 44$.

This is so because the families having two categories of dogs are added twice and the families having three categories of dogs are added thrice in the above sum.

Hence, the correct answer is (D).

67. **Level of Difficulty:** Easy

Topic: Ratios, rates, and proportions

The correct answer is (D).

The ratio of number of one-dollar coins to quarters to dimes with John = $3 : 8 : 10$.

Thus, let the number of one-dollar coins, quarters and dimes with John be $3k, 8k$, and $10k$ respectively, where k is some constant.

Let us calculate the total amount with John in dollars.

Thus: $3k$ one-dollar coins amount to $\$3k$.

$8k$ quarters amount to $\$\dfrac{8k}{4} = \$2k$.

$10k$ dimes amount to $\$\dfrac{10k}{10} = \$k$.

Thus, total amount with John = $\$(3k + 2k + k) = \$6k$.

Hence, we have: $6k = 210 => k = 35$.

Thus, the number of quarters with him = $8k = 8 \times 35 = 280$.

Hence, the answer is (D).

68. **Level of Difficulty:** Easy

The correct answer is (C).

We know that each gift set is identical.

Thus, the maximum number of children among whom the gifts could be distributed would be the HCF of 96 and 72 i.e. 24.

Thus, each gift set should have $\dfrac{96}{24} = 4$ pens and $\dfrac{72}{24} = 3$ pencils i.e. a total of $4 + 3 = 7$ items.

Hence, the answer is (C).

69. **Level of Difficulty:** Medium

Topic: Percents

The correct answer is 72.

Let the number of candidates who appeared for the TAS be 100 and the number of candidates who appeared for the TCA be 50 (since half the number of candidates appeared in the TCA as compared to the TAS).

Thus, number of candidates selected in the TAS = 15% of 100 = 15, and the number of candidates selected in the TCA = 20% of 50 = 10.

Thus, total number of candidates who were selected = 15 + 10 = 25.

However, we know that these 25 are actually equal to 18000.

We need to find the actual number of students who appeared in TAS i.e. the actual number of students corresponding to 100.

Since $25 \equiv 18000$, we have $100 \equiv \dfrac{18000}{25} \times 100 = 72000$ i.e. 72 thousands.

Hence, the answer is 72.

70. **Level of Difficulty:** Difficult

Topic: Ratios, rates, and proportions

The correct answer is (D).

Here, the relation between four integers, w, x, y, z is given.

Since $2w = \dfrac{3}{2}x = y = \dfrac{5}{3}z$, let us assume that all of these are equal to k.

Thus, $w = \dfrac{k}{2}, x = \dfrac{2k}{3}, y = k, z = \dfrac{3k}{5}$.

So, the ratio $w : x : y : z = \dfrac{k}{2} : \dfrac{2k}{3} : k : \dfrac{3k}{5} = \dfrac{1}{2} : \dfrac{2}{3} : 1 : \dfrac{3}{5}$.

To make the ratio as integers, we multiply it with the LCM of the denominators i.e. $2, 3, 5 = 30$.

Thus, the ratio $w : x : y : z = \dfrac{30}{2} : \dfrac{60}{3} : 30 : \dfrac{90}{5} = 15 : 20 : 30 : 18$.

Thus, from the ratio, we have: $w = 15m, x = 20m, y = 30m, z = 18m$ where m is some constant.

Now, we need to substitute the values of w, x, y, z in the options to check which option can result in an integer.

Option (A): $\dfrac{wx}{yz} = \dfrac{(15m)(20m)}{(30m)(18m)} = \dfrac{5}{9}$. This is not an integer.

Option (B): $\dfrac{x}{w} = \dfrac{20m}{15m} = \dfrac{4}{3}$. This is not an integer.

Option (C): $\dfrac{4x}{y} = \dfrac{4(20m)}{30m} = \dfrac{8}{3}$. This is not an integer.

Hence, option (D) must be the one which can be an integer. In fact, $\dfrac{x^2}{y} = \dfrac{(20m)^2}{30m} = \dfrac{40m}{3}$. This can become an integer if we choose m as a multiple of 3.

Hence, the answer is (D).

71. **Level of Difficulty:** Medium

Topic: Data inferences

The correct answer is (D).

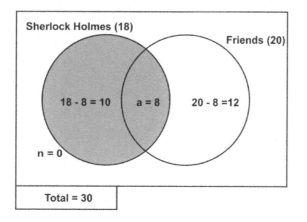

We have: $30 = 18 + 20 - a => a = 8$

Thus, 8 people liked both shows.

Also, 10 people preferred Sherlock Holmes over Friends and 12 people preferred Friends over Sherlock Holmes.

Thus, $10 + 12 = 22$ people preferred one show over the other.

Also, 22 people liked only one show.

Thus, statements I and II are correct.

Hence, the correct answer is (D).

72. **Level of Difficulty:** Medium

The correct answer is (B).

The first few terms are shown below:

$t_1 = 1$

$t_2 = 1 + 3 = 4$

$t_3 = 4 \times (-1) = -4$

$t_4 = -4 + 3 = -1$

$t_5 = -1 \times (-1) = 1$

$t_6 = 1 + 3 = 4$

$t_7 = 4 \times (-1) = -4$

$t_8 = -4 + 3 = -1$

Thus, we see that the same four terms $1, 4, -4$, and -1 keep repeating.

The sum of the above four terms is $1 + 4 + (-4) + (-1) = 0$.

Since for every four terms the sum becomes zero, the sum of the first 32 terms (32 is a multiple of 4) is also zero.

Hence, the correct answer is (B).

73. **Level of Difficulty:** Easy

Topic: Data inferences

The correct answer is 50.

The different regions are shown in the Venn diagram below:

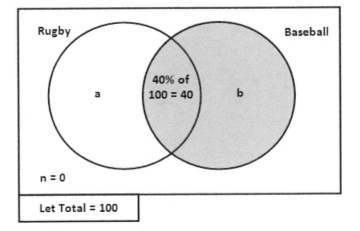

Since all students play at least one of the two games rugby and baseball, we have $n = 0$.

We know that 20% of the students who play baseball do not play rugby.

Thus: $\frac{20}{100} \times (40 + b) = b => 8 + \frac{b}{5} = b => b = 10$.

Thus, total number of students who play baseball $= 10 + 40 = 50$.

Thus, percentage of students who play baseball $= \frac{50}{100} \times 100 = 50\%$.

Hence, the correct answer is 50.

74. **Level of Difficulty:** Medium

   Topic: Ratios, rates, and proportions

   The correct answer is (C).

   We can use the concept of addendo which states:

   If $\frac{x}{y} = \frac{p}{q} = m$, then m also equals $\frac{x+p}{y+q}$.

   Thus, we have: $\frac{a}{7} = \frac{3a}{3 \times 7} = \frac{3a}{21}$ and $\frac{2b}{5} = \frac{2b \times (-2)}{5 \times (-2)} = \frac{-4b}{-10}$.

   Since multiplying the same number in both numerator and denominator does not alter the value of the fraction, we have:

   $\frac{3a}{21} = \frac{-4b}{-10} = \frac{3a-4b}{21-10} = \frac{3a-4b}{11}$ (using the concept of addendo).

   Hence, we have $k = 11$.

   Alternative: Let $\frac{a}{7} = \frac{2b}{5} = \frac{3a-4b}{k} = r => a = 7r, 2b = 5r, 3a - 4b = kr$.

   Substituting values of a and $2b$ in $3a - 4b = kr$, we get:

   $3(7r) - 2(5r) = kr => 11r = kr => k = 11$.

   Hence, the answer is (C).

75. **Level of Difficulty:** Difficult

   Topic: Data collection and conclusions

   The correct answer is (B).

   Number of households in 'no children' category $= 35\%$ of 120 million $= 42$ million

Thus, 20% of the households in 'no children' category = 20% of 42 million = 8.4 million

The ratio of households going in for 1, 2, and 3 children = 4 : 2 : 1

Thus, the number of additional households with 2 children

$$= \frac{2}{4+2+1} * 8.4 \text{ million} = 2.4 \text{ million}$$

Thus, total number of households with 2 children

= 20% of 120 million + 2.4 million = 26.4 million

Thus, the share of households having 2 children $= \frac{26.4}{120} \times 100 = 22\%$

76. **Level of Difficulty:** Difficult

Topic: Data collection and conclusions

The correct answer is (B).

Continuing from the previous problem:

Number of additional households with 1 children $= \frac{4}{4+2+1} \times 8.4 \text{ million} = 4.8 \text{ million}$

Thus, number of additional children born = 4.8 million.

Number of additional households with 2 children $= \frac{2}{4+2+1} \times 8.4 \text{ million} = 2.4 \text{ million}$

Thus, number of additional children born = 2 × 2.4 million = 4.8 million.

Number of additional households with 3 children $= \frac{1}{4+2+1} \times 8.4 \text{ million} = 1.2 \text{ million}$

Thus, number of additional children born = 3 × 1.2 $million$ = 3.6 $million$.

Thus, total number of additional children born = (4.8 + 4.8 + 3.6) million = 13.2 million

77. **Level of Difficulty:** Difficult

Topic: Data collection and conclusions

The correct answer is (A).

Percent increase in the number of households from 2000 to 2014

$$= \frac{145-120}{120} \times 100 = 20.83\%$$

This percent change happened over a period of 14 years.

Thus, the average annual percent increase in the number of households

$$= \frac{20.83}{14} \% = 1.49\% \approx 1.5\%$$

78. **Level of Difficulty:** Difficult

Topic: Data collection and conclusions

The correct answer is (C).

Total number of households in 2014 = 145 million

Number of households with 1 child = 22% of 145 million = 31.9 million

Thus, number of children = 31.9 million

Number of households with 2 children = 18% of 145 million = 26.1 million

Thus, number of children = 2 × 26.1 million = 52.2 million

Number of households with 3 children = 20% of 145 million = 29 million

Thus, number of children = 3 × 29 million = 87 million

Thus, total children = (31.9 + 52.2 + 87) million = 171.1 million

79. **Level of Difficulty:** Easy

The correct answer is (D).

When P is multiplied by 9, the resulting number becomes a multiple of 9.

Hence, from the divisibility rule for 9, we can say that the sum of the digits of the product should be divisible by 9.

We know that the product is a number consisting of 5 followed by some 7's.

Let the number of 7's be x.

Thus, the sum of the digits of the product = $5 + 7x$.

This would be a multiple of 9 when x takes the value of 7 (we obtain the value by trial and error, starting with x as 1. When we have $x = 7$, the total becomes $5 + 7 \times 7 = 54$, which is divisible by 9).

Thus, the minimum number of 7's is 7 and this corresponds to the minimum value of P as well.

Hence, the answer is (D).

80. **Level of Difficulty:** Medium

Topic: Linear and exponential growth

The correct answer is 5.

Plugging in the values from the table in the equation, we have:

$24 = kn^3$ ... (i)

$48 = kn^4$ ... (ii)

Dividing: $n = 2$

Substituting: $k = \dfrac{24}{2^3} = 3$

$k + n = 5$

Chapter 3

Heart of Algebra

---

1 The use of calculator is **not permitted**.

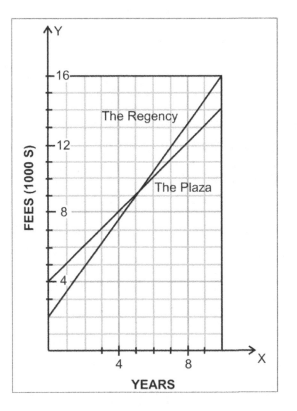

The membership plans of two health clubs, The Plaza and The Regency for ten years are shown in the graph below (membership fees are in thousand dollars). For the initial registration, each club requires an upfront payment of registration fees and every year thereafter one needs to pay a fixed annual membership fee. What is the difference between the annual charges of the two clubs (in dollars)?

(A) $0

(B) $200

(C) $400

(D) $1400

A B C D
O O O O

---

2 The use of calculator is **not permitted**.

$f(x) = x^2 + px + q$. If $p = 2q$ and the function has a value of 16 at $x = 3$, what is the value of p?

---

3 The use of calculator is **permitted**.

The average of the temperatures recorded by the National Climatic Centre in New York in a particular week for Monday, Tuesday, Wednesday and Thursday was 60°F. The average for Tuesday, Wednesday, Thursday and Friday in the same week was 55°F. If the ratio of the temperatures for Monday and Friday was 13 : 9, what was the temperature on Monday?

(A) 45 °F

(B) 55 °F

(C) 60 °F

(D) 65 °F

A B C D
O O O O

4   The use of calculator is **not permitted**.

abcd is a four-digit number. If $a + b = c + d$, $a + c = 2(b + d)$ and $a + b + c + d = 24$, how many such numbers are possible if the digits a, b, c, d are all distinct?

(A) 9

(B) 8

(C) 7

(D) 2

A   B   C   D
○   ○   ○   ○

5   The use of calculator is **not permitted**.

N is a two-digit number having sum of digits as S and product of digits as P. How many such two-digit numbers exist such that $2N = 2S + 3P$?

(A) 0

(B) 1

(C) 9

(D) 12

A   B   C   D
○   ○   ○   ○

6   The use of calculator is **not permitted**.

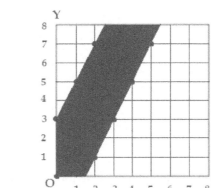

A part of the graph shown beside has been shaded. The lines which form the boundary are the two axes and two lines (the integer coordinates through which the lines pass are shown by dots). Which of the following options correctly depicts the shaded region?

(A) $|y - 2x| = 5$

(B) $|y - 2x| > 3$

(C) $|y - x| < 2$

(D) $|y - 2x| \leq 3$

A   B   C   D
○   ○   ○   ○

7 The use of calculator is **permitted**.

Abe reads a book every day, some pages in the morning and some in the evening. He reads 23 pages every morning and 31 pages every evening. The number of pages, N, completed by Abe after some number of days can be written as a function of the number of mornings, M, and the number evenings, E. Which of the following will be the number of pages read by Abe just after 11 mornings have passed?

56.3

8 The use of calculator is **permitted**.

Twelve friends raised some funds among themselves for a dinner party. Ten of them contributed $80 each while the other two subscribed $80 and $120 more than the average of all twelve friends. What was the average contribution of all the friends taken together?

(A) $220

(B) $180

(C) $100

(D) $80

A   B   C   D
O   O   O   O

9 The use of calculator is **permitted**.

The profit of a company is determined by the following equation: $P = 50.2 \times N - 236.8$, where 'P' represents the profit of the company and 'N' represents number of units manufactured by the company. What is the minimum number of units produced so as to have no loss incurred?

(A) Minimum number of units manufactured is 3

(B) Minimum number of units manufactured is 4

(C) Minimum number of units manufactured is 5

(D) Minimum number of units manufactured is 6

A   B   C   D
O   O   O   O

10 The use of calculator is **permitted**.

M is a point on AB extended such that 3. AM = 7. BM. The co-ordinates of A and M are (3, 0) and (– 4, 7) respectively. What are the co-ordinates of B?

(A) (1, 3)

(B) (0, 3)

(C) (0, 5)

(D) (– 1, 4)

A   B   C   D
○   ○   ○   ○

11 The use of calculator is **not permitted**.

Adam bought 23 pencils, 15 erasers and 20 sharpeners from a stationery shop and spent a total of $111. Bob bought 12 erasers, 4 pencils and 7 sharpeners from the same stationery shop and spent $51. What is the price of 1 pencil, 1 eraser and 1 sharpener, respectively?

(A) $4, $2, $1

(B) $5, $1, $2

(C) $2, $5, $2

(D) $2, $3, $1

A   B   C   D
○   ○   ○   ○

12 The use of calculator is **permitted**.

If $3a - 7b = 5c + 9$ and $5a + 2b + 4 = 7c$, what is the value of $(a - b)$ in terms of c?

(A) $\dfrac{55c - 67}{41}$

(B) $\dfrac{43c + 67}{41}$

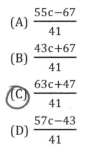 (C) $\dfrac{63c + 47}{41}$

(D) $\dfrac{57c - 43}{41}$

A   B   C   D
○   ○   ○   ○

13 The use of calculator is **not permitted**.

If $a + 2b + 3c = 24$ and $3a + 2b + c = 36$, what is the value of $(a + b + c)$?

(A) 8

(B) 12

(C) 15

(D) 60

14 The use of calculator is **permitted**.

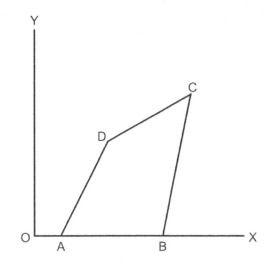

The coordinates of A, B, C and D as shown in the figure are $(2, 0)$, $(9, 0)$, $(11, p)$ and $(q, 6)$ respectively. If the slope of lines AD and CD are 2 and 0.5 respectively, what is the length of BC?

(A) $3\sqrt{10}$

(B) $\sqrt{85}$

(C) $4\sqrt{5}$

(D) $2\sqrt{13}$

15 The use of calculator is **permitted**.

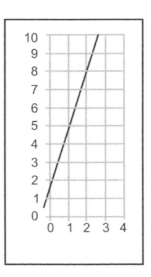

The graph above depicts a straight line. Which of the following options could be the correct equation of the line shown?

(A) $y = x - 1$

(B) $y = 2x + 1$

(C) $y = \frac{15}{4}x + 1$

(D) $y = 4 + 1$

A   B   C   D
○   ○   ○   ○

16 The use of calculator is **not permitted**.

A man earns $40 per hour as a consultant. Additionally, he also earns $6 per hour as a content writer. He is only allowed to work 15 hours per week, but wants to make $450 per week. If n represents the integer number of hours he works as a consultant, what is the least integer value of n?

17   The use of calculator is **not permitted**.

Joseph, the primary school teacher of Illinois Public School, distributed some sweets among the students of his class on his birthday. After distributing three sweets to every student, he found some sweets were still left over with him. He doubled the number of sweets with each student and found that he still had M sweets left over. However, instead of doubling, had he given only one sweet extra to every student, he would have been left with N sweets ($N > M$). How many students are there in his class?

(A) $6S + M$

(B) $4S + N$

(C) $N - M$

(D) $\dfrac{N-M}{2}$

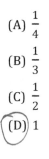

A	B	C	D
○	○	○	○

18   The use of calculator is **permitted**.

The demand of a particular product decreases as the price goes up. A company researched that when the product price is $45, the demand for the product is 1000. For every $5 increase in the price of the product, the demand falls by 15. What will be the demand for the product when the price is set at $80?

(A) 890

(B) 895

(C) 985

(D) 995

A	B	C	D
○	○	○	○

19   The use of calculator is **permitted**.

In a game of marbles between Ron and Jacob, at one-point Ron gave Jacob one-third of his marbles to Jacob and Jacob returned one-fourth of his total of marbles to Ron. It was found that the initial ratio of the number of marbles with Ron and Jacob remained the same after this exchange. What is the ratio of the number of marbles with Ron and Jacob?

(A) $\dfrac{1}{4}$

(B) $\dfrac{1}{3}$

(C) $\dfrac{1}{2}$

(D) 1

A	B	C	D
○	○	○	○

20   The use of calculator is **not permitted**.

In a fraction $\dfrac{x}{y}$ which is reduced to its lowest form where x and y are positive integers, if two is subtracted from numerator and three is added to the denominator, the fraction becomes $\dfrac{3}{5}$. What is the largest possible value of the original fraction?

$$\frac{5}{2}$$

21   The use of calculator is **not permitted**.

In a factory, the number of units manufactured in a month follows the linear function $N = 231D$, where N is the number of units produced in the month and D is the number of days elapsed in the month. Which of the following represents 231 in the above equation?

(A) The number of units manufactured only in the first day

(B) The number of workers working in the factory

(C) The number of units manufactured each day of the month

(D) The increase in the number of workers in the factory per day

A   B   C   D

22   The use of calculator is **permitted**.

If $2a + 3b - c = a + 2b + c = 3a - b - c$, then what is the ratio of $a : b : c$?

(A) $4 : 1 : 5$

(B) $8 : 2 : 5$

(C) $4 : 2 : 1$

(D) $8 : 2 : 1$

A   B   C   D

23 The use of calculator is **not permitted**.

The average of thrice the cube of a number and twice the square of the same number equals eight times the same number. Given that the number is a positive integer, what is the number?

24 The use of calculator is **permitted**.

Fences are to be placed at gaps of 2 feet to cover a length of l meters. If the width of each stick used to make the fence is 1.5 inches, which of the following is the correct expression for the number of sticks to be used to make the fence? ($1\ foot = 12\ inches$)

(A) $\dfrac{8l}{17}$

(B) $\dfrac{2l}{7}$

(C) $\dfrac{8(l+2)}{17}$

(D) $\dfrac{2(l+2)}{7}$

25 The use of calculator is **not permitted**.

How many integer values of x satisfy $5 + 2|2x - 3| < 19$?

(A) 8

(B) 6

(C) 4

(D) 3

26 The use of calculator is **permitted**.

Which of the following figures is generated using the four points $(1, 3), (1, 9), (1 + 3\sqrt{3}, 12)$ *and* $(1 + 3\sqrt{3}, 6)$ taken in the order as mentioned?

(A) Rectangle

(B) Rhombus

(C) Square

(D) Trapezium

A	B	C	D
○	○	○	○

27 The use of calculator is **not permitted**.

The minimum possible ratio of a two-digit number and the sum of its digits is __

(A) 1.0

(B) 1.9

(C) 2.5

(D) 5.5

A	B	C	D
○	○	○	○

28 The use of calculator is **permitted**.

The entry fee of an amusement park is $10. Each ride in the park costs $2.50. If Chad has $25 with him, what is the maximum number of rides he can get on?

(A) 6

(B) 8

(C) 9

(D) 10

A	B	C	D
○	○	○	○

29 The use of calculator is **permitted**.

If $a + b + c + d = 24, a + b = c + d, a + c = 2(b + d)$ and $a = b$, what is the value of c?

(A) 2

(B) 6

(C) 8

(D) 10

A	B	C	D
○	○	○	○

30   The use of calculator is **permitted**.

The reduction in speed, r, in miles per hour, of an engine having n bogies attached to it is given as: $r = 4\sqrt{n}$. The final speed, s, in miles per hour, at which the engine can pull the n bogies attached is given as: $s = 40 - r$. What is the speed of the train, to the nearest tenths, in miles per hour, when there are 15 bogies attached?

24.5

31   The use of calculator is **not permitted**.

Four friends, Ann, Bob, Charlie and David together have $200. The amount with Charlie is twice of that with Bob. The amount with Ann and Bob together is $40 less than the amount with David. Charlie has $30 less than what David has. What is the amount with Ann?

(A) $20

(B) $30

(C) $40

(D) $60

A   B   C   D
O   O   O   O

32   The use of calculator is **permitted**.

The distance, d, in feet, covered by a ball in the nth second after being dropped from the top of a building is given by $d = 6n + 1$. What is the total distance, in feet, covered by the ball in the first 5 seconds?

(A) 27

(B) 31

(C) 65

(D) 95

A   B   C   D
O   O   O   O

33 The use of calculator is **permitted**.

The relation between the temperature readings of the Celsius (C) and Fahrenheit (F) scales is given by:
$F = \frac{9}{5}C + 32$. If the temperature in Fahrenheit increases by 36 degrees, what is the corresponding increase in the Celsius scale?

(A) 12^0

(B) 20^0

(C) 32^0

(D) 52^0

A	B	C	D
○	○	○	○

34 The use of calculator is **permitted**.

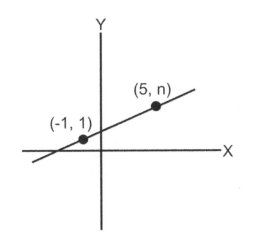

The graph above depicts a straight line passing through $(-1, 1)$ and $(5, n)$. What is the least integer value of n if the slope is greater than $\frac{2}{3}$?

6

	/	○	○	
	.	○	○	○	○
0	○	○	○	○
1	○	○	○	○
2	○	○	○	○
3	○	○	○	○
4	○	○	○	○
5	○	○	○	○
6	○	○	○	○
7	○	○	○	○
8	○	○	○	○
9	○	○	○	○

35 The use of calculator is **permitted**.

The cost of 3 chocolates, 2 candies and 1 bubblegum is \$14. If the cost of 1 chocolate, 3 candies and 5 bubblegum is \$14, what is the cost of 1 chocolate, 1 candy and 1 bubblegum?

(A) \$3

(B) \$6

(C) \$8

(D) \$9

A   B   C   D
○   ○   ○   ○

36 The use of calculator is **permitted**.

N is a point on PQ extended such that 3. PN = 7. QN. The co-ordinates of P and Q are (6, 0) and (− 2, 8) respectively. What are the co-ordinates of N?

(A) (3, 6)

(B) (9, 6)

(C) (− 8, 14)

(D) (8, − 14)

A   B   C   D
○   ○   ○   ○

37 The use of calculator is **not permitted**.

If $a + 5b + 9c = 24$ and $5a + 3b + c = 10$, what is the value of $(a + b + c)$?

(A) 3

(B) 4

(C) 5

(D) 6

A   B   C   D
○   ○   ○   ○

38 The use of calculator is **permitted**.

The average score of S students of a class in a Physics test was $2S$. If the lowest three scores were excluded, the average score of the class would have increased by three. Which of the following gives the correct expression of the average score of the five students?

(A) S − 3

(B) S + 3

(C) 2S − 3

(D) 2S + 3

A   B   C   D
○   ○   ○   ○

39   The use of calculator is **not permitted**.

What is the minimum value of the expression $|x + 3| + |x - 1|$?

4

40   The use of calculator is **not permitted**.

For how many positive integer values of n will $(n^2 + 5n + 12)$ be divisible by $(n + 5)$?

(A) 1

(B) 2

(C) 3

(D) 5

41   The use of calculator is **not permitted**.

The sum of a two-digit number and twice its reverse is 150. Given that the reverse of the original number is also another two-digit number, what is the maximum value of the sum of digits of the number?

(A) 3

(B) 6

(C) 8

(D) 11

42   The use of calculator is **permitted**.

The waiting time, t, in minutes, for the nth person in a queue, is given by the relation: $t = 12.5n - 15$. If each person takes 10 minutes to be serviced, what is the time gap, in minutes, between when the service for a person is completed and the service for the next person begins?

(A) 1.5

(B) 2.5

(C) 3

(D) 4

43 The use of calculator is **permitted**.

A man covers a distance of d miles at a speed of s miles per hour and another distance, D at $3s$ miles per hour. If $D > 2d$, and the man makes the entire journey within 2 hours, and $d < ks$, what is the value of k?

44 The use of calculator is **not permitted**.

Joe distributed some pens among the other students of his class. The number of students among whom he distributed pens was 3 more than the number of pens each got. If the total number of pens distributed is less than 21, which of the following is the correct inequality for the total number of students, s, in the class?

(A) $s^2 - 5s - 16 < 0$

(B) $s^2 + s - 23 < 0$

(C) $s^2 - 5s - 17 < 0$

(D) $s^2 - 3s - 21 < 0$

45 The use of calculator is **permitted**.

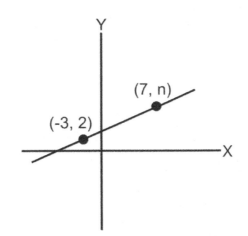

The graph above depicts a straight line passing through $(-3, 2)$ and $(7, n)$. If the Y-intercept of the line is given by k, which of the following is the correct expression of k in terms of n?

(A) $k = 2$

(B) $k = 0.3n - 0.6$

(C) $k = 0.3n + 1.4$

(D) $k = 0.1n + 1.8$

A	B	C	D
O	O	O	O

46 The use of calculator is **permitted**.

Chad decides to save at least \$105 over a period of 15 days. Initially, for the first n days, he saves \$3 every day; for the next $2n$ days, he saves 75 cents more per day than what he was saving initially. If, for the remaining days, he saves \$s per day, which of the following gives the correct relation between n and s?

(A) $s > 3.5 \left(\frac{10 - n}{5 - n} \right)$

(B) $s \geq 3.5 \left(\frac{10 - n}{5 - n} \right)$

(C) $s \leq 3.5 \left(\frac{10 - n}{5 - n} \right)$

(D) $s < 3.5 \left(\frac{10 - n}{5 - n} \right)$

A	B	C	D
O	O	O	O

47 The use of calculator is **permitted**.

A square garden is to be fenced using wooden posts five inches wide. These posts are to be placed at a gap of one foot (one foot is twelve inches). If there are 50 wooden posts available and the fences on each side of the garden begin and end with a wooden post, what could be the maximum length (in inches) of a side of the garden?

48 The use of calculator is **not permitted**.

Jacob was asked to add two numbers M and N, each having two digits such that M is ten more than N. However, Jacob ended up adding the numbers obtained by reversing the digits of M and N (which were also two-digit numbers). If the total he actually obtained is nine less than the total he was supposed to get, what is the maximum value of the sum of digits of N?

(A) 18

(B) 16

(C) 15

(D) 9

A	B	C	D
○	○	○	○

49 The use of calculator is **not permitted**.

On his birthday, Joseph bought some lozenges to distribute among his N friends. He tried giving x lozenges to each friend but had 7 lozenges left over. Had he tried giving one more lozenge to each friend, three of his friends would have been left without any lozenges; however, no lozenges would be left over. Which of the following is the correct relation between N and x?

(A) $N = 3x + 10$

(B) $N = 3x + 7$

(C) $N = x + 10$

(D) $N = x + 7$

A	B	C	D
○	○	○	○

50 The use of calculator is **not permitted**.

abcd is a four-digit number such that $a + b + c = d$ and $a + c = 5b$. What is the value of $a + b + c + d$?

51 The use of calculator is **not permitted**.

What is the sum of all the possible values of x if $|x - 1| + |x - 7| = 10$?

(A) 0

(B) 3

(C) 6

(D) 8

A   B   C   D

52 The use of calculator is **permitted**.

Harry got $350 as his salary. He puts $M in his savings account, and then spends the rest of the money on buying presents for his family members. If Harry has 8 family members and he spends $A amount on each member, which of the following equations represents the amount Harry spends on each member?

(A) $(45 - M)$

(B) $(350 - 0.125M)$

(C) $(43.75 - M)$

(D) $(43.75 - 0.125M)$

A   B   C   D

53 The use of calculator is **permitted**.

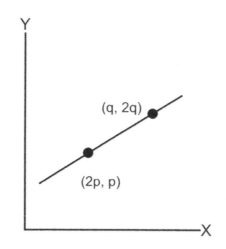

The graph above depicts a straight line. If $q > 2p$, which of the following options could be the slope of the line shown?

(A) $\dfrac{1}{2}$

(B) 1

(C) 2

(D) $\dfrac{7}{2}$

A B C D
O O O O

54 The use of calculator is **not permitted**.

The IKEA Store made a special promotion where the price of a set of 7 chairs and 13 tables would cost $1060, while the price of 13 chairs and 7 tables would be $940. If all chairs and tables are identical, what is the combined cost of two chairs and one table?

(A) $40

(B) $60

(C) $100

(D) $140

A B C D
O O O O

55 The use of calculator is **permitted**.

Amy completes a work in t days and with Bob, Amy takes n days for the same work. If, Bob can complete twice the same work inside of 16 days, which of the following gives the correct relation between t and n?

(A) $n < \frac{8t}{8+t}$

(B) $n < \frac{8+t}{8t}$

(C) $n > \frac{t}{8t+1}$

(D) $n > \frac{t}{8+t}$

A   B   C   D
○   ○   ○   ○

56 The use of calculator is **permitted**.

A, B, C and D are four distinct positive integers lying between 1 and 5, both inclusive; such that C + D = A and D − C = B. What is the maximum possible value of (A + B + C + D) if none of the numbers is 4?

57 The use of calculator is **not permitted**.

With $30 in his pocket, Ron wanted to buy some chocolates priced at $3 per piece and some pencils priced at $4 per piece. What is the different number of ways in which he can purchase the items if he must buy at least one chocolate and one pencil and he must spend the entire amount he has?

(A) 1

(B) 2

(C) 3

(D) 4

A   B   C   D
○   ○   ○   ○

58   The use of calculator is **permitted**.

A grid is made up of 13 rows of squares, each having 14 identical squares. Bob comes and wants to draw some more squares to the grid. So, he draws 3 additional rows and adds 'S' additional squares in each row, including the ones he added himself. Which of the following expression correctly represents the increase in the total number of squares in the grid?

(A) $11 + 5n$

(B) $42 + 16n$

(C) $60 + 12n$

(D) $224 + 16n$

A   B   C   D
○   ○   ○   ○

59   The use of calculator is **not permitted**.

A man buys a apples and g oranges, each costing 80 cents and 60 cents respectively. If the man buys less than 18 fruits and spends less than $12, which of the following is the correct inequality representing the above information?

(A) $a + g = 18$

    $4a + 3g = 60$

(B) $a + g < 18$

    $4a + 3g < 60$

(C) $a + g \leq 18$

    $4a + 3g \leq 60$

(D) $a + g \leq 18$

    $4a + 3g = 60$

A   B   C   D
○   ○   ○   ○

60   The use of calculator is **permitted**.

A class of 50 students belonging to the Kindergarten is divided in two sections A and B, having students in the ratio 2: 3 respectively. The average weight of the students of the entire class is 40 lbs. The average weight of the students of section A is 2 lbs. less than that of the students of section B. What is the average weight of the students of section B?

(A) 32.6 lbs.

(B) 36.4 lbs.

(C) 38.8 lbs.

(D) 40.8 lbs.

A   B   C   D
○   ○   ○   ○

61 The use of calculator is **permitted**.

The reduction in speed, r, in miles per hour, of an engine having n bogies attached to it is given as: $r = 4\sqrt{n}$.
The final speed, s, in miles per hour, at which the engine can pull the n bogies attached is given as: $s = 40 - r$.
What is the maximum number of bogies that the engine can pull?

62 The use of calculator is **permitted**.

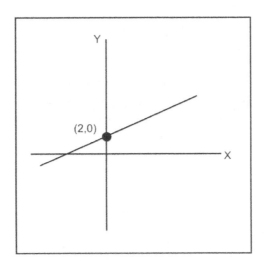

The graph above depicts a straight line having the equation $y = mx + n$. What can be said about the line given by the equation $y = nx + m$?

(A) The line passes through the 1st, 2nd and 3rd quadrants

(B) The line passes through the 1st, 2nd and 4th quadrants

(C) The line passes through the 1st, 3rd and 4th quadrants

(D) The line passes through the 2nd, 3rd and 4th quadrants

A   B   C   D
○   ○   ○   ○

63 The use of calculator is **permitted**.

To complete a particular task Dave charged $50 for the first 3 hours and thereafter $10 per hour. If '$A$' represents the amount that Dave receives after working for 'H' hours, which of the following expresses the amount he earns after working for 'H' hours, where $H > 3$?

(A) A = 10H

(B) A = 10H + 10

(C) A = 10H + 20

(D) A = 10H + 50

A   B   C   D
O   O   O   O

64 The use of calculator is **not permitted**.

If $x^2 - 4x - 32 > 0$ and $|x - 2| < 7$, how many integer solutions of x exist?

(A) 0

(B) 9

(C) 13

(D) 15

A   B   C   D
O   O   O   O

65 The use of calculator is **permitted**.

Harry got $350 as his salary. He puts $\left(\frac{1}{n}\right)^{th}$ of his salary in his savings account, and then spends the rest of the money on buying presents for his family members. If Harry has 8 family members and he spends an amount, the same as what he saved, equally on each member, what is the value of n?

(A) 6

(B) 8

(C) 9

(D) 12

A   B   C   D
O   O   O   O

66 The use of calculator is **permitted**.

In an exam, 3.5 points are awarded for every correct answer and 0.45 points are deducted for every wrong answer. If out of N questions, a boy answers at least 4 questions wrong and at most 8 questions wrong, which of the following correctly gives the correct range of scores, S, he can get in the exam?

(A) $3.5N - 31.6 \leq S \leq 3.5N - 15.8$

(B) $3.5N - 31.6 \leq S \leq 3.5N$

(C) $15.8 \leq S \leq 3.5N - 31.6$

(D) $3.5N \leq S \leq 31.6$

A   B   C   D
O   O   O   O

67 The use of calculator is **not permitted**.

Given that the system of equations $3x + ky = 1$ and $6x + 3y = 2$. For what value of k does this system have infinite solutions?

68 The use of calculator is **permitted**.

During the NBA playoffs, Chicago Bulls, last year's basketball champion, scored 88 points in their fifth game of the season. As a result, their average points increased by an integer value from what it initially was in that season. Which of the following could have been their initial average points i.e. average of the points scored in the initial four games in the season?

(A) 67

(B) 78

(C) 91

(D) 93

69 The use of calculator is **not permitted**.

In the TAS aptitude test, three marks are awarded for a correct response and one mark is deducted for an incorrect response. John took the test and secured 76 marks. If there are 40 questions in the test and John attempted all questions, how many of his responses were incorrect?

70 The use of calculator is **not permitted**.

Fred visits a car showroom. Being concerned about safety, he wanted cars with automatic braking system (ABS) or adaptive cruise control (ACC). Among the cars he checked, six did not have ABS and seven did not have ACC. Also, nine cars had one of the safety features and none had both features built-in. How many cars did Fred check?

(A) 5

(B) 10

(C) 11

(D) 13

A   B   C   D
○   ○   ○   ○

71 The use of calculator is **permitted**.

The demand of a particular product decreases as a linear function as the price goes up. A company researched that when the product price is $45, the demand for the product is 1000. For every $5 increase in the price of the product, the demand falls by 5. Which of the following correctly represents the demand, D, for the product as a function of the product price, p?

(A) $D(p) = 1000 - \left(\frac{-4}{5}\right)p$

(B) $D(p) = 1000 - (p + 45)$

(C) $D(p) = \frac{1000}{45} - \frac{5}{4}p$

(D) $D(p) = 1000 - \frac{5}{4}\left(\frac{4p}{5} - 36\right)$

A   B   C   D
○   ○   ○   ○

72 The use of calculator is **permitted**.

A man travels by bus to work. For each trip, the man pays $x. He has an option of purchasing a monthly pass for $P which would reduce the fare for each trip by$r. If n be the number of trips he must make per month so that purchasing the pass is a profitable to him, which of the following is the correct inequality satisfying the above information?

(A) $n < \frac{P}{r}$

(B) $n > \frac{P}{r}$

(C) $n < \frac{P}{x-r}$

(D) $n > \frac{P}{x-r}$

A   B   C   D
○   ○   ○   ○

73 The use of calculator is **not permitted**.

Ron had \$35 with which he wanted to buy some chocolates priced at \$2 per piece, some pens priced at \$5 per piece and some pencils priced at \$4 per piece. What is the difference between the maximum number of total items he can buy and the minimum number of total items he can buy, if he must buy at least one chocolate, one pen and one pencil and he must to spend the entire amount with him?

(A) 5

(B) 6

(C) 7

(D) 8

A B C D
○ ○ ○ ○

74 The use of calculator is **permitted**.

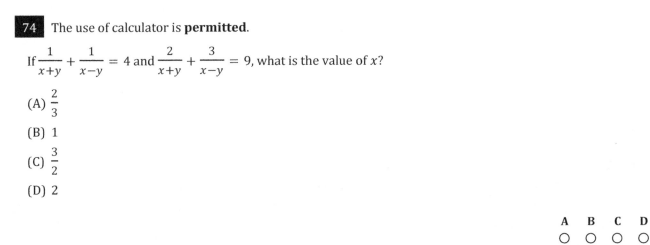

If $\dfrac{1}{x+y} + \dfrac{1}{x-y} = 4$ and $\dfrac{2}{x+y} + \dfrac{3}{x-y} = 9$, what is the value of x?

(A) $\dfrac{2}{3}$

(B) 1

(C) $\dfrac{3}{2}$

(D) 2

A B C D
○ ○ ○ ○

75 The use of calculator is **not permitted**.

The cost, in dollars, of producing tires by a manufacturing firm is determined by the following equation: $C = 120 + 90 \times W + 78 \times N$, where '$C$' represents the cost incurred, 'W' represents the number of workers, 'N' represents the number of units produced. If 10 units have to be produced, what is the maximum number of workers that can be employed so that the total cost doesn't exceed \$2700?

(A) 18

(B) 19

(C) 20

(D) 21

A B C D
○ ○ ○ ○

76   The use of calculator is **not permitted**.

Peter, Rene and Andrew were playing a game of marbles. In the game, at a point of time, Peter gave one-fourth of his marbles to Rene, who in turn gave half of what she received to Andrew. If the difference between the marbles left with Peter and the marbles received by Andrew is 30, then how many marbles did Rene receive from Peter?

77   The use of calculator is **permitted**.

In an experiment, the temperature of the reactants was being carefully monitored. It was observed that the maximum and minimum temperatures recorded were 64.7° Fahrenheit and 79.4° Fahrenheit. Which of the following inequalities represents all possible temperature values, t, observed during the experiment?

(A) $|t - 72.05| > 7.35$

(B) $|t - 72.05| = 7.35$

(C) $|t - 72.05| \leq 7.35$

(D) $|t - 72.05| < 7.35$

A   B   C   D
O   O   O   O

78   The use of calculator is **not permitted**.

In five years, Alfred would be 20 years more than twice his son's age. Ten years back, Alfred was 30 years more than thrice his son's age. After how many years would Alfred be exactly twice as old as his son?

(A) 5

(B) 10

(C) 15

(D) 25

A   B   C   D
O   O   O   O

79 The use of calculator is **permitted**.

The number of inventory items, n, in a factory, at the end of each month starting from January in 2016, was given by the relation: $n = 60 + 15m$, where m represents the number of months completed after January in that year. If 80 items were procured in each month for the inventory, what is the total number of items used from the inventory till end of March in that year? Assume that there was no inventory carried forward from the previous year.

(A) 65

(B) 85

(C) 130

(D) 150

A   B   C   D
○ ○ ○ ○

80 The use of calculator is **permitted**.

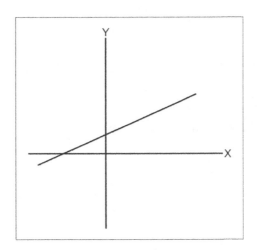

The graph below depicts the straight line $y = \frac{x}{2} + 3$. If the line is reflected about the X axis and the equation of the new line is $y = mx + n$, what is the value of $|m + n|$?

Answers and Explanations

1. **Level of Difficulty:** Medium

   Topic: Graphing linear equations

   The correct answer is (C).

   We can see that the registration fees of The Regency and The Plaza are $2000 and $4000 respectively.

   At the end of 5 years, the total amount spent for membership of either club is equal to $9000.

   Thus, the annual charge for The Regency = $\$\frac{9000-2000}{5} = \$1400$.

   The annual charge for The Plaza = $\$\frac{9000-4000}{5} = \$1000$.

   Hence, the difference between the annual charges of the two clubs = $1400 – $1000 = $400.

   Hence, the correct answer is (C).

2. **Level of Difficulty:** Easy

   Topic: Functions

   The correct answer is 2.

   Since $p = 2q$, we have: $f(x) = x^2 + 2qx + q$.

   Again, the function takes a value of 16 at $x = 3$, we have:

   $16 = 3^2 + 2q \times 3 + q => 16 = 9 + 7q => q = 1$.

   Thus, $p = 2q = 2$.

   Hence, the answer is 2.

3. **Level of Difficulty:** Medium

   Topic: Linear inequality and equation (word problems)

   The correct answer is (D).

   Let the temperatures on Monday, Tuesday, Wednesday, Thursday, and Friday be denoted by M,T, W, H, and F respectively.

   Since the average of M, T, W and H is 60, we have: $M + T + W + H = 60 \times 4 = 240$ ... (i)

   Again, since the average of T, W, H and F is 55, we have: $T + W + H + F = 55 \times 4 = 220$ ... (ii)

   Subtracting: (i) – (ii): $M - F = 20 => M = F + 20$ ... (iii)

   We know that $M : F = 13 : 9 => (F + 20) : F = 13 : 9 => \frac{F+20}{F} = \frac{13}{9} => 9F + 180 = 13F$

   $F = 45$.

   Thus, $M = F + 20 = 45 + 20 = 65$.

   Thus, the temperature on Monday was 65°F.

   Hence, the answer is (D).

4. **Level of Difficulty**: Difficult

    Topic: Solving linear equations and inequalities

    The correct answer is (D).

    $a + b + c + d = 24$ ... (i)

    $a + b = c + d$ ... (ii)

    Adding $c + d$ to both sides of (ii): $a + b + c + d = 2(c + d)$ => $2(c + d) = 24$ (from (i))

    $c + d = a + b = 12$ ... (iii)

    Again, $a + c = 2(b + d)$ ... (iv)

    Adding $b + d$ to both sides of (iv): $a + b + c + d = 3(b + d)$ => $3(b + d) = 24$ (from (i))

    $b + d = 8$ ... (v)

    $a + c = 2 \times 8 = 16$ ... (vi)

    Since there are three main relations given ((i), (ii) and (iv)), we cannot solve for all the variables.

    Since we need to find number of possible values of the number, we should start with that equation that provides the minimum number of possibilities (since we need to satisfy all the above equations simultaneously).

    Let us start from equation (vi):

    Possible cases where $a + c = 16$ are: $(a, c) = (7,9); (8,8); (9,7)$.

    Since all digits are distinct, we cannot include (8,8) as a solution.

    Thus, the possibilities of $(a, c) = (7,9)$ and $(9,7)$.

    Using (iii): $a + b = 12$.

    We know that $a = 7$ or 9.

    Thus, we have $b = 12 - a = 5$ or 3.

    Thus, the possible cases are: $(a, b) = (7,5)$ and $(9,3)$.

    Finally, we can use (v): $b + d = 8$.

    We know that $b = 5$ or 3.

    Thus, we have $d = 8 - b = 3$ or 5.

    Thus, the possible cases are: $(b, d) = (5,3)$ and $(3,5)$.

    Hence, the complete set of solutions for $abcd$ is 7593 or 9375.

    Thus, there are two solutions possible.

    Hence, the answer is (D).

5. **Level of Difficulty:** Difficult

    Topic: Linear inequality and equation (word problems)

    The correct answer is (C).

    Let the two-digit number be $N = 10x + y$ where x and y are the digits.

We know that $1 \leq x \leq 9$ and $0 \leq y \leq 9$.

The sum of the digits of the number $= S = x + y$.

The product of the digits $= P = xy$.

Thus, we have: $2(10x + y) = 2(x + y) + 3xy => 20x + 2y = 2x + 2y + 3xy$

$18x = 3xy => y = 6$.

Since we cannot determine the value of x, it implies that x can take any value from 1 to 9.

Thus, the possible numbers are 16, 26, 36, 46, 56, 66, 76, 86, and 96.

Thus, there are 9 such numbers.

Hence, the correct answer is (C).

6. **Level of Difficulty:** Difficult

   Topic: Graphing linear equations

   The correct answer is (D).

   Let us work with the options.

   Option (A): $|y - 2x| = 5 => y - 2x = \pm 5 => y = 2x + 5$ or $y = 2x - 5$.

   Thus, we get a pair of lines and not a region as shown in the graph. Thus, option (A) is not correct.

   Option (B): $|y - 2x| > 3 => y - 2x > 3$ or $y - 2x < -3 => y > 2x + 3$ or $y < 2x - 3$.

   This is an unbounded region and hence, is not the true representation of the shaded (bounded) region.

   Let us take a point on in the shaded region, say $(x, y) = (3, 4)$. This point does not satisfy either of the above two inequalities. Thus, option (B) is incorrect.

   Option (C): $|y - x| < 2 => -2 < y - x < 2 => x - 2 < y < x + 2$.

   Thus, this is a bounded region between the lines $y = x + 2$ and $y = x - 2$.

   However, the lines bounding the shaded region in the graph are not the lines as given above.

   Let us take a point on any of the two lines, say $(x, y) = (0, 3)$. This point does not satisfy either of the above two lines. Thus, option (C) is incorrect.

   Hence, option (D) must be correct. $|y - 2x| \leq 3 => -3 \leq y - 2x \leq 3 => 2x - 3 \leq y \leq 2x + 3$.

   Thus, this is a bounded region between the lines $y = 2x - 3$ and $y = 2x + 3$.

   Let us take a few points on both the lines, say $(x, y) = (0, 3); (1, 5); (2, 1); (3, 3)$.

   The first two points satisfy $y = 2x + 3$ and the latter two points satisfy $y = 2x - 3$.

   Since two points are sufficient to determine a line, we can say that the lines bounding the shaded region in the graph are the same lines as given above.

   Hence, the correct answer is (D).

7. **Level of Difficulty:** Medium

   Topic: Linear function (word problems)

   The correct answer is 56.3.

As Abe reads 23 pages every morning, thus after 'M' mornings he should have read '23M' pages

Also, as Abe reads 31 pages every evening, after 'E' evenings he should have read '31E' pages

So, the total pages read by Abe by that time should be given by $N = 23M + 31E$

After exactly 11 mornings have passed, M = 11 and E = 10, we get $N = 253 + 310 = 563$

The correct answer is 563.

8. **Level of Difficulty:** Difficult

    Topic: Linear inequality and equation (word problems)

    The correct answer is (C).

    Let the average contribution of all 12 friends be x

    Thus, total contributions of all 12 friends = $12x$.

    Average of 10 friends is $80.

    Thus, total contributions of these 10 friends = $80 × 10 = $800.

    Also, contributions from the last two friends are $(x + 80)$ and $(x + 120)$.

    Thus, we have: $12x = 800 + (x + 80) + (x + 120) => 12x = 1000 + 2x => x = 100$.

    Thus, average contribution of all the friends taken together = $100.

    Hence, the answer is (C).

9. **Level of Difficulty:** Easy

    Topic: Interpreting linear functions

    The correct answer is (C).

    Since there is no loss, we have:

    $P > 0 : 50.2 × N - 236.8 > 0$

    $N > 4.72$

    Minimum integer value of N should be 5

    The correct answer is option C.

10. **Level of Difficulty:** Easy

    The correct answer is (D).

    We have: $3. AM = 7. BM => \dfrac{AM}{BM} = \dfrac{7}{3}$.

    The diagram showing the points is given.

    Thus, we have point B dividing MA in the ratio 3 : 4.

    Hence, the coordinates of B are: $\left(\dfrac{(3 × 3 + 4 × (-4))}{4+3}, \dfrac{3 × 0 + 4 × 7}{4+3} \right) = (-1, 4)$.

    Hence, the correct answer is (D).

11. **Level of Difficulty:** Medium

    Topic: Linear function (word problems)

    The correct answer is (D).

    Let the cost of a pencil be 'a', the cost an eraser be 'b', the cost of a sharpener be 'c', then Adam should have spent $23a + 15b + 20c$, which must be equal to $111

    $23a + 15b + 20c = 111$ ... (i)

    Also, Bob must have spent $12b + 4a + 7c$ and as he spent $51, we have:

    $4a + 12b + 7c = 51$ ... (ii)

    Adding, we have: $27a + 27b + 27c = 162 => a + b + c = 6$ ... (iii)

    Only option D satisfies (iii).

    The correct answer is option D.

12. **Level of Difficulty:** Difficult

    Topic: Solving systems of linear equations

    The correct answer is (C).

    $3a - 7b = 5c + 9$ ... (i)

    $5a + 2b = 7c - 4$ ... (ii)

    From $5 \times$ (i) $- 3 \times$ (ii):

    $$-41b = 4c + 57 => b = -\left(\frac{4c + 57}{41}\right)$$

    Substituting: $a = \frac{1}{3}\left\{(5c + 9) - \frac{7(4c+57)}{41}\right\} = \frac{\frac{1}{3}(177c-30)}{41} = \left(\frac{59c-10}{41}\right)$

    $$a - b = \frac{63c + 47}{41}$$

    The correct answer is option C.

13. **Level of Difficulty:** Easy

    Topic: Solving linear equations and inequalities

    The correct answer is (C).

    $a + 2b + 3c = 24$ ... (i)

    $3a + 2b + c = 36$ ... (ii)

    Adding: $4(a + b + c) = 60$

    $a + b + c = 15$

    The correct answer is option C.

14. **Level of Difficulty:** Medium

The correct answer is (B).

Slope of AD: $\dfrac{6-0}{q-2} = 2 => 6 = 2q - 4 => q = 5 \ldots$ (i)

Slope of DC: $\dfrac{6-p}{q-11} = 0.5 => \dfrac{6-p}{5-11} = 0.5 => 6 - p = -3 => p = 9 \ldots$ (ii)

Thus, the coordinates of C are $(11, 9)$.

Hence, the length of BC $= \sqrt{(11-9)^2 + (9-0)^2} = \sqrt{85}$.

Hence, the correct answer is (B).

15. **Level of Difficulty:** Difficult

Topic: Graphing linear equations

The correct answer is (C).

At $x = 0, y = 1$

Option A doesn't satisfy hence can be eliminated.

The slope of the line based on the points A $(0, 1)$ and B; where the x-coordinate of B is 1 and the *y*-coordinate of B is greater than 4.

If B were $(1, 4)$, the slope of AB $= \dfrac{4-1}{1-0} = 3$.

Since B is above $(1, 4)$, the slope is greater than 3.

If B were $(1, 5)$, the slope of AB $= \dfrac{5-1}{1-0} = 4$.

Since B is below $(1, 5)$, the slope is less than 4.

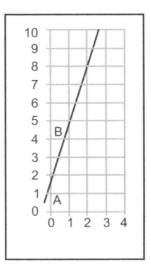

Thus, the correct answer is option C.

16. **Level of Difficulty:** Medium

    Topic: Systems of linear inequalities (word problems)

    The correct answer is 11.

    The man works n hours as a consultant. Let he work x hours as a content writer.

    Thus: $n + x \leq 15$ ... (i)

    Also: $40n + 6x = 450$ ... (ii)

    Multiplying (i) with 6 and subtracting (ii):

    $-34n \leq -360$

    $n \geq \dfrac{360}{34}$

    $n \geq 10.59$

    Since n is an integer, we have: $n \geq 11$

    The correct answer is '11'.

17. **Level of Difficulty:** Medium

    Topic: Linear inequality and equation (word problems)

    The correct answer is (D).

    Let the number of students in the class be S.

    After doubling the number of sweets with each student, each student receives 6 sweets (initially they had 3 sweets each, which when doubled would imply 6 sweets for each student).

    Thus, total sweets given away by Joseph = 6S.

    Since there were M sweets left, total number of sweets with Joseph = 6S + M.

    Had Joseph given one extra sweet to each student, he would have given 4 sweets to each student.

    Thus, total sweets given away by Joseph = 4S.

    Since there were N sweets left, total number of sweets with Joseph = 4S + N.

    Thus, we have: $6S + M = 4S + N \implies 2S = N - M \implies S = \dfrac{N-M}{2}$.

    Thus, the number of students in the class $= \dfrac{N-M}{2}$.

    Hence, the correct answer is (D).

18. **Level of Difficulty:** Medium

    Topic: Linear function (word problems)

    The correct answer is (B).

    We know that, when the price is \$45, the demand is 1000 units.

    For every \$5 increase in price, the demand falls by 15 units.

Thus, when the price is $70, the price has gone up by $(80 − 45) = $35

Thus, the demand falls by $\frac{35}{5} \times 15 = 105$ units

Thus, the demand = 1000 − 105 = 895

The correct answer is Option B.

19. **Level of Difficulty:** Difficult

Topic: Linear inequality and equation (word problems)

The correct answer is (D).

Let the number of marbles with Ron and Jacob be $12x$ and $4y$ respectively (we take 12x marbles for Ron since we need to take one-third and then one-fourth of that number; we take 4y marbles for Jacob since we need to take one-fourth of that number).

Thus, initial ratio of the number of marbles with Ron and Jacob $= \frac{12x}{4y} = \frac{3x}{y}$.

Number of marbles Ron gives to Jacob $= \frac{1}{3} \times 12x = 4x$.

Number of marbles left with Ron $= 12x - 4x = 8x$.

Number of marbles with Jacob $= 4y + 4x = 4(x + y)$.

Number of marbles Jacob returns to Ron $= \frac{1}{4} \times 4(x + y) = x + y$.

Number of marbles left with Jacob $= 4(x + y) - (x + y) = 3(x + y)$.

Number of marbles with Ron $= 8x + (x + y) = 9x + y$.

Since the ratio of the number of marbles with Ron and Jacob remains the same, we have:

$\frac{3x}{y} = \frac{9x+y}{3(x+y)} => \frac{9x}{3y} = \frac{9x+y}{3x+3y}$ (multiplying 3 to both numerator and denominator on the left)

$\frac{9x}{3y} = \frac{9x+y}{3x+3y} = \frac{9x+y-9x}{3x+3y-3y} = \frac{y}{3x}$

(using the properties of ratios that if two ratios $\frac{p}{q} = \frac{m}{n}$, then the ratios are also equal to $\frac{p-m}{q-n}$

$\frac{9x}{3y} = \frac{y}{3x} => \frac{x^2}{y^2} = \frac{1}{9} => \frac{x}{y} = \frac{1}{3}$ (taking square root on both sides).

Thus, the required ratio of the number of marbles with Ron and Jacob $= \frac{3x}{y} = 3 \times \left(\frac{x}{y}\right) = 3 \times \frac{1}{3} = 1$.

Hence, the correct answer is (D).

20. **Level of Difficulty:** Difficult

Topic: Linear inequality and equation (word problems)

The correct answer is $\frac{5}{2}$.

We have the fraction as $\frac{x}{y}$ where x and y have no factor common except 1.

Thus, we have: $\frac{x-2}{y+3} = \frac{3}{5} => 5x - 10 = 3y + 9 => 5x - 3y = 19$.

Since both x and y are positive integers, we need to find a starting solution for x and y and using that, get the other possible solutions.

By trial and error, we see that $x = 5$ (smallest possible value of x) satisfies and the corresponding value of $y = \frac{5x-19}{3} = \frac{25-19}{3} = 2$.

To get the other positive integer solutions, we increase y by the coefficient of x, i.e. 5 and decrease x by the coefficient of y, i.e. -3 i.e. effectively increasing x by 3.

The possible values of x and y are shown below:

x	y	Fraction $= \frac{x}{y}$
5	2	$\frac{5}{2}$
8	7	$\frac{8}{7}$
11	12	$\frac{11}{12}$
etc...		

We can see that each successive fraction becomes smaller in value.

Thus, the maximum value of the fraction $\frac{x}{y} = \frac{5}{2}$.

Hence, the correct answer is $\frac{5}{2}$

21. **Level of Difficulty:** Easy

Topic: Interpreting linear Functions

The correct answer is (C).

As 'N' represents the number of units produced in the month and 'D' represents the number of days elapsed in the month, the 231 getting multiplied to the number of days implies:

$N = 231$, for D $= 1$

$N = 462$, for D $= 2$

And so on...

This means that the number of units manufactured each day of the month is 231

Hence option (C)

22. **Level of Difficulty:** Medium

    Topic: Solving systems of linear equations

    The correct answer is (B).

    $2a + 3b - c = a + 2b + c$

    $=> a + b = 2c \ ... \ (i)$

    $2a + 3b - c = 3a - b - c$

    $a = 4b \ ... \ (ii)$

    Thus: $4b + b = 2c => b = \dfrac{2c}{5}$

    $a = 4b = \dfrac{8c}{5}$

    $a: b: c = \dfrac{8c}{5} : \dfrac{2c}{5} : c = 8 : 2 : 5$

    The correct answer is option B.

23. **Level of Difficulty:** Medium

    Topic: Quadratic and exponential (word problems)

    The correct answer is 2.

    Let the number be x.

    Thus, we have: $\dfrac{3x^3 + 2x^2}{2} = 8x => 3x^3 + 2x^2 - 16x = 0 => x\left(3x^2 + 2x - 16\right) = 0$

    $x(3x^2 + 8x - 6x - 16) = 0 => x\{x(3x + 8) - 2(3x + 8)\} = 0$

    $x(x - 2)(3x + 8) = 0 => x = 0, 2, -\dfrac{8}{3}.$

    Since x is non-zero and an integer, we have $C = 2$.

    Hence, the correct answer is 2.

24. **Level of Difficulty:** Difficult

    Topic: Interpreting linear functions

    The correct answer is (C).

    Let the number of sticks used, each 1.5 inches $= \dfrac{1.5}{12}$ feet wide, be n.

    Thus, there are $(n - 1)$ gaps, each 2 feet wide.

    Thus, we have: $\dfrac{1.5}{12}n + 2\left(n - 1\right) = l$

    $\dfrac{n}{8} + 2n - 2 = l$

    $\dfrac{17n}{8} = (l + 2)$

$$n = \frac{8(l + 2)}{17}$$

The correct answer is option C.

25. **Level of Difficulty:** Easy

Topic: Solving linear equations and inequalities

The correct answer is (B).

$5 + 2|2x - 3| < 19 \Rightarrow 2|2x - 3| < 14 \Rightarrow |2 - 3| < 7$

$-7 < 2x - 3 < 7 \Rightarrow -7 + 3 < 2x < 7 + 3 \Rightarrow -4 < 2x < 10 \Rightarrow -2 < x < 5.$

Thus, the possible integer values of x are: $\{-1, 0, 1, 2, 3, 4\}$

Hence, there are 6 possible integer values of x satisfying the inequality.

Hence, the correct answer is (B).

26. **Level of Difficulty:** Difficult

The correct answer is (B).

Let us name the points: A $(1, 3)$, B $(1, 9)$, C $(1 + 3\sqrt{3}, 12)$ and D $(1 + 3\sqrt{3}, 6)$.

We know that in any quadrilateral, if the diagonals bisect each other, it must be a parallelogram.

Since the first three options are all parallelograms, let us first check whether the diagonals bisect each other.

For the figure ABCD, the diagonals would be AC and BD.

Mid-point of AC $= \left(\frac{(1)+(1+3\sqrt{3})}{2}, \frac{(3)+(12)}{2}\right) = \left(\frac{2+3\sqrt{3}}{2}, \frac{15}{2}\right).$

Mid-point of BD $= \left(\frac{(1)+(1+3\sqrt{3})}{2}, \frac{(9)+(6)}{2}\right) = \left(\frac{2+3\sqrt{3}}{2}, \frac{15}{2}\right).$

Since the midpoints are the same, we can say that ABCD is a parallelogram.

Hence, option (D) is not possible.

In a square and rhombus, the diagonals are perpendicular to one another, while it is not so in a rectangle. So, we check whether the diagonals AC and BD are perpendicular to one another.

Slope of AC $= \frac{(12)-(3)}{(1+3\sqrt{3})-(1)} = \frac{9}{3\sqrt{3}} = \sqrt{3}.$

Slope of BD $= \frac{(6)-(9)}{(1+3\sqrt{3})-(1)} = \frac{-3}{3\sqrt{3}} = -\frac{1}{\sqrt{3}}.$

Product of the slopes of AC and BD $= (\sqrt{3}) \times \left(-\frac{1}{\sqrt{3}}\right) = -1.$

Hence, we can say that the diagonals AC and BD are perpendicular.

Hence, the answer must be either option (B) or (C).

Option (A) is not possible.

In a square, any two adjacent sides are perpendicular while it is not so in the case of a rhombus.

Let us find the slopes of AB and AD. If their product is (– 1), ABCD is a square, else a rhombus.

We can see that A (1, 3) and B (1, 9) form a line that is parallel to the X-axis.

However, A (1, 3) and D (1 + 3√3, 6) do not form a line parallel to the Y-axis.

Thus, AB and AD are not perpendicular to one another. Thus, ABCD is a rhombus and not a square.

Hence, the correct answer is (B).

27. **Level of Difficulty:** Difficult

Topic: Linear inequality and equation (word problems)

The correct answer is (B).

Let the two-digit number be $10x + y$ where x and y are the digits of the number.

We know that $1 \leq x \leq 9$ and $0 \leq y \leq 9$.

The sum of the digits of the number $= x + y$.

We need to find the minimum ratio of $\dfrac{10x+y}{x+y}$.

We have: $\dfrac{10x+y}{x+y} = \dfrac{x+y+9x}{x+y} = \dfrac{x+y}{x+y} + \dfrac{9x}{x+y} = 1 + \dfrac{9x}{x+y}$.

We need to minimize this ratio.

Since x is multiplied with 9, we need to choose the least possible value of x to minimize the numerator. Also, since we have y in the denominator, we need to maximize y in order to minimize the ratio.

Thus, we choose $x = 1$ and $y = 9$.

Hence, the ratio $= 1 + \dfrac{9 \times 1}{1+9} = 1 + \dfrac{9}{10} = 1.9$.

Hence, the correct answer is (B).

28. **Level of Difficulty:** Medium

Topic: Linear function (word problems)

The correct answer is (A).

If Chad takes 'R' rides in the park and spends 'A' amount on it, then $A = 10 + 2.5 \times R$

Here, $A = 25 \Rightarrow R = \dfrac{25-10}{2.5} = 6$

The correct answer is option 'A'

29. **Level of Difficulty:** Medium

Topic: Solving systems of linear equations

The correct answer is (D).

$a + b + c + d = 24$

Since: $a + b = c + d \Rightarrow 2(a + b) = 24 \Rightarrow a + b = 12$

$a = b \Rightarrow 2a = 12 \Rightarrow a = b = 6$

Since: $a + c = 2(b + d) \Rightarrow 3(b + d) = 24 \Rightarrow b + d = 8$

$a + c = 2 \times 8 = 16$

$c = 16 - a = 10$

The correct answer is option D.

30. **Level of Difficulty:** Easy

Topic: Interpreting linear functions

The correct answer is 24.5.

$r = 4\sqrt{n}$

Also: $s = 40 - r = 40 - 4\sqrt{n}$

For $n = 15$: $s = 40 - 4\sqrt{15} = 24.508 \approx 24.5$

The correct answer is 24.5

31. **Level of Difficulty:** Difficult

Topic: Linear inequality and equation (word problems)

The correct answer is (A).

Let the amounts with Ann, Bob, Charlie and David be \$$a$, \$$b$, \$$c$ and \$$d$ respectively.

Thus, we have:

$a + b + c + d = 200$ ... (i)

$c = 2b$ ... (ii)

$a + b = d - 40$ ... (iii)

$c = d - 30$ ... (iv)

Substituting (iii) and (iv) in (i): $(d - 40) + (d - 30) + d = 200 \Rightarrow 3d = 270 \Rightarrow d = 90$ ... (v)

From (iv): $c = d - 30 = 90 - 30 = 60$.

From (ii): $2b = c = 60 \Rightarrow b = 30$.

From (iii): $a + b = d - 40 \Rightarrow a + 30 = 90 - 40 \Rightarrow a = 20$.

Hence, the answer is (A).

32. **Level of Difficulty:** Difficult

Topic: Interpreting linear functions

The correct answer is (D).

Distance covered in the 1st second: $d = 6 \times 1 + 1 = 7$

Distance covered in the 2nd second: $d = 6 \times 2 + 1 = 13$

Distance covered in the 3rd second: $d = 6 \times 3 + 1 = 19$

Distance covered in the 4th second: $d = 6 \times 4 + 1 = 25$

Distance covered in the 5th second: $d = 6 \times 5 + 1 = 31$

Thus, total distance $= 7 + 13 + 19 + 25 + 31 = 95 \, feet$.

The correct answer is option D.

33. **Level of Difficulty:** Medium

Topic: Interpreting linear functions

The correct answer is (B).

$$F = \frac{9}{5}C + 32$$

$$\frac{9}{5}C = F - 32$$

$$C = \frac{5}{9}(F - 32)$$

Thus, difference between two Celsius readings based on two Fahrenheit readings

$$= C_1 - C_2 = \frac{5}{9}\big((F_1 - 32) - (F_2 - 32)\big) = \frac{5}{9}(F_1 - F_2)$$

Change in Fahrenheit scale $= 36°$

Thus, difference in Celsius scale $= \frac{5}{9}(F_1 - F_2) = \frac{5}{9} \times 36 = 20^0$

The correct answer is option B.

34. **Level of Difficulty:** Easy

Topic: Graphing linear equations

The correct answer is 6.

Slope of the line $= \frac{n-1}{5+1} = \frac{n-1}{6} > \frac{n-1}{6} > \frac{2}{3}$

$n - 1 > 4$

$n > 5$

Thus, the least integer value of n is 6.

The correct answer is '6'.

35. **Level of Difficulty:** Difficult

Topic: Linear function (word problems)

The correct answer is (B).

Let the cost of 1 chocolate, 1 candy and 1 bubblegum be $\$x$, $\$y$ and $\$z$, respectively.

Thus: $3x + 2y + z = 14 \dots$ (i)

$x + 3y + 5z = 14 \dots$ (ii)

Adding (i) and (ii): $4x + 5y + 6z = 28 \dots$ (iii)

Adding (i) and (iii): $7x + 7y + 7z = 42 \Rightarrow x + y + z = 6$

The correct answer is option B.

36. **Level of Difficulty:** Easy

The correct answer is (C).

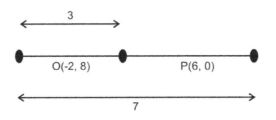

We have: $3 . \text{PN} = 7 . \text{QN} \Rightarrow \dfrac{\text{PN}}{\text{QN}} = \dfrac{7}{3}$.

The diagram showing the points is given.

Thus, we have point N dividing PQ extended in the ratio 7 : 3.

Hence, the coordinates of N are: $\left(\dfrac{(3 \times 6 - 7 \times (-2))}{3-7}, \dfrac{3 \times 0 - 7 \times 8}{3-7} \right) = (-8, 14)$.

Hence, the correct answer is (C).

37. **Level of Difficulty:** Difficult

Topic: Solving systems of linear equations

The correct answer is (B).

$a + 5b + 9c = 24 \dots$ (i)

$5a + 3b + c = 10 \dots$ (ii)

From (ii) $\times$ 2 + (i):

$11a + 11b + 11c = 44$

$a + b + c = 4$

The correct answer is option B.

38. **Level of Difficulty:** Difficult

Topic: Linear inequality and equation (word problems)

The correct answer is (B).

Let the average score of the three students be A. Thus, total score of the three students = 3A.

Initial total score of the S students in the class = $S \times 2S = 2S^2$.

Final average of the $(S - 3)$ students = $(2S + 3)$.

Thus, final total score of the $(S - 3)$ students = $(2S + 3)(S - 3) = 2S^2 - 3S - 9$.

Hence, we have: $2S^2 - 3A = 2S^2 - 3S - 9 => 3A = 3S + 9 => A = S + 3$.

Hence, the answer is (B).

39. **Level of Difficulty:** Medium

   Topic: Solving linear equations and inequalities

   The correct answer is 4.

   We know that $|x - a|$ refers to the distance of the point x from the point a on the number line.

   Based on the above expression, we can divide the number line in four regions as shown below:

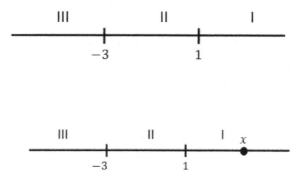

   Region I:

   $|x + 3|$ and $|x - 1|$ refer to the distances of the points -3 and 1 from x respectively. The distances between any two consecutive points have been marked (in bold) in the diagram.

   Thus, $|x + 3| + |x - 1| = (d + 4) + d = 2d + 4 \geq 4$ (since $d \geq 0$).

   Region II:

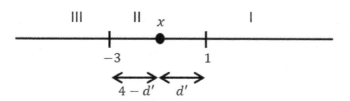

Here, $|x + 3| + |x - 1| = (4 - d`) + d` = \mathbf{4}$.

Region III:

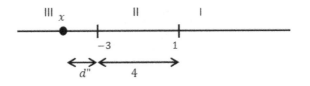

Here, $|x + 3| + |x - 1| = (d") + (4 + d") = 4 + 2d" \geq 4$.

Thus, from the above, we can conclude that the minimum value of the expression is 4 (which occurs at any value of x from -3 to 1).

Hence, the correct answer is 4.

40. **Level of Difficulty:** Medium

   Topic: Quadratic and exponential (word problems)

   The correct answer is (B).

   We can see that $n^2 + 5n + 12 = n(n + 5) + 12$.

   Thus, we see that the first term i.e. $n(n + 5)$ is divisible by $(n + 5)$.

   In order that the entire expression i.e. $n(n + 5) + 12$ has to be divisible by $n + 5$, we must ensure that 12 is also divisible by $n + 5$.

   Thus, $n + 5$ must be the factors of 12.

   Since n is a positive integer, $n + 5$ can either be 6 or 12.

   Thus, $n = 6 - 5 = 1$ or $n = 12 - 5 = 7$.

   Thus, there are two values of n which satisfy the condition given.

   Hence, the answer is (B).

41. **Level of Difficulty:** Difficult

   Topic: Linear inequality and equation (word problems)

   The correct answer is (D).

   Let the two-digit number be $N = 10x + y$ where x and y are the digits.

   Thus, the reverse of the above two-digit number is $10y + x$.

   Since the reverse is also a two-digit number, we have: $1 \leq x \leq 9$ and $1 \leq y \leq 9$.

   According to the problem: $10x + y + 2(10y + x) = 150 => 12x + 21y = 150$

   $4x + 7y = 50$.

   Since $4x$ and 50 are even, $7y$ must be even as well, implying that y is even.

   Since both x and y are positive integers, we need to find a starting solution for x and y and using that, get the other possible solutions.

   By trial and error, we see that $y = 2$ (smallest possible value of y) satisfies and the corresponding value of

$$x = \frac{50-7y}{4} = \frac{50-14}{4} = 9.$$

It is clear that we need to increase y and as a result, the value of x would decrease. Thus, to get the other solutions, we increase y by the coefficient of x, i.e. 4 and decrease x by the coefficient of y, i.e. 7.

The possible values of x and y are shown below:

x	y	$N = 10x + y$	Sum of digits $= x + y$
9	2	98	11
2	6	26	8

Beyond this, the value of x would become negative and hence inadmissible.

Thus, the maximum value of $x + y = 11$.

Hence, the correct answer is (D).

42. **Level of Difficulty:** Easy

    Topic: Interpreting linear functions

    The correct answer is (B).

    For the nth person, there are $(n - 1)$persons ahead of him.

    So, time for servicing $= 10(n - 1)$

    For those $(n - 1)$ persons, there would be $(n - 2)$ gaps

    If each gap is of k minutes, we have:

    $$10(n - 1) + k(n - 2) = 12.5n - 15$$

    $$k(n - 2) = 2.5n - 5 = 2.5(n - 2)$$

    $$k = 2.5$$

    The correct answer is option B.

43. **Level of Difficulty:** Difficult

    Topic: Systems of linear inequalities (word problems)

    The correct answer is $\left(\frac{6}{7}\right)$.

    Time taken to cover d miles at s miles per hour $= \frac{d}{s}$ hours

    Time taken to cover D miles at $3s$ miles per hour $= \frac{D}{3s}$ hours

    $$\frac{d}{s} + \frac{D}{3s} = 2$$

    $$3d + 2D = 6s \ldots \text{(i)}$$

    Since $D > 2d \Rightarrow 2D > 4d$

Thus, the LHS of (i) is greater than 3d + 4d i.e. 7d, which in turn equals 6s

Thus, 7d must be less than 6s

$7d < 6s$

$d < \dfrac{6s}{7}$

44. **Level of Difficulty:** Medium

   Topic: Systems of linear inequalities (word problems)

   The correct answer is (C).

   Total students in the class $= s$

   Thus, number of students other than Joe $= (s - 1)$

   Thus, number of pens each student got $= (s - 1 - 3) = (s - 4)$

   Thus, total number of pens $= (s - 1)(s - 4)$

   $(s - 1)(s - 4) < 21$

   $s^2 - 5s - 17 < 0$

   The correct answer is option C.

45. **Level of Difficulty:** Medium

   Topic: Graphing linear equations

   The correct answer is (C).

   Equation of the line:

   $\dfrac{y - 2}{x + 3} = \dfrac{n - 2}{7 + 3}$

   $\dfrac{y - 2}{x + 3} = \dfrac{n - 2}{10}$

   $y = \dfrac{n - 2}{10}(x + 3) + 2$

   $y = \left(\dfrac{n - 2}{10}\right) \times + \dfrac{3(n - 2)}{10} + 2$

   $y = \left(\dfrac{n - 2}{10}\right) \times + \dfrac{3n}{10} - \dfrac{6}{10} + 2$

   $y = \left(\dfrac{n - 1}{6}\right) \times + \left(\dfrac{3n}{10} + 1.4\right)$

   Thus, the Y-intercept $= k = (0.3n + 1.4)$

   The correct answer is Option C.

46. **Level of Difficulty:** Medium

   Topic: Systems of linear inequalities (word problems)

The correct answer is (B).

Amount saved in the first n days $= \$(3n)$

Amount saved in the next$(2n)$ days $= \$(3.75 \times 2n) = \$(7.5n)$

Days remaining $= 15 - n - 2n = 15 - 3n$

Thus: $3n + 7.5n + s(15 - 3n) \geq 105$

$10.5n + 15s - 3ns \geq 105$

$21n + 30s - 6ns \geq 210$

$7n + 10s - 2ns \geq 70$

$s(10 - 2n) \geq 70 - 7n$

$s \geq \dfrac{7(10 - n)}{2(5 - n)}$

$s \geq 3.5 \left(\dfrac{10 - n}{5 - n} \right)$

The correct answer is option B.

47. **Level of Difficulty:** Difficult

   Topic: Linear inequality and equation (word problems)

   The correct answer is 209.

   Let there be n posts along each side of the garden.

   Since we need to find the maximum length of a side of the garden, we should try to use all the posts.

   Thus, it appears as if there should have been 4n posts used in all. However, in that case, we would be counting the posts at each corner twice (since two sides of the square would share the same corner).

   Thus, the number of posts used actually $= (4n - 4)$.

   But, $(4n - 4) = 4(n - 1)$ is a multiple of 4 while 50 (the number of posts available) is not.

   Thus, we need to take a multiple of 4 less than 50, i.e. 48.

   Hence, $4n - 4 = 48 => n = 13$.

   Thus, there are 13 posts along each side of the square garden.

   So, for 13 posts, there would be 12 gaps in between.

   So, the width of the 12 gaps $= 12$ feet (since each gap is one foot) $= 12 \times 12 = 144"$.

   Also, the width of the 13 posts $= 13 \times 5" = 65"$.

   Thus, the length of each side $= 144 + 65 = 209"$.

   Hence, the answer is 209.

48. **Level of Difficulty:** Difficult

   Topic: Linear inequality and equation (word problems)

   The correct answer is (B).

Let the two-digit number be $N = 10x + y$ where x and y are the digits.

Thus, the reverse of the above two-digit number is $10y + x$.

The value of $M = 10 + 10x + y = 10(x + 1) + y$.

Thus, the reverse of the above two-digit number is $10y + (x + 1)$.

Since all the above numbers are two-digit numbers, we have: $1 \leq x \leq 8$ and $1 \leq y \leq 9$.

Thus, Jacob was asked to add $10x + y$ and $10(x + 1) + y$.

Instead, he added $10y + x$ and $10y + (x + 1)$.

According to the problem, we have:

$(10y + x) + \big(10y + (x + 1)\big) = (10x + y) + (10(x + 1) + y) - 9$

$20y + 2x + 1 = 20x + 2y + 10 - 9 => 18y = 18x => x = y.$

Thus, the maximum value of the sum of digits of N, i.e. $x + y$, will occur when $x = y = 8$ (since the value of x cannot be 9, else M will become a three-digit number).

Thus, maximum value of the sum of digits of N, i.e. $x + y = 8 + 8 = 16$.

Hence, the correct answer is (B).

49. **Level of Difficulty:** Difficult

   Topic: Linear inequality and equation (word problems)

   The correct answer is (A).

   We know that Joseph has N friends. Also, each friend receives x lozenges initially.

   There are 7 lozenges are left over.

   Thus, the number of lozenges $= Nx + 7$ ... (i)

   Had he tried giving one more lozenge to each friend, i.e. each friend received $(x + 1)$ lozenges; and he could have perfectly distributed them among $(N - 3)$ friends.

   Thus, the number of lozenges $= (N - 3)(x + 1) = Nx - 3x + N - 3$ ... (ii)

   Hence, from (i) and (ii) we have: $Nx - 3x + N - 3 = Nx + 7 => N - 3x = 10 => N = 3x + 10$.

   Hence, the answer is (A).

50. **Level of Difficulty:** Medium

   Topic: Solving linear equations and inequalities

   The correct answer is 12.

   We have:

   $a + b + c = d$ ... (i)

   $a + c = 5b$ ... (ii)

   From (i) and (ii): $b + 5b = d => 6b = d$ ... (iii)

Since b and d are single digits, the only possible solution is $b = 1$ and $d = 6$ (if $b = 2$ or higher, then $d = 12$ or higher, which is not a single digit).

Thus, we have: $a + b + c + d = (a + b + c) + d = d + d = 6 + 6 = 12$.

Hence, the answer is 12.

51. **Level of Difficulty:** Medium

   Topic: Solving linear equations and inequalities

   The correct answer is (D).

   We know that $|x - a|$ refers to the distance of the point x from the point a on the number line.

   Based on the above expression, we can divide the number line in three regions as shown below:

   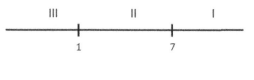

   Region I:

   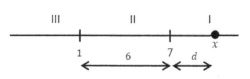

   $|x - 1|$ and $|x - 7|$ refer to the distances of the points 1 and 7 from x respectively. The distances between any two consecutive points have been marked (in bold) in the diagram.

   Thus, $|x - 1| + |x - 7| = 10 \Rightarrow (d + 6) + d = 10 \Rightarrow 2d + 6 = 10 \Rightarrow d = 2$.

   Hence, the value of $x = 7 + 2 = 9$.

   Region II:

   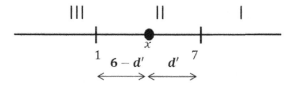

   Here, $|x - 1| + |x - 7| = (6 - d') + d' = 6 \neq 10$.

   Thus, no value of x is possible in this region.

   Region III:

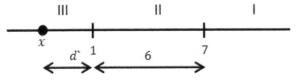

Here, $|x - 1| + |x - 7| = 10 \Rightarrow (d`) + (6 + d`) = 10 \Rightarrow 6 + 2d` = 10 \Rightarrow d` = 2$.

Hence, the value of $x = 1 - 2 = -1$ (we subtract since x is to the left of 1).

Thus, there are two possible values of x, namely $x = 9$ or $x = -1$.

Thus, the sum of all the possible values of $x = 9 + (-1) = 8$.

Hence, the correct answer is (D).

52. **Level of Difficulty:** Medium

    Topic: Linear function (word problems)

    The correct answer is (D).

    Harry gets a salary of $350 and saves $M from it.

    Thus, Harry is left with $$(350- M)$

    If he spends $A on each member, and there are 8 members, then total amount spent must be equal to $(8A)

    8A = (350 − M)

    Or, A $= \dfrac{350-M}{8} = 43.75 - 0.125M$

53. **Level of Difficulty:** Difficult

    Topic: Graphing linear equations

    The correct answer is (D).

    Slope of the line $= m = \dfrac{2q-p}{q-2p}$

    Since both points are in the first quadrant, $p > 0$ and $q > 0$

    Since $q > 2p$, let $q = 2p + k$, where $k > 0$

    Thus, slope $m = \dfrac{2(2p+k)-p}{(2p+k)-2p} = \dfrac{3p+2k}{k} = 3\left(\dfrac{p}{k}\right) + 2$

    Thus, the slope is greater than 2.

    The correct answer is option D.

54. **Level of Difficulty:** Medium

    Topic: Linear inequality and equation (word problems)

    The correct answer is (D).

    Let the price of a chair be $c and that of a table be $t.

    Thus, we have:

$7c + 13t = 1060 \dots \text{(i)}$

$13c + 7t = 940 \dots \text{(ii)}$

Since we see that in the equations, the coefficients have reversed positions, we would make two new equations by adding and subtracting the given equations.

Thus, by adding (i) and (ii), we have: $20c + 20t = 2000 \Rightarrow c + t = 100 \dots \text{(iii)}$

By subtracting (ii) from (i), we have: $-6c + 6t = 120 \Rightarrow -c + t = 20 \dots \text{(iv)}$

Adding (iii) and (iv): $2t = 120 \Rightarrow t = \$60$.

Substituting the value of t in (iii): $c = 100 - t = 100 - 60 = \$40$.

Thus, the price of two chairs and one table $= 2c + t = \$(2 \times 40 + 60) = \$140$.

Hence, the answer is (D).

55. **Level of Difficulty:** Difficult

Topic: Systems of linear inequalities (word problems)

The correct answer is (A).

Fraction of work done by Amy in 1 day $= \dfrac{1}{t}$

Fraction of work done by Amy and Bob together in 1 day $= \dfrac{1}{n}$

Thus, fraction of work completed by Bob in 1 day $= \left(\dfrac{1}{n} - \dfrac{1}{t}\right)$

Thus, time taken by Bob to complete the entire work $= \dfrac{1}{\left(\dfrac{1}{n} - \dfrac{1}{t}\right)} = \dfrac{nt}{t-n}$

Since Bob does twice the work in less than 16 days, he can complete that work in less than 8 days

$\dfrac{nt}{t-n} < 8$

$nt < 8t - 8n$

$n(t + 8) < 8t$

$n < \dfrac{8t}{8 + t}$

The correct answer is option A.

56. **Level of Difficulty:** Difficult

Topic: Solving linear equations and inequalities

The correct answer is 11.

We have:

$C + D = A \dots \text{(i)}$

$D - C = B \dots \text{(ii)}$

Adding the above two equations: $2D = A + B \dots \text{(iii)}$

Since 2D is even, A + B must be even. Thus, A and B are either both even or both odd.

Since we need to maximize the sum A + B + C + D, we should choose the maximum possible values of A and B.

Thus, let A = 5, B = 3 (both odd).

Hence, 2D = 5 + 3 = 8 => D = 4.

However, we cannot have any number as 4.

Hence, let us take A = 5, B = 1.

Hence, 2D = 5 + 1 = 6 => D = 3.

Since C + D = A => A + B + (C + D) = A + B + A = 2A + B = 2 × 5 + 1 = 11.

Hence, we have: A + B + C + D = 11.

Hence, the answer is 11.

57. **Level of Difficulty:** Difficult

Topic: Linear inequality and equation (word problems)

The correct answer is (B).

Let Ron buy c chocolates and p pencils.

Thus: $3c + 4p = 30$ ... (i)

The number of chocolates and pens must be positive integers. To find the integer solutions to the above equation, we need to find any one solution (by trial and error) and use that to find the other solutions.

The first solution is easily obtainable: $c = 10, p = 0$ (it does not matter that p is not a positive integer).

It is clear that we need to increase p and as a result, the value of c would decrease. Thus, to get the other solutions, we increase p by the coefficient of c, i.e. 3 and decrease c by the coefficient of p, i.e. 4.

The other solutions of the above equation are shown below:

c	p
10	0
6	3
2	6

Beyond this, the value of c would become negative and hence inadmissible.

Thus, there are only two ways in which Ron can spend the amount to buy chocolates and pencils (the first solution in the table above is inadmissible since the number of pencils is zero while the problem states that he needs to buy at least one of each).

Hence, the answer is (B).

58. **Level of Difficulty:** Medium

    Topic: Linear function (word problems)

    The correct answer is (B).

    Number of squares initially $= 13 \times 14 = 182$

    After Bob draws the additional squares, the grid has $(13 + 3) = 16$ rows

    There are $(14 + n)$ squares in each row

    Thus, the total number of squares $= 16(14 + n) = 224 + 16n$

    Thus, increase in the number of squares $= (224 + 16n) - 182 = 42 + 16n$

59. **Level of Difficulty:** Easy

    Topic: Systems of linear inequalities (word problems)

    The correct answer is (B).

    Since total number of fruits is less than 15, we have: $a + g < 18$

    Since total amount spent is less than \$12, we have: $80a + 60g < 1200 => 4a + 3g < 60$

60. **Level of Difficulty:** Medium

    Topic: Linear inequality and equation (word problems)

    The correct answer is (D).

    Ratio of the number of students in section A and B is $2: 3$.

    Also, the average weight of the students of section A is 2 lbs less than that of the students of section B.

    Let the average weight of the students of section B be x lbs.

    Thus, the average weight of the students of section A $= (x - 2)$ lbs.

    Thus, overall average weight of all 50 students $= \dfrac{2(x-2)+3x}{2+3} = \dfrac{5x-4}{5}$.

    Thus, $\dfrac{5x-4}{5} = 40 => x = 40.8$

    Thus, the average weight of the students of section B $= 40.8$ lbs.

    Hence, the answer is (D).

61. **Level of Difficulty:** Medium

    Topic: Interpreting linear functions

    The correct answer is 99.

    $r = 4\sqrt{n}$

    Also: $s = 40 - r = 40 - 4\sqrt{n}$

    The maximum number of bogies will be that value of n for the speed is just above '0' miles per hour. Thus, we have:

$40 - 4\sqrt{n} = 0$

$n = 100$

Thus, will 100 bogies, the final speed becomes '0'; hence, the maximum number of bogies the engine can pull will be 1 less, i.e. 99.

62. **Level of Difficulty:** Difficult

Topic: Graphing linear equations

The correct answer is (A).

From the diagram it is clear that the line $y = \text{m}x + n$ is a flat line, the slope is less than 1.

Thus, the value of $0 < m < 1$

Also, the Y-intercept is 2, i.e. $n = 2$

Thus, in the line $y = \text{n}x + m$, the slope is $n = 2$, the Y-intercept is a positive fraction.

Thus, the line would be as shown:

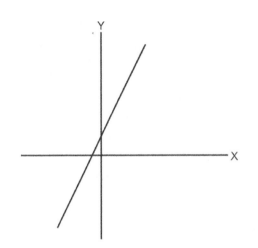

The correct answer is option A.

63. **Level of Difficulty:** Medium

Topic: Linear function (word problems)

The correct answer is (C).

For the first 3 hours, the Amount charged is 50

For more than 3 hours, the number of chargeable hours at the rate of 10, should be $(H - 3)$

Thus, the Amount collected should be $50 + (H - 3) \times 10 = 10H + 20$

The correct answer is option 'C'

64. **Level of Difficulty:** Medium

Topic: Solving linear equations and inequalities

The correct answer is (A).

$x^2 - 4x - 32 > 0 => (x - 8)(x + 4) > 0 => x > 8$ or $x < -4$ ... (i)

(Note: if the above had been an equation, the roots would have been 8 or – 4. Since the inequality is of 'more than' type, the solution can be remembered easily as: "greater than the greatest or less than the least". Here, the bigger root is 8, hence $x > 8$ while the smaller root is – 4, hence we have: $x < -4$).

$|x - 2| < 7 => -7 < x - 2 < 7 => -5 < x < 9$ ... (ii)

(Note: if the above had been an equation, the roots would have been 9 or – 5. Since the inequality is of 'less than' type, the solution can be remembered easily as: "in between the greatest and the least". Here, the bigger root is 9 while the smaller root is – 5, hence we have: $-5 < x < 9$).

Now, we need to combine the solutions from (i) and (ii) and find the common region (intersection) as shown in the number line below:

Hence, we see that the common regions are: $8 < x < 9$ or $-5 < x < -4$.

However, in the above regions, there is no integer value present.

Thus, there are no integer solutions for x.

Hence, the answer is (A).

65. **Level of Difficulty:** Medium

   Topic: Linear function (word problems)

   The correct answer is (C).

   Harry gets a salary of $360 and saves $\$\left(\frac{360}{n}\right)$

   Amount left = $\$\left(360 - \frac{360}{n}\right)$

   Amount he spends on each member = $\$\left(\frac{360}{n}\right)$

   So, we have $8\left(\frac{360}{n}\right) = 360 - \frac{360}{n}$

   $9\left(\frac{360}{n}\right) = 360 => n = 9$

   The correct answer is option C.

66. **Level of Difficulty:** Medium

   Topic: Systems of linear inequalities (word problems)

   The correct answer is (A).

Let the number of wrong answers = w => $4 \le w \le 8$

Number of correct answers = $(N - w)$

Thus, total score:

$S = 3.5(N - w) - 0.45w = 3.5N - 3.95w$

Minimum score happens when $w = 8$: $S = 3.5N - 3.95 \times 8 = 3.5N - 31.6$

Maximum score happens when $w = 4$: $S = 3.5N - 3.95 \times 4 = 3.5N - 15.8$

$3.5N - 31.6 \le S \le 3.5N - 15.8$

The correct answer is option A.

67. **Level of Difficulty:** Medium

Topic: Solving systems of linear equations

The correct answer is 1.5.

$Ax + By = C$

$Px + Qy = R$

For infinite solutions: $\dfrac{A}{P} = \dfrac{B}{Q} = \dfrac{C}{R}$

$\dfrac{3}{6} = \dfrac{k}{3} = \dfrac{1}{2} => k = \dfrac{3}{2} = 1.5$

The correct answer is 1.5

68. **Level of Difficulty:** Difficult

Topic: Linear inequality and equation (word problems)

The correct answer is (B).

Let the average in the first four games be x points.

Thus, total points across the four games = $4x$.

Since the team scored 88 points in their fifth game, the total points across the five games = $(4x + 88)$.

Thus, average across five games = $\dfrac{4x+88}{5}$.

Thus, increase in average = $\dfrac{4x+88}{5} - x = \dfrac{88-x}{5}$.

This increase is given to be an integer.

Now, when 88 is divided by 5, the remainder is 3.

Thus, x should be a number such that when it is divided by 5, the remainder is 3 as well so that the remainders cancel each other out in $(88 - x)$.

From the options, we can see that options (B) and (D) leave a remainder 3 when divided by 5. However, according to the question, the initial average must have been less than 88 as only then the average would increase.

Hence, the answer is (B).

69. **Level of Difficulty:** Easy

    Topic: Linear inequality and equation (word problems)

    The correct answer is 11.

    Let the number of responses that John got correct be c and the responses that he got incorrect be i.

    Thus: $c + i = 40$ ... (i)

    Also, since he secured 76 marks, we have: $3c - i = 76$ ... (ii)

    Adding (i) and (ii): $4c = 116 => c = 29$.

    Thus, $i = 40 - c = 40 - 29 = 11$.

    Hence, 11 of John's responses were incorrect.

    Hence, the answer is 11.

70. **Level of Difficulty:** Medium

    Topic: Linear inequality and equation (word problems)

    The correct answer is (C).

    Let the number of cars that Fred checked be x.

    Number of cars that did not have ABS $= 6$.

    Thus, the number of cars that had ABS $= x - 6$.

    Again, the number of cars that did not have ACC $= 7$.

    Thus, the number of cars that had ACC $= x - 7$.

    Since no car had both features, we can say that the cars having ABS and the cars having ACC are all different cars.

    Thus, total number of cars having a safety feature $= (x - 6) + (x - 7) = 2x - 13$.

    According to the problem, we have: $2x - 13 = 9 => 2x = 22 => x = 11$.

    Therefore, Fred had checked 11 cars.

    Hence, the correct answer is (C).

71. **Level of Difficulty:** Medium

    Topic: Linear function (word problems)

    The correct answer is (D).

    Let the linear function be: $D(p) = kp + l$, where k and l are constants

    At $p = 45, D = 1000 => 1000 = 45k + l$

    After $5 increase, new demand decreases by 5

    If $p = 50, D = 995 => 995 = 50k + l$

    Subtracting the 2 equations: $5k = -5 => k = -1$

    $l = 1045$

Thus: $D(p) = -p + 1045$

Only Option D, on simplification, leads to the same function.

Alternative:

At $p = 45$, the Demand must be 1000.

Only option that satisfies this condition is Option (D)

Hence the answer is Option 'D'

72. **Level of Difficulty:** Medium

Topic: Systems of linear inequalities (word problems)

The correct answer is (B).

The man travels n times per month.

Normal travel: Total cost = $\$(nx)$

With the pass: Total cost = $\${P + (x - r)n\}$

Thus, the pass will be profitable if:

$P + (x - r)n < nx$

$P < n\{x - (xsssss - r)\}$

$P < rn$

$n > \dfrac{P}{r}$

The correct answer is option B.

73. **Level of Difficulty:** Difficult

Topic: Linear inequality and equation (word problems)

The correct answer is (C).

Since Ron has to buy at least one of each item, he spends $\$(2 + 5 + 4) = \$11$.

Amount left with him = $\$(35 - 11) = \$24$.

He will be able to buy the maximum number of items if he purchases the items priced the least.

Thus, to maximize the number of items, he buys only chocolates with the remaining amount.

Number of chocolates he can buy $= \dfrac{24}{2} = 12$.

Thus, total number of items $= 3 + 12 = 15$ (maximum).

Similarly, he will be able to buy the minimum number of items if he purchases items priced the most.

Thus, to minimize the number of items, he should buy only pens with the remaining amount. However, since he needs to spend the entire amount, he cannot buy only pens since they are priced at $5 per piece whereas he has $24 left which is not a multiple of 5.

Thus, he needs to buy a combination of pens and pencils.

Let he buy x pens and y pencils.

Thus: $5x + 4y = 24 \dots$ (i)

Since 4y and 24 are even, $5x$ must be even, hence, x must be even.

Trying with $x = 4$, we get $y = 1$.

Thus, he can buy a minimum of $4 + 1 = 5$ items (since pens are priced maximum, we need to buy as many pens as possible in order to minimize the number of items).

Thus, total number of items $= 3 + 5 = 8$ (minimum).

Thus, the difference between the maximum and minimum number of items $= 15 - 8 = 7$.

Hence, the answer is (C).

74. **Level of Difficulty:** Difficult

Topic: Solving systems of linear equations

The correct answer is (A).

Let $\dfrac{1}{(x+y)} = a$ and $\dfrac{1}{(x-y)} = b$

$a + b = 4 \dots$ (i)

$2a + 3b = 9 \dots$ (ii)

From (ii) – 2 x (i): $b = 1$ and $a = 3$

$\dfrac{1}{x+y} = 3 => x + y = \dfrac{1}{3}$

Also: $\dfrac{1}{x-y} = 1 => x - y = 1$

Adding, we have: $2x = \dfrac{1}{3} + 1 = \dfrac{4}{3} => x = \dfrac{2}{3}$

The correct answer is option A.

75. **Level of Difficulty:** Medium

Topic: Interpreting linear functions

The correct answer is (C).

$C = 120 + 90 \times W + 78 \times N$

For 10 units, total cost $= 120 + 90W + 780 = 900 + 90W$

Thus: $900 + 90W \le 2700$

$W \le 20$

The correct answer is option C.

76. **Level of Difficulty:** Medium

    Topic: Linear inequality and equation (word problems)

    The correct answer is 12.

    Let the number of marbles with Peter be 8p (we assumed the number of marbles with Peter as 8p since Peter would give one-fourth of his marbles to Rene who would give away half of that to Andrew. It would be Easy to work if we assume the number of marbles with him as a multiple of $4 \times 2 = 8$).

    When Peter gives one-fourth of his marbles to Rene, he gives away $\frac{1}{4} \times 8p = 2p$ marbles to Rene.

    Thus, number of marbles left with Peter $= 8p - 2p = 6p$.

    Rene gives away half of what she received to Andrew, i.e. $\frac{1}{2} \times 2p = p$.

    Thus, the number of marbles received by Andrew $= p$.

    Thus, we have: $6p - p = 30 => 5p = 30 => p = 6$.

    Thus, the number of marbles Rene received from Peter $= 2p = 2 \times 6 = 12$.

    Hence, the answer is 12.

77. **Level of Difficulty:** Medium

    Topic: Systems of linear inequalities (word problems)

    The correct answer is (C).

    Maximum and minimum temperatures = 64.7° Fahrenheit and 79.4° Fahrenheit

    Average of the two values $= \dfrac{64.7 + 79.4}{2} = 72.05°$ Fahrenheit

    Difference between the above average and the maximum (or minimum) temperatures

    $= 79.4° - 72.05° = 7.35°$ Fahrenheit (this represents the maximum gap between any temperature and the average value obtained).

    Thus, we have: $|t - 72.05| \leq 7.35$

    The correct answer is option C.

78. **Level of Difficulty:** Difficult

    Topic: Linear inequality and equation (word problems)

    The correct answer is (D).

    Let the age of Alfred's son ten years back be x years.

    Hence, Alfred's age at that time was $3x + 30$ years.

    Thus, the present age of Alfred $= 3x + 30 + 10 = (3x + 40)$ years.

    Also, the present age of Alfred's son $= (x + 10)$ years.

    Now, in five years, Alfred would be $(3x + 40 + 5) = (3x + 45)$ years old.

    Also, in five years, Alfred's son would be $(x + 10 + 5) = (x + 15)$ years old.

Thus, $3x + 45 = 20 + 2(x + 15) => x = 5$.

Thus, the present age of Alfred $= 3x + 40 = 55$ years and the present age of Alfred's son $= x + 10 = 15$ years.

Let in y years, Alfred would become exactly twice as old as his son.

Thus, we have: $55 + y = 2(15 + y) => y = 25$.

Thus, Alfred would become twice as old as his son in 25 years (the ages of Alfred and his son would be 80 and 40 respectively).

Hence, the answer is (D).

79. **Level of Difficulty:** Difficult

Topic: Interpreting linear functions

The correct answer is (D).

For January: $m = 0$

Thus, number of items $= 60$

Since 80 items were procured in January, $80 - 60 = 20$ items were used up in January.

For February: $m = 1$

Thus, number of items $= 60 + 15 = 75$ => Number of additional items $= 75 - 60 = 15$

Since 80 items were procured in February, $80 - 15 = 65$ items were used up in February.

For March: $m = 2$

Thus, number of items $= 60 + 15 \times 2 = 90$ => Number of additional items $= 90 - 75 = 15$

Since 80 items were procured in March, $80 - 15 = 65$ items were used up in March.

Thus, total items used up $= 20 + 65 + 65 = 150$

The correct answer is option D.

80. **Level of Difficulty:** Difficult

Topic: Graphing linear equations

The correct answer is 3.5.

Equation of the line: $y = \frac{x}{2} + 3$

$2y - x = 3$

Thus, the X-intercept $(y = 0)$: $\frac{x}{2} = -3 => x = -6 =>$ The point is $(-6, 0)$

Y-intercept $(x = 0)$: $y = 3 =>$ The point is $(0, 3)$

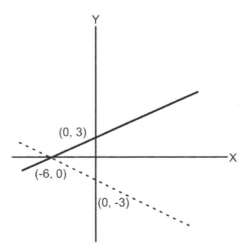

When this line is reflected about the X-axis, the X-intercept remains at $(-6, 0)$ while the Y-intercept changes to $(0, -3)$

Thus, the equation of the line through these points:

$$\frac{y - 0}{x + 6} = \frac{-3 - 0}{0 + 6}$$

$$\frac{y}{x + 6} = -\frac{1}{2}$$

$$y = -\frac{1}{2}x - 3$$

$$m = -\frac{1}{2}, n = -3 => m + n = -3.5$$

$$|m + n| = 3.5$$

Chapter 4

Passport to Advanced Math

---

1 The use of calculator is **permitted**.

Let $\leftrightarrow$ be an operation on p and q defined as $p \leftrightarrow q = (2^p - q)$. If $p \leftrightarrow 12 = p$, then find the value of p.

(A) 2

(B) 4

(C) 8

(D) 12

A   B   C   D
○   ○   ○   ○

2 The use of calculator is **permitted**.

The number of units sold, N, of a product follows the relation $N = 120 - C$, where $\$C$ is the selling price per unit. The cost to setup the manufacturing facility is $150 and the cost per unit is $5. If all units are sold, what should be the least selling price, in dollars, per unit to have a profit of $400?

3 The use of calculator is **not permitted**.

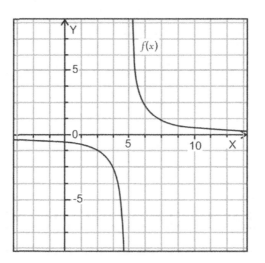

The graph of $f(x) = \dfrac{3}{x-5}$ is shown above:

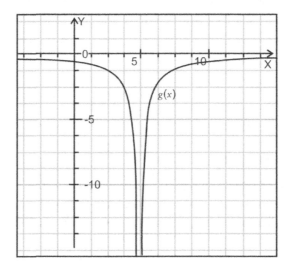

Which option gives the correct expression for $g(x)$ as shown below?

(A) $|f(x)|$

(B) $-|f(x)|$

(C) $-f(x)$

(D) $f(|x|)$

A   B   C   D
○   ○   ○   ○

4 The use of calculator is **permitted**.

For all non-negative numbers x, let $f(x) = x^3 - 8$ and $g(x) = x - 2$. For how many integer values of x is $f(x) = g(x)$? NC

(A) 0

(B) 1

(C) 2

(D) 3

A   B   C   D
○   ○   ○   ○

5 The use of calculator is **permitted**.

If $a^6 b^3 = 4816$ and $\dfrac{a^{10}}{b} = 301$, what is the value of $\dfrac{a^2}{b^2}$?

(A) 301

(B) 64

(C) 16

(D) 4

A   B   C   D
○   ○   ○   ○

6 The use of calculator is **not permitted**.

Let $\cong$ be an operation on a and b defined as $a \cong b = ab + b^2$. If $p \cong q = 0$ where p and q are non-zero integers, which of the following options is true?

(A) $p + q = 1$

(B) $p + 2q = 0$

(C) $p + 3q = 2p$

(D) $p - 2q = -3q$

A   B   C   D
○   ○   ○   ○

7 The use of calculator is **permitted**.

If $x^2 > x^3 > x$, which of the following statements must be correct?

I. $x^6 > x^7$

II. x can take any value between 0 and 1

III. $-1 < x < 0$

(A) Only I

(B) Only II

(C) Only III

(D) Both I and III

A   B   C   D
○   ○   ○   ○

8 The use of calculator is **permitted**.

A man puts $P in a bank which offers $n\%$ interest compounded annually. After 2 years, the amount of money in the bank is $M. Which of the following is the value of r if $M = \$1728$ and $P = 1200$?

9 The use of calculator is **permitted**.

After multiplying by 5, each of the following numbers will have the same number of perfect square factors EXCEPT

(A) 350

(B) 290

(C) 250

(D) 12

10 The use of calculator is **permitted**.

How many two-digit numbers exist such that the difference of the squares of its digits is 24?

(A) 2

(B) 4

(C) 6

(D) 8

11 The use of calculator is **not permitted**.

If p and q are the roots of $x^2 - 4x + 1 = 0$, choose from the options below, the correct equation whose roots are given by $(p + q)^2$ and $(p - q)^2$.

(A) $x^2 - 12x + 168 = 0$

(B) $x^2 - 10x + 90 = 0$

(C) $x^2 - 28x + 192 = 0$

(D) $x^2 - 36x + 320 = 0$

A	B	C	D
○	○	○	○

12 The use of calculator is **not permitted**.

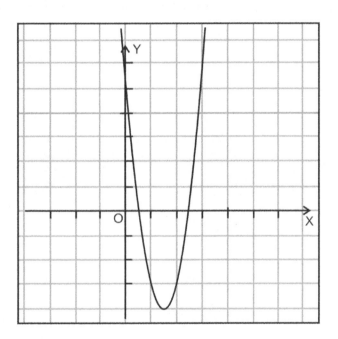

The graph of a quadratic expression $ax^2 + bx + c$ is shown beside. Which of the following is correct?

(A) $ab > 0, bc < 0, ac > 0$

(B) $ab > 0, bc > 0, ac > 0$

(C) $ab > 0, bc > 0, ac < 0$

(D) $ab < 0, bc < 0, ac > 0$

A	B	C	D
○	○	○	○

13 The use of calculator is **not permitted**.

If $f(x) = x^3 - kx^2 + 2x$ and $f(-x) = -f(x)$, the value of k is __

(A) – 2

(B) 0

(C) 1

(D) 2

A	B	C	D
◯	◯	◯	◯

14 The use of calculator is **permitted**.

Joe throws a ball upwards from a height of 12 feet from ground level. The height of the ball above the ground after time t seconds from when the ball was thrown is given by the expression $h(t) = -t^2 + at + b$. The ball comes back to the ground after 8 seconds. What is the value of $(a + b)$?

(A) 6.5

(B) 12.0

(C) 18.5

(D) 19.0

A	B	C	D
◯	◯	◯	◯

15 The use of calculator is **permitted**.

Which of the following correctly shows the range of the function $f(x) = \sqrt{-x^2 + 4x + 12}$?

(A) $0 < y < 4$

(B) $-1 \leq y \leq 4$

(C) $-1 < y < 5$

(D) $0 \leq y \leq 4$

A	B	C	D
◯	◯	◯	◯

16 The use of calculator is **not permitted**.

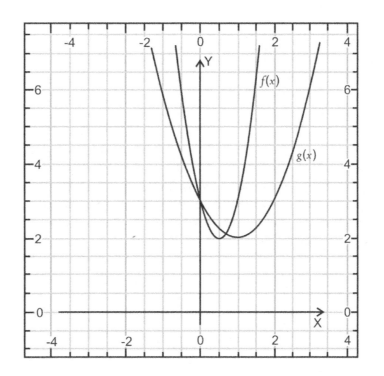

The graphs of $f(x)$ and $g(x)$ are shown below. Which option is true?

(A) $f(x) = g(x + 1)$

(B) $f(x) = g(x) + 1$

(C) $f(x) = 2g(x)$

(D) $f(x) = g(2x)$

A	B	C	D
○	○	○	○

17 The use of calculator is **not permitted**.

If $f(x + 2) = 3x + 11$ and $g(f(x)) = 2x$, find the value of $g(5)$.

(A) 0

(B) 1

(C) 3

(D) 5

A	B	C	D
○	○	○	○

18 The use of calculator is **permitted**.

If a and b are positive integers satisfying $(a + 3)^2 + (b + 1)^2 = 85$, what is the minimum value of $(2a + b)$?

(A) 6

(B) 7

(C) 11

(D) 12

A B C D
○ ○ ○ ○

19 The use of calculator is **permitted**.

Joe throws a ball upwards from a certain height above the ground level. The height of the ball above the ground after time t seconds from when the ball was thrown is given by the expression $h(t) = -(t - a)^2 + b$. The ball reaches a maximum height of 25 feet after 4 seconds. After how much time (in seconds) will the ball reach the ground level?

(A) 6

(B) 7

(C) 8

(D) 9

A B C D
○ ○ ○ ○

20 The use of calculator is **not permitted**.

If $f(x) = ax^2 + bx + c$ and $f(x + 1) = f(x) + x + 1$, then the value of $(a + b)$ is __

(A) – 2

(B) – 1

(C) 0

(D) 1

A B C D
○ ○ ○ ○

21 The use of calculator is **permitted**.

After multiplying by 2, each of the following numbers becomes a perfect square EXCEPT

(A) 72

(B) 162

(C) 392

(D) 500

A B C D
○ ○ ○ ○

22 The use of calculator is **permitted**.

$f(x) = x^2 + 16$. For what value of k is $f(2k + 1) = 2f(k) + 1$ if k is a positive integer?

23 The use of calculator is **not permitted**.

Which of the following statements are true regarding the expression $f(x) = x^2 - 6x + 11$?

I. The expression has a least value of 11

II. The value of the expression is always positive for any value of x

III. The roots of $f(x) = 0$ are real

(A) Only I

(B) Only II

(C) Both I and II

(D) Both II and III

24 The use of calculator is **not permitted**.

Let $\emptyset$ be an operation on x and y defined as $x \emptyset y = \dfrac{x^{-2}+y^{-2}}{x^{-1}+y^{-1}}$. Find the value of $(1 \emptyset 1) \emptyset 3$?

(A) 0.83

(B) 1.00

(C) 2.50

(D) 2.67

25 The use of calculator is **permitted**.

If $9^x - 2.3^x - 3 = 0$, what is the value of x?

26 The use of calculator is **not permitted**.

Find the sum of the first 20 terms of the sequence shown below:

$$\frac{1}{1(1+1)} + \frac{1}{2(2+1)} + \frac{1}{3(3+1)} + \frac{1}{4(4+1)} + \dots + \frac{1}{20(20+1)}.$$

(A) $\frac{1}{2}$

(B) $\frac{3}{4}$

(C) $\frac{9}{10}$

(D) $\frac{20}{21}$

A B C D

27 The use of calculator is **permitted**.

Let $\nexists$ be an operation on a and b defined as $a \nexists b = a^b$. If $p = 4 \nexists a, q = 4 \nexists b, r = 2 \nexists (2c)$ and $a + b + c = 4$, find the value of pqr.

(A) 4

(B) 16

(C) 64

(D) 256

A B C D

28 The use of calculator is **not permitted**.

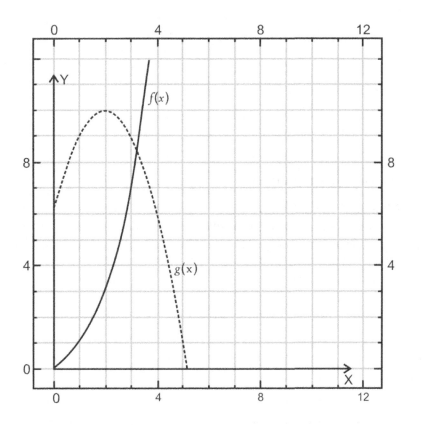

The graphs of $f(x)$ and $g(x)$ are shown below. If $3f(g(k) + 1) = g(f(m))$, where k and m are positive integers from 1 to 5, what is the maximum value of $(k + m)$?

29 The use of calculator is **not permitted**.

What is the value of x that satisfies the equation: $\sqrt{x-3} = \sqrt{2x+2} - 2$?

(A) 4

(B) 7

(C) 9

(D) 12

A   B   C   D
○   ○   ○   ○

30 The use of calculator is **not permitted**.

It was observed in an experiment that the number of bacteria doubles every hour. It was found that the number of bacteria twelve hours from the start of observation was 40960. After how many hours from the start of the experiment would the number of bacteria has been one-fourth the final number of bacteria?

(A) 11

(B) 10

(C) 8

(D) 6

A   B   C   D
○   ○   ○   ○

31 The use of calculator is **not permitted**.

Let $\forall$ be an operation on a defined as $\forall a = (a^2 - 3a - 4)$. If $\forall k$ also equals $(k - 4)$, find the positive value of k.

(A) -5

(B)

(C) 4

(D) 1

A   B   C   D
○   ○   ○   ○

32 The use of calculator is **permitted**.

If $x > x^3$, then all the options may be correct EXCEPT

(A) $x^3 > x^5$

(B) $x^2 > x$

(C) $x^2 > x^3$

(D) $\dfrac{1}{x} > \dfrac{1}{x^2}$

A   B   C   D
○   ○   ○   ○

33 The use of calculator is **not permitted**.

A sequence is defined as: $t_{n+1} = t_n - t_{n-1}$, where t_n denotes the nth term of the sequence. If $t_1 = 1$ and $t_2 = 5$, find the sum of the first 100 terms of the above sequence.

(A) 1

(B) 9

(C) 10

(D) 20

A B C D
○ ○ ○ ○

34 The use of calculator is **not permitted**.

Let ! be an operation on p and q defined as $q \mathbin{!} p = p^2 - 4pq + q^4$. If $x \mathbin{!} 1 = -3$, what is the value of $x \mathbin{!} (x + 1)$?

(A) -11

(B) 1

(C) 2

(D) 61

A B C D
○ ○ ○ ○

35 The use of calculator is **not permitted**.

What is the positive value of x that satisfies the equation: $\dfrac{6}{x+1} = \dfrac{3}{x-1} - 1$?

(A) 1

(B) 2

(C) 3

(D) 4

A B C D
○ ○ ○ ○

36 The use of calculator is **permitted**.

Let ■ be an operation on p defined as $■p = p^2 - 3$. Which of the following correctly represents the value of $■(■(■2))$?

(A) $■(■(■1))$

(B) $■\big(■(■(■(-2)))\big)$

(C) $■\big(■(■(-1))\big)$

(D) $■\big(■(■(■1))\big)$

A B C D
○ ○ ○ ○

37 The use of calculator is **not permitted**.

How many solutions exist for the equation $2|x - 1|^2 + 4 = 0$?

38 The use of calculator is **permitted**.

Let n be the value of the least integer ($0 < n < 5$) so that $3^{2n} + 4$ is not prime. What is the value of the remainder when $3^{2n} + 4$ is divided by n?

(A) 1

(B) 2

(C) 3

(D) 4

39 The use of calculator is **permitted**.

In the quadratic equation $ax^2 + bx + 2 = 0$, both a and b belong to the set $P = \{3, 4, 5\}$. How many different quadratic equations can be formed using the values from the set P for a and b so that the roots of the equation are real?

(A) 3

(B) 5

(C) 6

(D) 8

40 The use of calculator is **not permitted**.

Which of the following statements are true regarding the expression $f(x) = 2x^2 + 4x + 9$?

I.   The expression has a least value of 7

II. The value of the expression is always positive for any value of x

III. The roots of $f(x) = 0$ are irrational

(A) Only I

(B) Only II

(C) Only III

(D) Both I and II

<table>
<tr><td>A</td><td>B</td><td>C</td><td>D</td></tr>
<tr><td>○</td><td>○</td><td>○</td><td>○</td></tr>
</table>

41 The use of calculator is **not permitted**.

If $x - 2y = 2$ and $x^2 - y^2 = 9$, what is the value of $(x^3 - 2y^3 - xy^2 + 2x^2y)$?

42 The use of calculator is **permitted**.

In the formula $\dfrac{2}{3a} - \dfrac{4}{5b} = \dfrac{5}{4c}$, what is the correct expression of a in terms of b and c?

(A) $\dfrac{40bc}{3(16b+25c)}$

(B) $\dfrac{40bc}{3(16b+25c)}$

(C) $\dfrac{40bc}{3(25b+16c)}$

(D) $\dfrac{40bc}{3(25b-16c)}$

<table>
<tr><td>A</td><td>B</td><td>C</td><td>D</td></tr>
<tr><td>○</td><td>○</td><td>○</td><td>○</td></tr>
</table>

43   The use of calculator is **not permitted**.

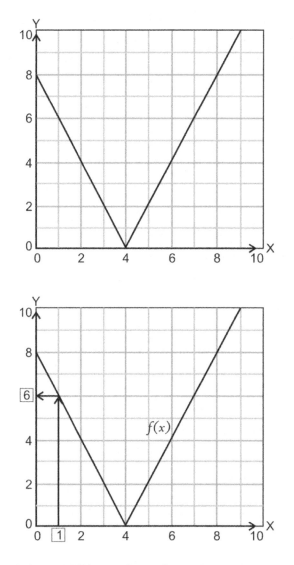

The graph of $y = f(x)$ is shown below. If $f(k) = 6$, then what is the minimum value of m so that $f(m) = k$?

44 	 The use of calculator is **permitted**.

How many values of x exist if $4^x - 12.2^x - 64 = 0$?

(A) 8

(B) 4

(C) 2

(D) 1

A 	 B 	 C 	 D
○ 	 ○ 	 ○ 	 ○

45 	 The use of calculator is **not permitted**.

If $(x) = \dfrac{a^x - 1}{a^x + 1}$, choose the correct statement.

I. 	 $f(-x) = f(x)$

II. 	 $f(-x) = -f(x)$

III. 	 $f(2x) = 2f(x)$

(A) Only I

(B) Only II

(C) Only III

(D) Both II and III

A 	 B 	 C 	 D
○ 	 ○ 	 ○ 	 ○

46 The use of calculator is **permitted**.

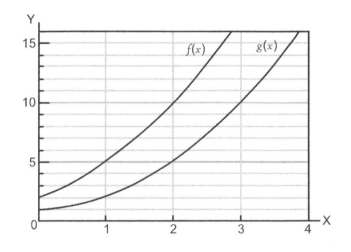

The graphs of $f(x)$ and $g(x)$ are shown below. Which option is true?

(A) $f(x) = (x + 2)^2$

(B) $f(x) = x^2 + 1$

(C) $g(x) = x^2$

(D) $g(x) = x^2 + 1$

A	B	C	D
○	○	○	○

47 The use of calculator is **not permitted**.

The function $f(x)$ is defined as follows:

$f(x) = x^2 - 1$ if $x \le 3$

$f(x) = 2x + 2$ if $3 < x \le 9$

$f(x) = 4x - 8$ if $x > 9$

What is the value of k if $f\left(f\big(f(3)\big)\right) = (k + 1)^2$ where k is a positive integer?

48 The use of calculator is **permitted**.

If $\dfrac{2x+3}{(x+1)(x+2)} = \dfrac{A}{x+1} + \dfrac{B}{x+2}$ for all real values of $x(\neq -1, -2)$, what is the value of $(A + B)$?

(A) 1

(B) 2

(C) 3

(D) 4

A   B   C   D
○   ○   ○   ○

49 The use of calculator is **permitted**.

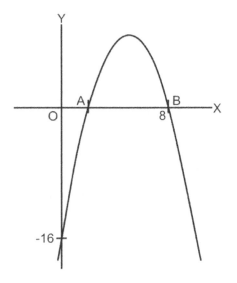

The graph of $f(x) = -x^2 + ax + b$ is shown below. What is the area of the square constructed with side AB?

50 The use of calculator is **not permitted**.

$f(x) = \frac{x-k}{5}$ and $g(x) = 5x + 7$. If $f(g(x)) = g(f(x))$, what is the value of k?

(A) 2

(B) 4

(C) 5

(D) 7

A	B	C	D
○	○	○	○

51 The use of calculator is **not permitted**.

Choose the correct option if it is known that one root of the quadratic equation $ax^2 + bx + c = 0$ is three times the other root?

(A) $b^2 = 3ac$

(B) $3b^2 = 16ac$

(C) $a^2 = 9b^2c$

(D) $4c^2 = 9ab$

A	B	C	D
○	○	○	○

52 The use of calculator is **not permitted**.

$f(x) = 2|x| + x$. Which of the options is the correct value of $f(-2) + f(-4)$?

(A) $f(-3)$

(B) $f(-1)$

(C) $f(0)$

(D) $f(2)$

A	B	C	D
○	○	○	○

53 The use of calculator is **permitted**.

If $f(x) = x^2 + 1$ and $f(g(2)) = 1$, then which of the following could be a possible expression for $g(x)$? C

(A) $5x - 1$

(B) $2x - 4$

(C) $6x + 3$

(D) $x - 1$

A	B	C	D
○	○	○	○

54 The use of calculator is **permitted**.

If $x = 4 + \frac{1}{a}$ and $y = 2 - \frac{1}{2a}$, what is the value of $(x^3 + 6x^2y + 12xy^2 + 8y^3)$?

55 The use of calculator is **permitted**.

If the quadratic equation $2x^2 + 5x + 1 = 0$ has roots p and q, what is the value of the expression $(2 - p)(2 - q)$?

(A) 0

(B) $2\sqrt{3}$

(C) $\sqrt{17}$

(D) 9.5

56 The use of calculator is **permitted**.

If $9^x - 2.3^x - 3 = 0$, what is the value of x?

57 The use of calculator is **not permitted**.

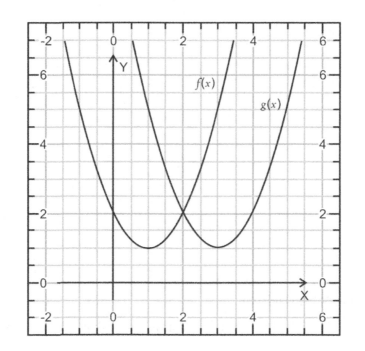

The graphs of $f(x)$ and $g(x)$ are shown below. Which option is true?

(A) $g(x) = f(x - 2)$

(B) $g(x) = f(x) + 1$

(C) $g(x) = f(x - 1)$

(D) $g(x) = f(x) - 2$

A   B   C   D
○   ○   ○   ○

58 The use of calculator is **permitted**.

$f(x)$ is defined to be the sum of all the digits in a number x. If x is a three-digit number, what is the difference between the largest and the smallest values of x such that $f(x) = 11$?

(A) 81

(B) 101

(C) 791

(D) 801

A   B   C   D
○   ○   ○   ○

59 The use of calculator is **not permitted**.

A symbol is defined below:

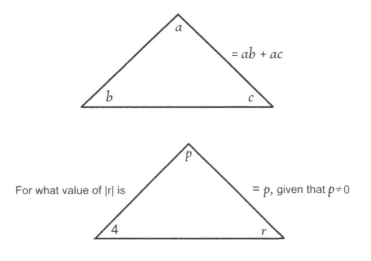

For what value of |r| is ⟨triangle with p, 4, r⟩ = p, given that $p \neq 0$

Find the value of $|r|$ given that $p \neq 0$?

60 The use of calculator is **not permitted**.

If the quadratic equations $x^2 - ax + 30 = 0$ and $x^2 - 12x + 20 = 0$ have exactly one root common, find the sum of the possible values of a.

(A) 3

(B) 10

(C) 13

(D) 17

61   The use of calculator is **not permitted**.

$f(x) = 3\sqrt[3]{x} - 5$ and $g(x) = 2px + q^2$. If $f\big(g(2)\big) = 7$, what is the minimum value of $(p + q)$ if p is a positive integer?

62   The use of calculator is **not permitted**.

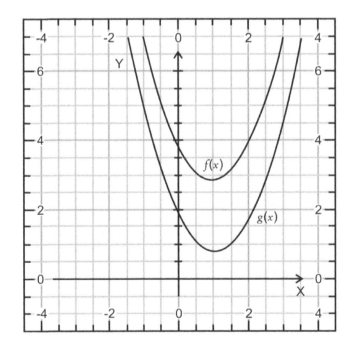

The graphs of $f(x)$ and $g(x)$ are shown below. Which option is true?

(A) $f(x) = g(x + 2)$

(B) $f(x) = g(x) + 2$

(C) $f(x) = g(x - 2)$

(D) $f(x) = g(x) - 2$

63 The use of calculator is **not permitted**.

The product of three consecutive positive integers is 8 times the sum of the three numbers. What is the sum of the three integers?

64 The use of calculator is **permitted**.

The harmonic mean of two quantities a and b is defined as $\dfrac{2ab}{a+b}$. If the harmonic mean of the quantities x and 12 is one less than the average of the same two quantities, which of the following can be the value of the sum of digits in x?

(A) 1

(B) 2

(C) 4

(D) 5

A B C D
○ ○ ○ ○

65 The use of calculator is **not permitted**.

If $2x = a - \dfrac{1}{a}$, where $a > 0$, what is the value of $\sqrt{(x^2 + 1)} + x$?

(A) 1

(B) $\dfrac{1}{a}$

(C) a

(D) $\dfrac{1}{2}\left(a + \dfrac{1}{a}\right)$

A B C D
○ ○ ○ ○

66 The use of calculator is **not permitted**.

$P = \left(1 + \frac{1}{x}\right)\left(1 + \frac{1}{x+1}\right)\left(1 + \frac{1}{x+2}\right) \ldots \left(1 + \frac{1}{x+20}\right)$. What is the value of P if $x = 9$?

(A) 1.50

(B) 2.25

(C) 2.75

(D) 3.33

A   B   C   D
○ ○ ○ ○

67 The use of calculator is **permitted**.

If $(x - 3)^2 < 25$ and $(y - 5)^2 < 4$, what is sum of the maximum and minimum possible values of $\frac{x}{y}$ given that x and y are integers?

(A) 2.67

(B) 2.00

(C) 1.50

(D) 1.20

A   B   C   D
○ ○ ○ ○

68 The use of calculator is **permitted**.

At how many points does the line $y = 2x - 1$ intersect the circle $(x - 4)^2 + (y - 6)^2 = 2$?

69 The use of calculator is **not permitted**.

If $h(x) = 2^{kx-1}$, what is the value of $\dfrac{h(a)h(b)}{h(a+b)}$?

(A) 4

(B) 2

(C) 1

(D) 0.5

A   B   C   D
○   ○   ○   ○

70 The use of calculator is **permitted**.

It is observed that the number of ants living in a colony increase by 25% every week. After four weeks of observation, total ants were found to be 6250. How many ants were found when the observation was first made?

(A) 1250

(B) 2560

(C) 3125

(D) 3250

A   B   C   D
○   ○   ○   ○

71 The use of calculator is **not permitted**.

If $N = a^2 b^4$ is divisible by 8 and 27. If a and b are positive integers not having any common factors except one, what is the minimum value of the least common multiple of a and b?

(A) 6

(B) 8

(C) 9

(D) 12

A   B   C   D
○   ○   ○   ○

72 The use of calculator is **not permitted**.

Find the sum of the possible integer values of m:

$2m + n = 10$
$m(n - 1) = 9$

73 The use of calculator is **permitted**.

In a series, the first term is k. Each term thereafter is three times the preceding term. The sum of the first six terms is 728. What is the sum of the first three terms of the series?

(A) 2

(B) 13

(C) 26

(D) 80

74 The use of calculator is **not permitted**.

In the formula $s = ut - \frac{a}{2}t^2$, which of the following is NOT the correct expression of a in terms of s, u and t?

(A) $\frac{2u}{t} - \frac{s}{t^2}$

(B) $\frac{2(ut - s)}{t^2}$

(C) $\frac{u - st}{2t}$

(D) $\frac{1}{t}\left(2u - \frac{s}{t}\right)$

75 The use of calculator is **permitted**.

If $f(x) = 8 - x^2$ where $-3 < x < 3$, what is the range of values of $f(x)$?

(A) $0 < y < 7$

(B) $-1 \leq y \leq 8$

(C) $8 < y < 17$

(D) $-1 < y \leq 8$

A   B   C   D
O   O   O   O

76 The use of calculator is **not permitted**.

A quadratic function $f(x)$ intersects the X-axis at points $(6, 0)$ and $(8, 0)$. If $f(a) = f(2) = 24$, what is the value of a $(a \neq 2)$?

77 The use of calculator is **permitted**.

In a sequence of terms, the first term is (-1). Each term thereafter is obtained by multiplying the previous number with (-2). How many of the first 50 terms of the series are less than 50?

(A) 3

(B) 25

(C) 28

(D) 32

A   B   C   D
O   O   O   O

78 The use of calculator is **permitted**.

If $f(x)$ be a function such that $f(-x) = -f(x)$, $g(x)$ be a function such that $g(-x) = -g(x)$ and $h(x)$ be a function such that $h(-x) = h(x)$, then choose the correct statement:

I. $h\big(f(g(-x))\big) = -h\big(f(g(x))\big)$

II. $f\big(g(h(-x))\big) = f\big(g(h(x))\big)$

III. $g(f(-x)) = g(f(x))$

(A) Only I

(B) Only II

(C) Only III

(D) Both I and II

A   B   C   D
○   ○   ○   ○

79 The use of calculator is **not permitted**.

If $\sqrt{x + 3} + \sqrt{7 - x} = 4$, what is the positive value of x^3?

(A) 1

(B) 8

(C) 27

(D) 216

A   B   C   D
○   ○   ○   ○

80 The use of calculator is **not permitted**.

If $f(x) = |x - 2| + x^2 - 1$ and $g(x) + f(x) = x^2 + 3$, find the maximum value of $g(x)$.

Answers and Explanations

1. **Level of Difficulty:** Medium

   Topic: Functions

   The correct answer is (B).

   We have: $p \leftrightarrow 12 = p$

   Going by the option:

   Option (A): $p \leftrightarrow 12 = p => 2^p - 12 = p => 2^2 - 12 = 2 =>$ which is not true.

   Option (B): $p \leftrightarrow 12 = p => 2^p - 12 = p => 2^4 - 12 = 4 =>$ which is true.

   Hence, (B) must be the correct option (we can verify the other options as not correct).

   Option (C): $p \leftrightarrow 12 = p => 2^p - 12 = p => 2^8 - 12 = 8 =>$ which is not true.

   Option (D): $p \leftrightarrow 12 = p => 2^p - 12 = p => 2^{12} - 12 = 12 =>$ which is not true.

   Hence, the correct answer is (B).

2. **Level of Difficulty:** Easy

   Topic: Linear and quadratic systems

   The correct answer is 10.

   For N units sold at $\$C$, total selling price $= \$(CN)$

   $= \$C(120 - C)$

   Total cost $= \$(150 + 5N) = \$(150 + 5(120 - C)) = \$(750 - 5C)$

   Selling price $=$ Cost price $+ \$400$

   $C(120 - C) = 750 - 5C + 400$

   $C^2 - 125C + 1150 = 0$

   $C^2 - 115C - 10C + 1150 = 0$

   $(C - 115)(C - 10) = 0$

   $C = 10$ or 115

   Thus, the minimum selling price $= \$10$.

3. **Level of Difficulty:** Difficult

   Topic: Nonlinear equation graphs

   The correct answer is (B).

   We have to find $g(x)$ in terms of $f(x)$.

   We can observe that the graph has not been shifted nor has the graph been magnified or minimized.

   The change is the part of the graph above the X-axis has been reflected down about the X-axis.

   So, if we take $|f(x)|$, then thenegative part of the graph (i.e. the part below the X-axis) would be reflected up about the X-axis.

Then if we negate the above graph, the entire graph would be reflected again about the X-axis and we would obtain the final form as given for $g(x)$.

Thus, the steps are: $f(x) \rightarrow |f(x)| \rightarrow -|f(x)|$.

Hence, we have $g(x) = -|f(x)|$.

Hence, the correct answer is (B).

4. **Level of Difficulty:** Difficult

   Topic: Linear and quadratic systems

   The correct answer is (B).

   $f(x) = x^3 - 8$

   $g(x) = x - 2$

   We have:

   $f(x) = g(x)$

   $x^3 - 8 = x - 2$

   $(x - 2)(x^2 + 2x + 4) - (x - 2) = 0$

   $(x - 2)(x^2 + 2x + 4) = 0$

   $x = 2$ OR $x^2 + 2x + 4 = 0$ (which has imaginary solutions)

   Thus, there is 1 possible value of x.

   The correct answer is option B.

5. **Level of Difficulty:** Easy

   Topic: Radicals and rational exponents

   The correct answer is (D).

   We have:

   $a^6 b^3 = 4816 \dots$ (i) and $\dfrac{a^{10}}{b} = 301 \dots$ (ii)

   Dividing (i) by (ii):

   $\dfrac{a^6 b^3}{\dfrac{a^{10}}{b}} = \dfrac{4816}{301} => (a^6 b^3) \times \left(\dfrac{b}{a^{10}}\right) = 16 => \dfrac{b^4}{a^4} = 16$

   Taking square root on both sides:

   $\dfrac{b^2}{a^2} = \sqrt{16} = 4.$

   Hence, the answer is (D).

6. **Level of Difficulty:** Difficult

    Topic: Functions

    The correct answer is (D).

    We have:

    $p \cong q = 0 => pq + q^2 = 0 => q(p + q) = 0 => p + q = 0.$

    Thus, options (A), and (B) are not true.

    Option (C): $p + 3q = p + q + 2q = 0 + 2q = 2q.$

    Hence, option (C) is not true.

    Option (D): $p - 2q = p + q - 3q = 0 - 3q = -3q.$

    Hence, option (D) is true.

    Hence, the correct answer is (D).

7. **Level of Difficulty:** Difficult

    Topic: Interpreting nonlinear expressions

    The correct answer is (D).

    While solving these types of questions, it is best to divide the number line in the four parts as shown below:

    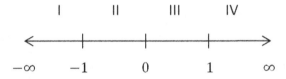

    We now need to pick a number from the regions (I, II, III and IV) and check which region(s) satisfy.

    However, to check statement I, we may follow a different strategy:

    Since $x^2 > x^3$, we can multiply both sides of the inequality by x^4: $x^2 \times x^4 > x^3 \times x^4 => x^6 > x^7$ (since x^4 is always non-negative, multiplying an inequality by x^4 will not reverse the inequality).

    Hence, the first statement is correct.

    To verify the second statement: Let us pick a number between 0 and 1, say 0.5 and see if it satisfies the condition. Thus, we have: $x^2 = 0.5^2 = 0.25, x^3 = 0.5^3 = 0.125.$

    Thus, we see that $x > x^2 > x^3.$

    Hence, the second statement is not correct.

    To verify the third statement: Let us pick one number between 0 and -1, say -0.5.

    Let us see if $x = -0.5$ satisfies the condition. Thus, we have: $x^2 = 0.25, x^3 = -0.125.$

    Thus, $x^2 > x^3 > x.$

    Hence, the condition is satisfied.

    Hence, the third statement is correct.

Hence, the answer is (D).

8. **Level of Difficulty:** Medium

   Topic: Isolating quantities

   The correct answer is 20.

   Amount after 2 years $= \$\left\{ P\left(1 + \frac{r}{100}\right)^2 \right\}$

   $$M = P\left(1 + \frac{r}{100}\right)^2$$

   $$\left(1 + \frac{r}{100}\right)^2 = \frac{M}{P}$$

   $$1 + \frac{r}{100} = \left(\frac{M}{P}\right)^{\left(\frac{1}{2}\right)}$$

   $$\frac{r}{100} = \left(\frac{M}{P}\right)^{\left(\frac{1}{2}\right)} - 1$$

   $$r = 100\left\{ \left(\frac{M}{P}\right)^{\left(\frac{1}{2}\right)} - 1 \right\}$$

   $$r = 100\left\{ \left(\frac{1728}{1200}\right)^{\left(\frac{1}{2}\right)} - 1 \right\}$$

   $$r = 20$$

9. **Level of Difficulty:** Difficult

   Topic: Radicals and rational exponents

   The correct answer is (C).

   We need to find the number of factors of each of the numbers which are perfect squares after the numbers are multiplied by 5. Thus, we need to break the numbers in their prime form. Working with options, we have:

   (A): $350 \times 5 = 2 \times 5^3 \times 7$.

   Hence, the factors which are perfect squares are 1 and 5^2. Thus, there are <u>two</u> such factors.

   (B): $290 \times 5 = 29 \times 2 \times 5^2$.

   Hence, the factors which are perfect squares are 1 and 5^2. Thus, there are <u>two</u> such factors.

   Since both options (A) and (B) have the same number of perfect square factors, any option that does not have two perfect square factors must be the answer.

   (C): $250 \times 5 = 2 \times 5^4$.

   Hence, the factors which are perfect squares are 1, 5^2 and 5^4. Thus, there are <u>three</u> such factors.

   Hence, we know that (C) must be the answer.

   It can be verified that options (D) does not have perfect square factor:

   (D): $12 \times 5 = 2^2 \times 3 \times 5 => 1$ and 2^2.

Hence, the answer is (C).

10. **Level of Difficulty:** Difficult

    Topic: Quadratic and exponential (word problems)

    The correct answer is (B).

    Let the two-digit number be $N = 10x + y$ where x and y are the digits.

    We know that $1 \le x \le 9$ and $0 \le y \le 9$.

    Thus, we have: $x^2 - y^2 = 24$ or $y^2 - x^2 = 24$.

    Let us work with the first condition: $x^2 - y^2 = 24$:

    $x^2 - y^2 = 24 => (x + y)(x - y) = 24$.

    Thus, we need to break 24 in two factors, one of which will be $x + y$ and the other will be $x - y$.

    Now, x and y must be integers.

    In order for this to happen, either $x + y$ and $x - y$ should both be even, or both be odd (if one is even and the other is odd, on adding them, we will get $2x$ which will be odd which is not possible for an integer).

    Since 24 is even, we cannot have both its factors as odd. Thus, both $x + y$ and $x - y$ must be even (while assigning values to $x + y$ and $x - y$, we must keep in mind that $x + y > x - y$).

    Thus, possible values of $x + y$ and $x - y$ are listed below:

$x + y$	$x - y$	x (add $x + y$ and $x - y$ and divide the result by 2)	y (subtract $x - y$ from $x + y$ and divide the result by 2)	$N = 10x + y$
12	2	7	5	75
6	4	5	1	51

    Thus, there are two values of N possible, 75 and 51.

    For the second case, i.e. $y^2 - x^2 = 24$, we will get the reverse numbers i.e. 57 and 15.

    Thus, there are 4 possible numbers.

    Hence, the correct answer is (B).

11. **Level of Difficulty:** Easy

    Topic: Solving quadratic equations

    The correct answer is (C).

    We know that in a quadratic equation $ax^2 + bx + c = 0$, the sum of the roots is given by $\left(-\frac{b}{a}\right)$ and the product of the roots is given by $\left(\frac{c}{a}\right)$.

    Thus, in the equation $x^2 - 4x + 1 = 0$, having roots as p and q, we have:

$$p + q = -\frac{-4}{1} = 4 \ldots \text{(i)}$$

$$pq = \frac{1}{1} = 1 \ldots \text{(ii)}$$

Thus: $(p + q)^2 = 4^2 = 16 \ldots \text{(iii)}$

Also, we have: $(p - q)^2 = (p + q)^2 - 4pq = 16 - 4 = 12 \ldots \text{(iv)}$

Thus, the new roots are 16 and 12.

Thus, the equation can be written as: $(x - 16)(x - 12) = 0 => x^2 - 28x + 192 = 0$.

Hence, the correct answer is (C).

12. **Level of Difficulty:** Difficult

    Topic: Polynomial factors and graphs

    The correct answer is (D).

    From the graph above, when $x = 0$, the value of y i.e. $f(0)$ is positive since the graph intersects the Y-axis above the origin.

    Substituting $x = 0$ in $f(x)$, we get: $f(0) = 0 + 0 + c = c$. Thus, the value of c must be positive.

    The graph intersects the X-axis at two points (the roots), both of which are positive. Hence, product of the roots is positive.

    We know that the product of the roots of the quadratic function $f(x) = ax^2 + bx + c$ is given by $\frac{c}{a}$.

    Thus, we can say that $\frac{c}{a}$ is positive.

    Since we know that c is positive, a must be positive.

    Alternatively, we can see that the graph is open upwards. Hence, the value of a must be positive.

    Since both roots are positive in the above graph, the sum of roots is also positive.

    We know that the sum of the roots of the quadratic function $f(x) = ax^2 + bx + c$ is given by $-\frac{b}{a}$.

    Thus, we can say that $-\frac{b}{a}$ is positive, hence, $\frac{b}{a}$ is negative.

    Since we know that a is positive, b must be negative.

    Thus, we have $a > 0, b < 0, c > 0$.

    Thus, $ab < 0, bc < 0, ac > 0$.

    Hence, the correct option is (D).

13. **Level of Difficulty:** Easy

    Topic: Functions

    The correct answer is (C).

    $f(-x) = (-x)^3 - k(-x)^2 + 2(-x) = -x^3 - kx^2 - 2x$.

    Since $f(-x) = -f(x) => -x^3 - kx^2 - 2x = -(x^3 - kx^2 + 2x) => 2kx^2 = 0 => k = 0$.

(Note: We should not conclude that $x = 0$ since according to the question, $f(-x) = -f(x)$ for all x in general).

Hence, the correct answer is (C).

14. **Level of Difficulty:** Difficult

    Topic: Quadratic and exponential (word problems)

    The correct answer is (C).

    $h(t) = -t^2 + at + b$.

    At $t = 0$, height of the ball above the ground level is 12 feet.

    Thus, $h(0) = 12 => b = 12$.

    Thus, $h(t) = -t^2 + at + 12$.

    Again, at $t = 8$, height of the ball above the ground level is zero.

    Thus, $h(8) = 0 => -64 + 8a + 12 = 0 => a = \frac{52}{8} = 6.5$.

    Thus, $h(t) = -t^2 + 6.5t + 12$.

    Thus, $a + b = 6.5 + 12 = 18.5$.

    Hence, the correct answer is (C).

15. **Level of Difficulty:** Difficult

    Topic: Functions

    The correct answer is (D).

    $-x^2 + 4x + 12 = -(x^2 - 4x) + 12 = -((x - 2)^2 - 4) + 12 = -(x - 2)^2 + 16$.

    Thus, $f(x) = \sqrt{-(x - 2)^2 + 16}$

    (For the function to exist, the part under the root must be non-negative.

    Thus, $-(x - 2)^2 + 16 \geq 0 => (x - 2)^2 \leq 16 => -4 \leq x - 2 \leq 4 => -2 \leq x \leq 6)$.

    The maximum value of $f(x)$ will occur when the term $-(x - 2)^2$ becomes zero (since the negative of a perfect square is non-positive and hence, when it becomes zero, the value of the function will be maximum).

    Thus, maximum value of $f(x) = \sqrt{16} = 4$.

    For the minimum value, we know that the "$\sqrt{}$" symbol only takes the positive square root.

    We can see that $-(x - 2)^2 + 16$ can be zero at $x = 6$.

    Thus, we can say that $f(x)$ is minimum zero and maximum 4.

    Hence, the range of $f(x)$ is given by: $0 \leq y \leq 4$.

    Hence, the correct answer is (D).

16. **Level of Difficulty:** Medium

    Topic: Nonlinear equation graphs

    The correct answer is (D).

    It appears that $f(x)$ has been made narrower compared to $g(x)$ keeping y values same.

    Let us pick a few values of y and check the values of x for each of $f(x)$ and $g(x)$.

    At $y = 2$: $x = 1$ for $g(x)$ while we have $x = 0.5$ for $f(x)$.

    At $y = 3$: $x = 0$ for both $g(x)$ and $f(x)$.

    At $y = 6$: $x = 3$ for $g(x)$ while we have $x = 1.5$ for $f(x)$.

    Thus, we see that for the same y values, the values of x in $f(x)$ are half of that of $g(x)$.

    Also, the minimum values of both $f(x)$ and $g(x)$ are the same.

    Thus, the graph of $f(x)$ is narrower than the graph of $g(x)$ by a factor of two.

    Thus, we can say that $f(x) = g(2x)$.

    Say $x = 1$: $f(x) = f(1) = 3$ and $g(2x) = g(2) = 3 => f(1) = g(2)$.

    Thus, the correct answer is (D).

17. **Level of Difficulty:** Medium

    Topic: Functions

    The correct answer is (A).

    $f(x + 2) = 3x + 11 = 3(x + 2) + 5$.

    Thus, we can say that: $f(x) = 3x + 5$.

    $g\big(f(x)\big) = g(3x + 5) = 2x = \frac{2}{3} \times (3x + 5) - \frac{10}{3} => g(3x + 5) = \frac{2}{3} \times (3x + 5) - \frac{10}{3}$.

    Thus, we can say that: $g(x) = \frac{2}{3}x - \frac{10}{3}$.

    Hence, $g(5) = \frac{2}{3} \times 5 - \frac{10}{3} = 0$.

    Hence, the correct answer is (A).

18. **Level of Difficulty:** Difficult

    Topic: Solving quadratic equations

    The correct answer is (D).

    Since a and b are positive integers, then $a + 3$ and $b + 1$ are positive integers as well.

    Thus, we need to find two integers whose sum of squares is 85.

    There are two such possibilities: $2^2 + 9^2 = 85$ or $6^2 + 7^2 = 85$.

    Thus, we can list the possible cases for a and b as shown in the table below:

$a + 3$	$b + 1$	a	b	$2a + b$
2	9	−1	Not possible	
9	2	6	1	13
6	7	3	6	12
7	6	4	5	13

Thus, we can see that the minimum value of $2a + b = 12$.

Hence, the correct answer is (D).

19. **Level of Difficulty:** Medium

Topic: Quadratic and exponential (word problems)

The correct answer is (D).

$h(t) = -(t - a)^2 + b$.

Since $(t - a)^2$ is a perfect square, it is always non-negative.

Thus, $-(t - a)^2$ is always non-positive.

Hence, for $h(t)$ to have the maximum value, the value of $-(t - a)^2$ should be zero; in that case the maximum height would be b.

Thus, $-(t - a)^2 = 0 => t = a$.

But we know that the maximum height was reached after 4 seconds.

Thus, $a = 4$.

Also, the maximum height reached is 25 feet.

Thus, $b = 25$.

Hence, $h(t) = -(t - 4)^2 + 25$.

Thus, we need to find when $h(t) = 0 => -(t - 4)^2 + 25 = 0 => (t - 4)^2 = 25$.

$t - 4 = \pm 5 => t = 4 \pm 5 => t = 9 \text{ or } -1$.

Since time cannot be negative, we get $t = 9$.

Thus, the ball reaches the ground level after 9 seconds.

Hence, the correct answer is (D).

20. **Level of Difficulty:** Medium

Topic: Functions

The correct answer is (D).

$f(x + 1) = f(x) + x + 1 => a(x + 1)^2 + b(x + 1) + c = ax^2 + bx + c + x + 1$

$a((x + 1)^2 - x^2) + b((x + 1) - x) = (x + 1)$

$a(2x + 1) + b = x + 1$.

The above is an identity, hence would be true for all values of x.

Since we need $a + b$, we substitute $x = 0$ in the above identity so that we get $2x + 1 = 1$.

Thus, we have: $a(2 \times 0 + 1) + b = 0 + 1 => a + b = 1$.

Hence, the correct answer is (D).

21. **Level of Difficulty:** Easy

Topic: Radicals and rational exponents

The correct answer is (D).

We need to find the number which when multiplied by 2 becomes a perfect square. Thus, we need to break the numbers in their prime form and check if the exponent of each prime is an even number (since perfect squares must have even exponents of each prime factor). Working with options, we have:

(A): $72 \times 2 = 2^4 \times 3^2$.

Since the exponents are even, the resulting number will be a perfect square.

(B): $162 \times 2 = 3^4 \times 2^2$.

Since the exponents are even, the resulting number will be a perfect square.

(C): $392 \times 2 = 2^4 \times 7^2$.

Since the exponents are even, the resulting number will be a perfect square.

(D): $500 \times 2 = 2^3 \times 5^3$.

Since the exponents are not even, the resulting number will not be a perfect square.

Hence, the answer should be (D).

Hence, the answer is (D).

22. **Level of Difficulty:** Easy

Topic: Functions

The correct answer is 2.

$f(2k + 1) = (2k + 1)^2 + 16 = 4k^2 + 4k + 17$.

$2f(k) + 1 = 2(k^2 + 16) + 1 = 2k^2 + 33$.

Thus, we have: $4k^2 + 4k + 17 = 2k^2 + 33 => 2k^2 + 4k - 16 = 0 => k^2 + 2k - 8 = 0$

$(k - 2)(k + 4) = 0 => k = 2$ or -4.

Since k is positive, we have $k = 2$.

Hence, the correct answer is 2.

23. **Level of Difficulty:** Difficult

Topic: Rational expressions and polynomials

The correct answer is (B).

We have $f(x) = x^2 - 6x + 11$

$(x - 3)^2 + 2$

Since $(x - 3)^2$ is a perfect square, it is non-negative.

Hence, the lease value of $f(x)$ occurs if the perfect square term becomes zero (which happens if $x = 3$).

In that case, the value of $f(x)$ becomes 2.

Thus, the least value of $f(x)$ is 2.

Hence, statement I is false.

Again, since $f(x) = (x - 3)^2 + 2$ and $(x - 3)^2$ is non-negative, we can conclude that the value of $f(x)$ for any value of x will always be positive.

Hence, statement II is true.

In a quadratic equation $ax^2 + bx + c = 0$, the roots are imaginary if $b^2 - 4ac < 0$.

Here, $a = 1, b = -6, c = 11$. Thus, $b^2 - 4ac = 36 - 44 = -8 < 0$.

Thus, the roots of the equation $f(x) = 0$ are imaginary.

Hence, statement III is false.

Hence, the correct answer is (B).

24. **Level of Difficulty:** Easy

    Topic: Functions

    The correct answer is (A).

    $$x \oslash y = \frac{x^{-2} + y^{-2}}{x^{-1} + y^{-1}} = \frac{\left(\dfrac{1}{x^2} + \dfrac{1}{y^2}\right)}{\left(\dfrac{1}{x} + \dfrac{1}{y}\right)} = \frac{x^2 + y^2}{xy(x + y)}.$$

    Thus, we have:

    $$(1 \oslash 1) \oslash 3 = \left(\frac{1^2 + 1^2}{1 \times 1 \times (1 + 1)}\right) \oslash 3 = 1 \oslash 3 = \frac{1^2 + 3^2}{1 \times 3 \times (1 + 3)} = \frac{10}{12} = \frac{5}{6} = 0.83.$$

    Hence, the correct answer is (A).

25. **Level of Difficulty:** Medium

    Topic: Rational expressions and polynomials

    The correct answer is 1.

    Let us assume $3^x = k$.

    Thus, $9^x = (3^x)^2 = k^2$

    Hence, our equation becomes:

    $k^2 - 2k - 3 = 0$

    $k^2 - 3k + k - 3 = 0$

    $k(k - 3) + 1(k - 3) = 0$

    $(k + 1)(k - 3) = 0$

$k = -1$ or 3

Thus, we have: $3^x = -1$ or $3^x = 3$.

Since 3^x is always positive, we can conclude that $3^x = 3$

$x = 1$

Hence, the correct answer is 1

26. **Level of Difficulty:** Difficult

The correct answer is (D).

$$\frac{1}{1(1+1)} = \frac{1}{1 \times 2} = \left(\frac{2-1}{1 \times 2}\right) = \left(\frac{1}{1} - \frac{1}{2}\right)$$

$$\frac{1}{2(2+1)} = \frac{1}{2 \times 3} = \left(\frac{3-2}{2 \times 3}\right) = \left(\frac{1}{2} - \frac{1}{3}\right)$$

$$\frac{1}{3(3+1)} = \frac{1}{3 \times 4} = \left(\frac{4-3}{3 \times 4}\right) = \left(\frac{1}{3} - \frac{1}{4}\right) \text{ and so on ...}$$

$$\frac{1}{19(19+1)} = \frac{1}{19 \times 20} = \left(\frac{20-19}{20 \times 21}\right) = \left(\frac{1}{19} - \frac{1}{20}\right).$$

$$\frac{1}{20(20+1)} = \frac{1}{20 \times 21} = \left(\frac{21-20}{20 \times 21}\right) = \left(\frac{1}{20} - \frac{1}{21}\right).$$

We can see that on adding these, terms in between get cancelled.

Thus, finally we are left with $\frac{1}{1} - \frac{1}{21} = \frac{20}{21}$.

Hence, the correct answer is (D).

27. **Level of Difficulty:** Difficult

Topic: Functions

The correct answer is (D).

We have:

$p = 4 ⌐ a = 4^a, q = 4 ⌐ b = 4^b, r = 2 ⌐ (2c) = 2^{2c} = (2^2)^c = 4^c.$

Thu pqr $= 4^a \times 4^b \times 4^c = 4^{a+b+c} = 4^4 = 256$.s,

Hence, the correct answer is (D).

28. **Level of Difficulty:** Difficult

Topic: Nonlinear equation graphs

The correct answer is 7.

We need to find the values of k and m so that $3f(g(k) + 1) = g(f(m))$.

Let $k = 1$: $g(k) = g(1) = 9$. So, $3f(g(k) + 1) = 3f(10)$. However, $f(10)$ is not shown on the graph.

Let $k = 2$: $g(k) = g(2) = 10$. So, $3f(g(k) + 1) = 3f(11)$. However, $f(11)$ is not shown on the graph.

Let $k = 3$: $g(k) = g(3) = 9$. So, $3f(g(k) + 1) = 3f(10)$. However, $f(10)$ is not shown on the graph.

Let $k = 4$: $g(k) = g(4) = 6$. So, $3f(g(k) + 1) = 3f(7)$. However, $f(7)$ is not shown on the graph.

Let $k = 5$: $g(k) = g(5) = 1$. So, $3f(g(k) + 1) = 3f(2) = 3 \times 3 = 9$.

Since we got only one value of $3f(g(k) + 1)$, we need to find m so that $g(f(m)) = 9$.

We can see that $g(1) = g(3) = 9$.

Thus, $f(m) = 1$ or $3 \Rightarrow m = 1$ or 2 respectively.

Thus, $g(f(1)) = g(f(2)) = 9$.

Hence, we have $k = 5$ and $m = 1$ or 2.

Hence, the maximum value of $k + m = 5 + 2 = 7$.

Hence, the correct answer is 7.

29. **Level of Difficulty:** Medium

Topic: Solving quadratic equations

The correct answer is (A).

Squaring both sides of the given equation, we have:

$$\left(\sqrt{x - 3}\right)^2 = \left(\sqrt{2x + 2} - 2\right)^2 \Rightarrow x - 3 = 2x + 2 - 4\sqrt{2x + 2} + 4 \Rightarrow 4\sqrt{2x + 2} = x + 9$$

Squaring both sides of the above equation:

$$16(2x + 2) = (x + 9)^2 \Rightarrow 32x + 32 = x^2 + 18x + 81 \Rightarrow x^2 - 14x + 49 = 0$$

$(x - 7)^2 = 0 \Rightarrow x = 7$.

Hence, the correct answer is (A).

30. **Level of Difficulty:** Easy

Topic: Quadratic and exponential (word problems)

The correct answer is (B).

Let the number of bacteria initially be N. The number of bacteria doubles in every hour.

Using the above information, we can calculate the number of bacteria in 12 hours and equate with the value mentioned. Then, we can calculate when the number of bacteria would have been one-fourth of the final value.

However, such calculations are unnecessary as we can solve the problem using a simple logic as mentioned below:

We know that the number of bacteria doubles every hour.

Thus, we can say that the time taken for the bacteria to double in value from $\frac{1}{2} \times 40960$ to 40960 would have taken only one hour.

Similarly, we can say that the time taken for the bacteria to double in value from $\frac{1}{4} \times 40960$ to $\frac{1}{2} \times 40960$ would also have taken only one hour.

Since the number of bacteria was 40960 after 12 hours from start of the experiment, the number of bacteria was one-fourth of that number two hours before i.e. 10 hours from the start of the experiment.

Hence, the correct answer is (B).

31. **Level of Difficulty:** Medium

    Topic: Functions

    The correct answer is (C).

    According to the definition for the symbol $\forall$, we have $\forall k = (k^2 - 3k - 4)$.

    Thus, $k^2 - 3k - 4 = k - 4 \Rightarrow k^2 - 4k = 0 \Rightarrow k(k - 4) = 0 \Rightarrow k = 0$ OR 4.

    Thus, the positive value of k is 4.

    Hence, the correct answer is (C)

32. **Level of Difficulty:** Difficult

    Topic: Interpreting nonlinear expressions

    The correct answer is (D).

    While solving these types of questions, it is best to divide the number line in the four parts as shown below:

    We now need to pick a number from the regions (I, II, III and IV) and check which region(s) satisfy.

    Region I: Say $x = -2$. Thus, $x^3 = -8$. Hence, $x > x^3$. Thus, region I satisfies the condition.

    Region II: Say $x = -0.5$. Thus, $x^3 = -0.125$. Hence, $x^3 > x$. Thus, region II doesn't satisfy the condition.

    Region III: Say $x = 0.5$. Thus, $x^3 = 0.125$. Hence, $x > x^3$. Thus, region III satisfies the condition.

    Region IV: Say $x = 2$. Thus, $x^3 = 8$. Hence, $x^3 > x$. Thus, region IV doesn't satisfy the condition.

    Thus, the regions satisfying the given condition are I and III.

    Going by options:

    (A): $x^3 > x^5$: This is satisfied by the point $x = -2$ in Region I since $(-2)^3 = -8 > (-2)^5 = -32$.

    (B): $x^2 > x$: This is satisfied by the point $x = -2$ in Region I since $(-2)^2 = 4 > -2$.

    (C): $x^2 > x^3$: This is satisfied by the point $x = 0.5$ in Region III since $(0.5)^2 = 0.25 > (0.5)^3 = 0.125$.

    This is also satisfied by the point $x = -2$ in Region I since $(-2)^2 = 4 > (-2)^3 = -8$.

    (D): $\frac{1}{x} > \frac{1}{x^2}$: Let us multiply x^2 to both sides (since x^2 is positive, it will not reverse the inequality).

As a result, we get: $\dfrac{x^2}{x} > \dfrac{x^2}{x^2} => x > 1$. However, we know that $x > 1$ (i.e. Region IV) is not a correct solution to the given condition. Thus, this option is not correct.

Hence, the answer is (D).

33. **Level of Difficulty:** Difficult

The correct answer is (B).

According to the definition of the sequence, we have:

For $n = 2$: $t_3 = t_2 - t_1 = 5 - 1 = 4$.

For $n = 3$: $t_4 = t_3 - t_2 = 4 - 5 = -1$.

For $n = 4$: $t_5 = t_4 - t_3 = -1 - 4 = -5$.

For $n = 5$: $t_6 = t_5 - t_4 = -5 - (-1) = -4$.

For $n = 6$: $t_7 = t_6 - t_5 = -4 - (-5) = 1$.

We find that $t_7 = t_1$.

Thus, the same sequence of numbers as above would follow.

Thus, we have a repetition of the following cycle: $1, 5, 4, -1, -5$ and -4.

Also, the sum of the above six numbers is zero.

Since the sum of every six numbers of the above sequence is zero, we can say that the sum of any 'multiple of six' terms is also zero.

Thus, the sum of the first $6 \times 16 = 96$ terms is zero.

Thus, we are left with the last four terms.

Again, the 97th term is the beginning of a new cycle, hence, is 1.

Thus, the last four terms are $1, 5, 4$ and -1.

The sum of these four terms $= 9$.

Hence, the sum of the first 100 terms is 9.

Hence, the correct answer is (B).

34. **Level of Difficulty:** Easy

Topic: Functions

The correct answer is (D).

$x \,!\, 1 = -3 => x^2 - 4x + 1 = -3 => x^2 - 4x + 4 = 0$

$(x - 2)^2 = 0 => x = 2$.

Thus, $x \,!\, (x + 1) = 2 \,!\, 3 = 2^2 - 4 \times 2 \times 3 + 3^4 = 4 - 24 + 81 = 61$.

35. **Level of Difficulty:** Easy

Topic: Solving quadratic equations

The correct answer is (B).

Simplifying the equation, we have:

$$\frac{6}{x+1} = \frac{3}{x-1} - 1 \Rightarrow \frac{6}{x+1} - \frac{3}{x-1} = -1 \Rightarrow \frac{6(x-1) - 3(x+1)}{(x+1)(x-1)} = -1$$

$$\frac{3x-9}{x^2-1} = -1 \Rightarrow 3x - 9 = 1 - x^2 \Rightarrow x^2 + 3x - 10 = 0 \Rightarrow x^2 + 5x - 2x - 10 = 0$$

$$(x+5)(x-2) = 0 \Rightarrow x = -5 \text{ or } 2.$$

Thus, the positive value of x is 2.

Hence, the correct answer is (B).

36. **Level of Difficulty:** Difficult

Topic: Functions

The correct answer is (D).

We have: $\blacksquare\big(\blacksquare(\blacksquare 2)\big) = \blacksquare\big(\blacksquare(2^2 - 3)\big) = \blacksquare(\blacksquare 1) = \blacksquare(1^2 - 3) = \blacksquare(-2) = (-2)^2 - 3 = 1.$

Thus, we can observe that: $\blacksquare 1 = -2$ and $\blacksquare(-2) = 1.$

Going by the options:

Option (A): $\blacksquare\big(\blacksquare(\blacksquare 1)\big) = \blacksquare\big(\blacksquare(-2)\big) = \blacksquare 1 = -2.$ Hence, this option is incorrect.

Option (B): $\blacksquare\big(\blacksquare(\blacksquare(\blacksquare(-2)))\big) = \blacksquare\big(\blacksquare(\blacksquare 1)\big) = \blacksquare\big(\blacksquare(-2)\big) = \blacksquare 1 = -2.$ Hence, this option is incorrect.

Option (C): $\blacksquare\big(\blacksquare(\blacksquare(-1))\big) = \blacksquare\big(\blacksquare((-1)^2 - 3)\big) = \blacksquare\big(\blacksquare(-2)\big) = \blacksquare 1 = -2.$ Hence, this option is incorrect.

Option (D): $\blacksquare\big(\blacksquare(\blacksquare(\blacksquare 1))\big) = \blacksquare\big(\blacksquare(\blacksquare(-2))\big) = \blacksquare(\blacksquare 1) = \blacksquare(-2) = 1.$ Hence, this option is correct.

Hence, the correct answer is (D).

37. **Level of Difficulty:** Medium

Topic: Solving quadratic equations

The correct answer is 1.

We have: $2|x-1|^2 + 4x + 6 = 0.$

Case I: If $x - 1 < 0 \Rightarrow |x-1| = -(x-1).$

Case II: If $x - 1 > 0 \Rightarrow |x-1| = (x-1).$

Thus, in either case, $|x-1|^2 = (x-1)^2 = x^2 - 2x + 1.$

Hence, we have:

$$x^2 - 2x + 1 + 4x = 0 \Rightarrow x^2 + 2x + 1 = 0 \Rightarrow (x+1)^2 = 0 \Rightarrow x = -1.$$

Thus, there is only one solution for x.

Hence, the correct answer is 1.

38. **Level of Difficulty:** Easy

Topic: Radicals and rational exponents

We need to try out a few values of n and check which value of n satisfies.

Since $0 < n < 5$ and we need the least value of n, we should try the values of n from 1 onwards (and not from 4 backwards).

With $n = 1$: $3^{2n} + 4 = 3^2 + 4 = 13$ is prime.

$n = 2$: $3^{2n} + 4 = 3^4 + 4 = 85$ is not a prime number.

Hence, the value of $n = 2$ and the corresponding value of $3^{2n} + 4 = 85$.

Thus, when $3^{2n} + 4$ is divided by n, i.e. 85 is divided by 2, the remainder comes as 1.

Hence, the answer is (A).

39. **Level of Difficulty:** Difficult

Topic: Solving quadratic equations

We know that in a quadratic equation $ax^2 + bx + c = 0$, the condition for real roots is given by: $b^2 - 4ac \geq 0$.

Here, the value of $c = 1$.

Thus, the condition is: $b^2 - 4a \geq 0$.

Using the above condition, we can choose the values of a and b from the set P in the following ways as shown in the table below:

a	b	$b^2 - 47a$
3	4	$16 - 12 = 4 \geq 0$
3	5	$25 - 12 = 13 \geq 0$
4	4	$16 - 16 = 0$
4	5	$25 - 16 = 9 \geq 0$
5	5	$25 - 20 = 5 \geq 0$

For each set of values for a and b, we get a different quadratic equation.

Thus, there are 5 different equations possible.

Hence, the correct answer is (B).

40. **Level of Difficulty:** Difficult

Topic: Functions

The correct answer is (D).

$f(x) = 2x^2 + 4x + 9 = 2(x^2 + 2x) + 9 = 2\{(x + 1)^2 - 1\} + 9 = 2(x + 1)^2 + 7.$

Since $(x + 1)^2$ is a perfect square, it is non-negative.

Hence, the lease value of $f(x)$ occurs if the perfect square term becomes zero (which happens if $x = -1$).

In that case, the value of $f(x)$ becomes 7.

Thus, the least value of $f(x)$ is 7.

Hence, statement I is true.

Again, since $f(x) = 2(x + 1)^2 + 7$ and $(x + 1)^2$ is non-negative, we can conclude that the value of $f(x)$ for any value of x will always be positive.

Hence, statement II is true.

In a quadratic equation $ax^2 + bx + c = 0$n, the roots are imaginary if $b^2 - 4ac < 0$.

Here, $a = 2, b = 4, c = 9$. Thus, $b^2 - 4ac = 16 - 72 = -56 < 0$.

Thus, the roots of the equation $f(x) = 0$ i.e. $2x^2 + 4x + 9 = 0$ are imaginary.

However, irrational numbers are real numbers.

Hence, statement III is not true.

Hence, the correct answer is (D).

41. **Level of Difficulty:** Medium

    Topic: Structure in expressions

    The correct answer is 18.

    We have:

    $x^3 - 2y^3 - xy^2 + 2x^2y$

    $= x^3 - 2x^2y - xy^2 + 2y^3$

    $= x^2(x - 2y) - y^2(x - 2y)$

    $= (x - 2y)(x^2 - y^2)$

    $= 2 \times 9 = 18$

42. **Level of Difficulty:** Medium

    Topic: Isolating quantities

    Plugging in $b = c = 1$, we have:

    $\dfrac{2}{3a} = \dfrac{4}{5} + \dfrac{5}{4} = \dfrac{41}{20}$

    $a = \dfrac{40}{123}$

    Plugging in $b = c = 1$ in each option, only option C gives $a = \dfrac{40}{123}$

Alternative:

$$\frac{2}{3a} - \frac{4}{5b} = \frac{5}{4c}$$

$$\frac{2}{3a} = \frac{5}{4c} + \frac{4}{5b} = \frac{25b + 16c}{20bc}$$

$$a = \frac{40bc}{3(25b + 16c)}$$

The correct answer is option C

43. **Level of Difficulty:** Difficult

Topic: Functions

The correct answer is 3.5.

From the graph, we can see that $f(1) = 6$.

Since $f(k) = 6 = f(1) => k = 1$.

Since we need to find the value of m so that: $f(m) = k$ i.e. $f(m) = 1$, we draw a horizontal line through $y = 1$ and read the x values of the points where the line intersects the graph of $f(x)$.

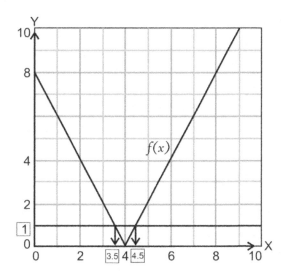

We see that $f(x)$ consists of two different lines meeting at $x = 4$. For both lines, if we move two units along the Y-axis, we move one unit along X-axis.

Thus, if we move one unit along the Y-axis, we would move half unit along X-axis.

Taking $x = 4$ as the reference, to reach the line through $y = 1$, we need to move one unit along Y-axis. Thus, on moving half unit along X-axis, we reach the points

$x = 4 - 0.5 = 3.5$ and $x = 4 + 3.5 = 4.5$.

Thus, possible values of $m = 3.5$ or 4.5, the minimum being 3.5.

Hence, the correct answer is 3.5.

44. **Level of Difficulty:** Medium

    Topic: Solving quadratic equations

    The correct answer is (D).

    Let us assume $2^x = k$.

    Thus, $4^x = \left(2^x\right)^2 = k^2$.

    Hence, our equation becomes: $k^2 - 12k - 64 = 0 => k^2 - 16k + 4k - 64 = 0$

    $k(k - 16) + 4(k - 16) = 0 => (k + 4)(k - 16) = 0 => k = -4$ or 16.

    Thus, we have: $2^x = -4$ or $2^x = 16$.

    Since 2^x is always positive, we can conclude that $2^x \neq -4$.

    Thus, $2^x = 16 = 2^4 => x = 4$.

    Thus, there is only one value possible for x.

    Hence, the correct answer is (D).

45. **Level of Difficulty:** Easy

    Topic: Functions

    The correct answer is (B).

    $$f(-x) = \frac{a^{-x} - 1}{a^{-x} + 1} = \frac{\frac{1}{a^x} - 1}{\frac{1}{a^x} + 1} = \frac{\frac{1-a^x}{a^x}}{\frac{1+a^x}{a^x}} = \frac{1-a^x}{1+a^x} = -\frac{a^x - 1}{a^x + 1} = -f(x).$$

    Hence, statement I is not true, and statement II is true.

    Again, $f(2x) = \frac{a^{2x} - 1}{a^{2x} + 1}$.

    While $2f(x) = 2\left(\frac{a^x - 1}{a^x + 1}\right) = \frac{2a^x - 2}{a^x + 1}$.

    Thus, $f(2x) \neq 2f(x)$.

    Hence, statement III is not true.

    Hence, the correct answer is (B).

46. **Level of Difficulty:** Easy

    Topic: Polynomial factors and graphs

    The correct answer is (D).

    Options (A) and (B) deal with $f(x)$.

    A set of points satisfying $f(x)$ can be given as: $\{(1, 5), (2, 10)\}$.

    Option (A): We put $x = 1$ which gives us $f(x) = 3^2 = 9$ which does not satisfy the point $(1, 5)$.

    Option (B): We put $x = 1$ which gives u $f(x) = 1^2 + 1 = 2$s which does not satisfy the point $(1, 5)$.

    Options (C), and (D) deal with $g(x)$.

A set of points satisfying $g(x)$ can be given as: $\{(1, 2), (2, 5), (3, 10)\}$.

Option (C): We put $x = 1$ which gives us $g(x) = 1^2 = 1$ which does not satisfy the point $(1, 2)$.

Option (D): We put $x = 1$ which gives us $g(x) = 1^2 + 1 = 2$ which satisfies the point $(1, 2)$.

Thus, checking the options, we can see that option (D) satisfies the above set of points.

Hence, the correct answer is (D).

47. **Level of Difficulty:** Medium

    Topic: Functions

    The correct answer is 7.

    $f(3) = 3^2 - 1 = 8$ (since $f(x) = x^2 - 1$ if $x \leq 3$)

    Thus, $f\big(f(3)\big) = f(8) = 2 \times 8 + 2 = 18$ (since $f(x) = 2 \times +2$ if $3 < x \leq 9$)

    Thus, $f\big(f(f(3))\big) = f(18) = 4 \times 18 - 8 = 64$ (since $f(x) = 4x - 8$ if $x > 9$)

    Thus, we have $f\big(f(f(3))\big) = 64 = (k + 1)^2$

    $k + 1 = 8$ (we do not take $k + 1 = -8$ since k is positive)

    $k = 7$.

    Hence, the correct answer is 7.

48. **Level of Difficulty:** Medium

    Topic: Structure in expressions

    The correct answer is (B).

    $2x + 3 = A(x + 2) + B(x + 1)$

    $2x + 3 = (A + B)x + (2A + B)$

    Since the above is true for all values of x, it is an identity.

    $A + B = 2$

    The correct answer is option B.

49. **Level of Difficulty:** Medium

    Topic: Polynomial factors and graphs

    The correct answer is 36.

    The graph represents $f(x) = -x^2 + ax + b$.

    The Y-intercept is $-16 \Rightarrow b = -16 \Rightarrow$ Product of roots $= \dfrac{b}{-1} = 16$

    Since one of the roots is 8 (X-intercept), the other root is $\dfrac{16}{8} = 2$. Thus, coordinates of point A are $(2, 0)$.

    Thus, the length of AB $= 8 - 2 = 6$

Thus, area of the square $= 6^2 = 36$

50. **Level of Difficulty:** Medium

    Topic: Functions

    The correct answer is (D).

    $f\big(g(x)\big) = \frac{g(x)-k}{5} = \frac{(5x+7)-k}{5} = \frac{5x+7-k}{5}$.

    $g\big(f(x)\big) = 5\big(f(x)\big) + 7 = 5 \; x \; \frac{(x-k)}{5} + 7 = x - k + 7$.

    Since $f\big(g(x)\big) = g\big(f(x)\big) => \frac{5x+7-k}{5} = x - k + 7 => 5x + 7 - k = 5x - 5k + 35$

    $4k = 28 => k = 7$.

    Hence, the correct answer is (D).

    Alternative:

    We know that $f\big(g(x)\big) = g\big(f(x)\big)$ is true only when one function is the inverse of the other i.e. $f(x) = g^{-1}(x)$ (in fact, $f\big(g(x)\big) = g\big(f(x)\big) = x$).

    Let us find the inverse of $g(x)$:

    We have: $y = 5x + 7 => 5x = y - 7 => x = \frac{y-7}{5}$.

    Interchanging x and y: $y = \frac{x-7}{5} => g^{-1}(x) = \frac{x-7}{5}$.

    Thus, we have $g^{-1}(x) = \frac{x-7}{5} = f(x) = \frac{x-k}{5}$.

    Comparing $g^{-1}(x)$ and $f(x)$, we get: $k = 7$.

    Hence, the correct answer is (D).

51. **Level of Difficulty:** Difficult

    Topic: Solving quadratic equations

    The correct answer is (B).

    Let the roots of the above quadratic be p and 3p.

    We know that in a quadratic equation $ax^2 + bx + c = 0$, the sum of the roots is given by $\left(-\frac{b}{a}\right)$ and the product of the roots is given by $\left(\frac{c}{a}\right)$.

    Thus: $-\frac{b}{a} = p + 3p => -\frac{b}{a} = 4p => b = -4ap$ ... (i)

    Also: $\frac{c}{a} = p \times 3p => \frac{c}{a} = 3p^2 => c = 3ap^2$ ... (ii)

    Squaring (ii) and dividing by (i) to eliminate p, we get:

    $\frac{b^2}{c} = \frac{(-4ap)^2}{3ap^2} => \frac{b^2}{c} = \frac{16a^2p^2}{3ap^2} => \frac{b^2}{c} = \frac{16a}{3} => 3b^2 = 16ac$.

Hence, the correct answer is (B).

52. **Level of Difficulty:** Easy

    Topic: Functions

    The correct answer is (D).

    $f(x) = 2|x| + x.$

    Thus, $f(-2) = 2|-2| + (-2) = 2 \times 2 - 2 = 2.$

    Also, $f(-4) = 2|-4| + (-4) = 2 \times 4 - 4 = 4.$

    Thus, $f(-2) + f(-4) = 2 + 4 = 6.$

    Hence, we need to choose that option whose value is 6.

    Going by the options, we get:

    Option (A): $f(-3) = 2|-3| + (-3) = 6 - 3 = 3 \neq 6.$

    Option (B): $f(-1) = 2|-1| + (-1) = 2 - 1 = 1 \neq 6.$

    Option (C): $f(0) = 2|0| + (0) = 0 \neq 6.$

    Hence, option (D) must be the answer. Let us verify:

    Option (D): $f(2) = 2|2| + (2) = 4 + 2 = 6.$

    Hence, the correct answer is (D).

53. **Level of Difficulty:** Easy

    Topic: Linear and quadratic systems

    The correct answer is (B).

    We know that:

    $f(x) = x^2 + 1$

    $f(g(2)) = (g(2))^2 + 1 = 1$

    $(g(2))^2 = 0$

    $g(2) = 0 \dots \text{(i)}$

    Working with the options:

    Option A: $g(x) = 5x - 1 => g(2) = 10 - 1 = 9$ – Does not satisfy (i)

    Option B: $g(x) = 2x - 4 => g(2) = 4 - 4 = 0$ – Satisfies (i)

    Option C: $g(x) = 6x - 3 => g(2) = 12 - 3 = 9$ – Does not satisfy (i)

    Option D: $g(x) = x - 1 => g(2) = 2 - 1 = 1$ – Does not satisfy (i)

54. **Level of Difficulty:** Difficult

    Topic: Structure in expressions

The correct answer is 512.

We have:

$$x = \left(4 + \frac{1}{a}\right)$$

$$y = \left(2 - \frac{1}{2a}\right) = \left(\frac{1}{2}\right)\left(4 - \frac{1}{a}\right)$$

$$x^3 + 6x^2y + 12xy^2 + 8y^3$$

$$= x^3 + 3x^2(2y) + 3x(2y)^2 + (2y)^3$$

$$= (x + 2y)^3$$

$$= \left\{\left(4 + \frac{1}{a}\right) + \left(4 - \frac{1}{a}\right)\right\}^3$$

$$= 8^3 = 512$$

55. **Level of Difficulty:** Difficult

Topic: Solving quadratic equations

The correct answer is (D).

We can see that the above quadratic cannot be factorized easily since it gives roots which are irrational numbers. Hence, we cannot simply calculate the values of p and q and substitute those values in the expression to get our answer.

Since the roots are p and q, and the coefficient of the second-degree term is 2, we can write the quadratic $2x^2 + 5x + 1$ as $2(x - p)(x - q)$.

Thus, we can say *that* $2x^2 + 5x + 1 = 2(x - p)(x - q)$ holds true for all values of x i.e. this is an identity.

If we plug in $x = 2$ in the above identity, it gives us:

$$(2 \times 2^2) + (5 \times 2) + 1 = 2(2 - p)(2 - q)$$

$$2(2 - p)(2 - q) = 19 => (2 - p)(2 - q) = \frac{19}{2} = 9.5.$$

Hence, the value of the expression $(2 - p)(2 - q) = 9.5$.

Hence, the correct answer is (D).

56. **Level of Difficulty:** Medium

Topic: Rational expressions and polynomials

The correct answer is 1.

Let us assume $3^x = k$.

Thus, $9^x = (3^x)^2 = k^2$

Hence, our equation becomes:

$$k^2 - 2k - 3 = 0$$

$$k^2 - 3k + k - 3 = 0$$

$$k(k - 3) + 1(k - 3) = 0$$

$(k + 1)(k - 3) = 0$

$k = -1$ or 3

Thus, we have: $3^x = -1$ or $3^x = 3$.

Since 3^x is always positive, we can conclude that $3^x = 3$

$x = 1$

Hence, the correct answer is 1

57. **Level of Difficulty:** Easy

Topic: Nonlinear equation graphs

The correct answer is (A).

It appears that the graph of $f(x)$ has been shifted right to get the graph of $g(x)$.

Let us pick a few values of y and check the values of x for each of $f(x)$ and $g(x)$.

At $y = 1$: $x = 1$ for $f(x)$ while we have $x = 3$ for $g(x)$.

At $y = 2$: $x = 0$ or 2 for $f(x)$ while we have $x = 2$ or 4 for $g(x)$.

At $y = 5$: $x = -1$ or 3 for $f(x)$ while we have $x = 1$ or 5 for $g(x)$.

Thus, we see that for the same y values, the values of x in $g(x)$ are two more than that of $f(x)$.

Thus, we can say that $g(x) = f(x - 2)$.

Say $x = 3$: $g(x) = g(3) = 1$ and $f(x - 2) = f(1) = 1 => g(3) = f(1)$.

Thus, the correct answer is (A).

58. **Level of Difficulty:** Difficult

Topic: Functions

The correct answer is (D).

We need to find the largest value of the three-digit number x such that the sum of the digits of the number is 11.

The largest three-digit number should have 9 in the hundreds' place.

Then we need to find two digits that add up to two.

Since we need the largest number, we place 2 in the tens' place and 0 in the units' place.

Thus, the largest value of x is 920.

We now need to find the smallest value of the three-digit number x such that the sum of the digits of the number is 11.

The smallest three-digit number should have 1 in the hundreds' place.

Then we need to find two digits that add up to ten.

Since we need the smallest number, we place 1 in the tens' place and 9 in the units' place (we cannot place 0 in the tens' place as then the units' digit should then be 10 which is not possible).

Thus, the smallest value of x is 119.

Thus, the difference between the largest and smallest values of x is $920 - 119 = 801$.

Hence, the correct answer is (D).

59. **Level of Difficulty:** Easy

    Topic: Functions

    The correct answer is 3.

    We have:

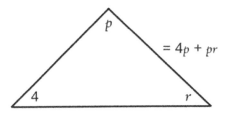

Thus, we have: $4p + pr = p => 3p = -pr => r = -3$ (since $p \neq 0$).

Hence, $|r| = |-3| = 3$.

Hence, the correct answer is 3.

60. **Level of Difficulty:** Easy

    Topic: Solving quadratic equations

    The correct answer is (C).

    $x^2 - 12x + 20 = 0 => (x - 2)(x - 10) = 0 => x = 2$ or 10.

    Since the equations have only one root common, the common root is either 2 or 10.

    Let the common root be 2.

    In the equation $x^2 - ax + 30 = 0$, the product of the roots $= \dfrac{30}{1} = 30$.

    Since one root is 2, the other root must be $\dfrac{30}{2} = 15$.

    The sum of the roots of $x^2 - ax + 30 = 0$ is given as $-\dfrac{-a}{1} = a$.

    Thus, we have $a = 2 + 15 = 17$.

    Thus, one possible value of a is 17.

    Let the common root be 10.

    In the equation $x^2 - ax + 30 = 0$, the product of the roots $= \dfrac{30}{1} = 30$.

    Since one root is 10, the other root must be $\dfrac{30}{10} = 3$.

    The sum of the roots of $x^2 - ax + 30 = 0$ is given as $\left(-\dfrac{-a}{1}\right) = a$.

Thus, we have $a = 10 + 3 = 13$.

Thus, the other possible value of a is 13.

Hence, sum of the possible values of $a = 13 + 17 = 30$.

Hence, the correct answer is (C).

61. **Level of Difficulty:** Difficult

Topic: Functions

The correct answer is 1.

$f(g(2)) = 7 => 3\sqrt[3]{g(2)} - 5 = 7 => 3\sqrt[3]{g(2)} = 12 => \sqrt[3]{g(2)} = 4 => g(2) = 4^3 = 64$.

Thus, $g(2) = 64 => 4p + q^2 = 64$.

Since p is an integer, q must also be an integer. We must choose a negative value of q since p is positive, so that the value of $(p + q)$ is minimum.

Also, since 4p and 64 are even, q^2 must be even i.e. q must be even.

Possible values of p and q are shown in the table below:

q^2	q	p	$p + q$
4	−2	15	13
16	−4	12	8
36	−6	7	1

Hence, the minimum value of $p + q = 1$.

Hence, the correct answer is 1.

62. **Level of Difficulty:** Easy

Topic: Nonlinear equation graphs

The correct answer is (B).

It appears that the graph of $g(x)$ has been shifted up to get the graph of $f(x)$.

Let us pick a few values of x and check the values of y for each of $f(x)$ and $g(x)$.

At $x = 0$: $y = 2$ for $g(x)$ while we have $y = 4$ for $f(x)$.

At $x = 1$: $y = 1$ for $g(x)$ while we have $y = 3$ for $f(x)$.

At $x = 3$: $y = 5$ for $g(x)$ while we have $y = 7$ for $f(x)$.

Thus, we see that for the same x values, the values of y in $f(x)$ are two more than that of $g(x)$.

Thus, we can say that $f(x) = g(x) + 2$.

Say $x = 1$: $f(x) = f(1) = 3$ and $g(x) = g(1) = 1 => f(1) = g(1) + 2$.

Thus, the correct answer is (B).

63. **Level of Difficulty:** Easy

    Topic: Solving quadratic equations

    The correct answer is 15.

    Let the three integers be $x - 1, x, x + 1$.

    Thus, we have: $(x - 1)x(x + 1) = 8\big((x - 1) + x + (x + 1)\big) => x(x^2 - 1) = 24x$

    $x^2 - 1 = 24 => x^2 = 25 => x = \pm5$.

    Since the numbers are positive, we take $x = 5$.

    Thus, the sum of the three numbers $= (x - 1) + x + (x + 1) = 3x = 3 \times 5 = 15$.

    Hence, the correct answer is 15.

64. **Level of Difficulty:** Difficult

    Topic: Quadratic and exponential (word problems)

    The correct answer is (B).

    The harmonic mean of x and 12 is given by $\dfrac{2 \times 12x}{x+12} = \dfrac{24x}{x+12}$.

    The average of x and 12 is given by $\dfrac{x+12}{2}$.

    Thus, we have: $\dfrac{24x}{x+12} = \dfrac{x+12}{2} - 1 => \dfrac{x+12}{2} - \dfrac{24x}{x+12} = 1 => \dfrac{(x+12)^2 - 48x}{2(x+12)} = 1$

    $(x^2 - 24x + 144) = 2x + 24 => x^2 - 26x + 120 = 0 => x^2 - 20x - 6x + 120 = 0$

    $(x - 20)(x - 6) = 0 => x = 20 \text{ or } 6$.

    If $x = 6$, the sum of digits is also 6.

    If $x = 20$, the sum of digits $= 2 + 0 = 2$.

    Thus, the sum of digits of x is either 6 or 2.

    Hence, the correct answer is (B).

65. **Level of Difficulty:** Easy

    Topic: Structure in expressions

    The correct answer is (C)

    We have:

    $x = \frac{1}{2}\left(a - \frac{1}{a}\right)$

    $x^2 + 1 = \left\{\frac{1}{2}\left(a - \frac{1}{a}\right)\right\}^2 + 1$

    $= \frac{1}{4}\left(a^2 + \frac{1}{a^2} - 2\right) + 1$

    $= \frac{1}{4}\left(a^2 + \frac{1}{a^2} + 2\right)$

$$= \frac{1}{4}\left(a + \frac{1}{a}\right)^2$$

$$\sqrt{(x^2 + 1)} = \frac{1}{2}\left(a + \frac{1}{a}\right)$$

$$\sqrt{(x^2 + 1)} + x = \frac{1}{2}\left(a + \frac{1}{a}\right) + \frac{1}{2}\left(a - \frac{1}{a}\right) = a$$

The correct answer is option C.

66. **Level of Difficulty:** Medium

Topic: Rational expressions and polynomials

The correct answer is (D)

$$P = \left(1 + \frac{1}{x}\right)\left(1 + \frac{1}{x+1}\right)\left(1 + \frac{1}{x+2}\right) \ldots \left(1 + \frac{1}{x+20}\right)$$

$$= \left(\frac{x+1}{x}\right)\left(\frac{(x+1)+1}{x+1}\right)\left(\frac{(x+2)+1}{x+2}\right) \ldots \left(\frac{(x+20)+1}{x+20}\right)$$

$$= \left(\frac{x+1}{x}\right)\left(\frac{x+2}{x+1}\right)\left(\frac{x+3}{x+2}\right) \ldots \left(\frac{x+21}{x+20}\right).$$

We can see that intermediate terms will cancel each other out.

Finally, we would be left with:

$$P = \left(\frac{x+1}{x}\right)\left(\frac{x+2}{x+1}\right)\left(\frac{x+3}{x+2}\right) \ldots \left(\frac{x+20}{x+20}\right)\left(\frac{x+21}{x+20}\right).$$

Thus, $P = \left(\frac{x+21}{x}\right)$.

Since $x = 9$, we have $P = \left(\frac{9+21}{9}\right) = \frac{30}{9} = \frac{10}{3} = 3.33$

Hence, the answer is (D).

67. **Level of Difficulty:** Difficult

Topic: Solving quadratic equations

The correct answer is (C).

We have:

$(x - 3)^2 < 25 => -5 < (x - 3) < 5 => -2 < x < 8.$

$(y - 5)^2 \leq 4 => -2 < (y - 5) < 2 => 3 < y < 7.$

The value of $\frac{x}{y}$ will be maximum when both x and y are of the same sign with magnitude of x as maximum and the magnitude of y as minimum.

Thus, we take $x = 7$ and $y = 4 => \frac{x}{y} = \frac{7}{4} = 1.75$ (since x is less than 8 and is an integer, we take x as 7 as the maximum value; similarly, since y is more than 3 and is an integer, we take y as 4 as the minimum value).

The value of $\frac{x}{y}$ will be maximum when x and y are of opposite signs with magnitude of x as maximum and the magnitude of y as minimum (since y is always positive, we must take x as negative).

Thus, we take $x = -1$ and $y = 4 => \frac{x}{y} = \frac{-1}{4} = -0.25$.

Hence, the sum of the maximum and minimum possible values of $\frac{x}{y}$ equals $1.75 + (-0.25) = 1.50$.

Hence, the correct answer is (C).

68. **Level of Difficulty:** Easy

Topic: Linear and quadratic systems

The correct answer is 2.

We have: $(x - 4)^2 + (y - 6)^2 = 2$ and $y = 2x - 1$

$(x - 4)^2 + (2x - 1 - 6)^2 = 2$

$(x - 4)^2 + (2x - 7)^2 = 2$

$x^2 - 8x + 16 + 4x^2 - 28x + 49 = 2$

$5x^2 - 36x + 63 = 0$

$5x^2 - 21x - 15x + 63 = 0$

$x(5x - 21) - 3(5x - 21) = 0$

$(x - 3)(5x - 21) = 0$

$x = 3 \text{ or } \frac{21}{5}$

Alternatively, one can use the quadratic-root formula to determine the roots.

Thus, there are 2 points of intersection.

The correct answer is 2.

69. **Level of Difficulty:** Easy

Topic: Functions

The correct answer is (D).

$\frac{h(a)h(b)}{h(a+b)} = \frac{\left(2^{ka-1}2^{kb-1}\right)}{2^{k(a+b)-1}} = \frac{2^{ka-1+kb-1}}{2^{k(a+b)-1}} = \frac{2^{k(a+b)-2}}{2^{k(a+b)-1}} = 2^{k(a+b)-2-(k(a+b)-1)} = 2^{-1} = \frac{1}{2} = 0.5.$

Hence, the correct answer is (D).

70. **Level of Difficulty:** Medium

Topic: Quadratic and exponential (word problems)

The correct answer is (B).

Let the number of ants initially be N.

The number of ants increases by 25% every week.

Thus, after one week, the number of ants would be: $N + 25\% \text{ of } N = N\left(1 + \frac{25}{100}\right) = N\left(1 + \frac{1}{4}\right) = \frac{5N}{4}.$

The number of ants at the end of every week is shown in the table below:

Time duration	Number of ants
1 week	$\dfrac{5}{4} \times N = \dfrac{5N}{4}$
2 weeks	$\dfrac{5}{4} \times \dfrac{5N}{4} = \dfrac{25N}{16}$
3 weeks	$\dfrac{5}{4} \times \dfrac{25N}{16} = \dfrac{125N}{64}$
4 weeks	$\dfrac{5}{4} \times \dfrac{125N}{64} = \dfrac{625N}{256}$

Thus, we have: $\dfrac{625N}{256} = 6250 => N = 6250 \times \dfrac{256}{625} = 2560$.

Hence, the correct answer is (B).

71. **Level of Difficulty:** Medium

    Topic: Radicals and rational exponents

    The correct answer is (D).

    Since $N = a^2 b^4$ is a perfect square (the exponents are even) and is a multiple of 8, it must be a multiple of 16 (since 8 is not a perfect square).

    Similarly, since N is a multiple of 27, it must be a multiple of 81 (since 27 is not a perfect square).

    81 can be expressed both as 9^2 as well as 3^4. Thus, either $a = 9$ or $b = 3$.

    Similarly, $16 = 2^4 = 4^2$, hence, $b = 2$ or $a = 4$.

    Thus, there are two possible cases:

    i) $N = 4^2 \times 3^4 => a = 4, b = 3 => \text{LCM of } a, b = 12$.

    ii) $N = 9^2 \times 2^4 => a = 9, b = 2 => \text{LCM of } a, b = 18$.

    Thus, minimum value of the LCM of $a, b = 12$.

    Hence, the answer is (D).

72. **Level of Difficulty:** Medium

    Topic: Quadratic equations

    The correct answer is 3.

    We have:

    $2m + n = 10 \text{ ... (i)}$

    $m(n - 1) = 9 \text{ ... (ii)}$

From (i): $n = 10 - 2m$.

Substituting the above in (ii): $m(n - 1) = 9 => m((10 - 2m) - 1) = 9$

$m(9 - 2m) = 9 => 9m - 2m^2 = 9 => 2m^2 - 9m + 9 = 0$

$2m^2 - 6m - 3m + 9 = 0 => 2m(m - 3) - 3(m - 3) = 0$

$(m - 3)(2m - 3) = 0 => m = 3 \text{ or } \dfrac{3}{2}$.

Since m is an integer, there is only one value of m possible.

Thus, sum of all integer values of m is 3.

Hence, the correct answer is 3.

73. **Level of Difficulty:** Easy

Topic: Quadratic and exponential (word problems)

The correct answer is (C).

The first 5 terms of the above series are: $k, 3k, 3^2k, 3^3k, 3^4k$ and 3^5k i.e. $k, 3k, 9k, 27k, 81k$ and $243k$.

Thus, we have: $k + 3k + 9k + 27k + 81k + 243k = 364k$.

Thus, $364k = 728 => k = \dfrac{728}{364} = 2$.

Thus, the sum of the first three terms $= k + 3k + 9k = 13k = 13 \times 2 = 26$.

Hence, the correct answer is (C).

74. **Level of Difficulty:** Medium

Topic: Isolating quantities

The correct answer is (C).

$s = \text{ut} - \dfrac{a}{2}t^2$

$\dfrac{a}{2}t^2 = \text{ut} - s$

$a = \dfrac{2(\text{ut} - s)}{t^2}$

$a = \dfrac{2\text{u}}{t} - \dfrac{s}{t^2}$

$a = \dfrac{1}{t}\left(2\text{u} - \dfrac{s}{t}\right)$

The correct answer is option C.

75. **Level of Difficulty:** Easy

Topic: Functions

The correct answer is (D).

Since $-3 < x < 3 => 0 \leq x^2 < 9 => -9 < -x^2 \leq 0$.

We have, $y = f(x) = 8 - x^2$.

Thus, $-9 + 8 < 8 - x^2 \leq 0 + 8 => -1 < 8 - x^2 \leq 8 => -1 < f(x) \leq 8$.

Hence, the range of the function is given by: $-1 < y \leq 8$.

Hence, the correct answer is (D).

76. **Level of Difficulty:** Medium

    Topic: Nonlinear equation graphs

    The correct answer is 12.

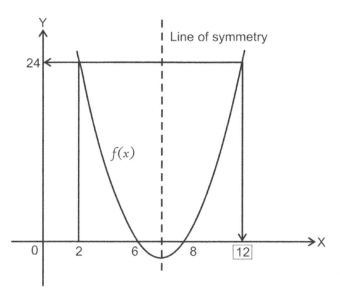

We know that a quadratic graph is symmetric about the line passing through the midpoint of the roots.

Thus, the graph is symmetric about the line $x = 7$.

Since $f(a) = f(2)$, both $x = a$ and $x = 2$ should be equidistant from the line $x = 7$.

Distance between $x = 2$ and $x = 7$ is 5 units.

Thus, distance between $x = a$ and $x = 7$ should also be equal to 5 units.

Thus, $a = 7 + 5 = 12$.

Hence, the correct answer is 12.

77. **Level of Difficulty:** Medium

    Topic: Quadratic and exponential (word problems)

    The correct answer is (C).

    Let us write the first few terms of the sequence:

    $t_1 = -1$

$$t_2 = (-1) \times (-2) = 2$$

$$t_3 = (2) \times (-2) = -4$$

$$t_4 = (-4) \times (-2) = 8$$

$$t_5 = (8) \times (-2) = -16 \text{ and so on.}$$

Thus, we can see that every odd positioned term, $t_1, t_3, t_5 \ldots t_{49}$ is negative and hence is less than 50.

There are $\dfrac{50}{2} = 25$ such terms. Again, the even positioned terms are positive. The first few terms are less than 50, however, as the magnitude increases, they would exceed 50. We need to find the number of such terms less than 50. We observe that successive such terms get multiplied with 4. Thus, we get:

$$t_2 = 2$$

$$t_4 = 2 \times 4 = 8$$

$$t_6 = 8 \times 4 = 32$$

$$t_8 = 32 \times 4 = 128.$$

Thus, we see that only 3 such terms are less than 50.

Thus, we have a total of $25 + 3 = 28$ terms which are less than 50.

Hence, the correct answer is (C).

78. **Level of Difficulty:** Medium

   Topic: Rational expressions and polynomials

   The correct answer is (D).

   Let us solve the given equation. We have

   $$\sqrt{x + 3} + \sqrt{7 - x} = 4$$

   Now, squaring both the sides we get,

   $$\left(\sqrt{x + 3} + \sqrt{7 - x}\right)^2 = 4^2$$

   $$(x + 3) + (7 - x) + 2.\sqrt{x + 3}.\sqrt{7 - x} = 16$$

   $$10 + 2\sqrt{x + 3}\sqrt{7 - x} = 16$$

   $$\sqrt{(x + 3)(7 - x)} = 3$$

   Again, squaring both sides, we get

   $$(x + 3)(7 - x) = 9$$

   $$(-x^2 + 4x + 21) = 9$$

   $$x^2 - 4x - 12 = 0$$

   $$(x - 6)(x + 2) = 0$$

   $$x = 6 \text{ OR} - 2$$

   Therefore, the positive value of $x^3 = (6)^3 = 216$.

   Hence, the correct answer is option (D).

79. **Level of Difficulty:** Difficult

    Topic: Functions

    The correct answer is (D).

    Let us work with the statements:

    Statement I:

    $$h\Big(f\big(g(-x)\big)\Big) = h\Big(f\big(-g(x)\big)\Big) \qquad \text{since } g(-x) = -g(x)$$

    $$= h\Big(-f\big(g(x)\big)\Big) \qquad \text{since } f(-x) = -f(x) => f\big(-g(x)\big) = -f\big(g(x)\big)$$

    $$= h\Big(f\big(g(x)\big)\Big) \qquad \text{since } h(-x) = h(x)$$

    Hence, statement I is true.

    Statement II:

    $$\mathbf{f}\Big(g\big(h(-x)\big)\Big) = f\Big(g\big(h(x)\big)\Big) \qquad \text{since } h(-x) = h(x)$$

    Hence, statement II is true.

    Statement III:

    $$g\big(f(-x)\big) = g\big(-f(x)\big) \qquad \text{since } f(-x) = -f(x)$$

    $$= -g\big(f(x)\big) \qquad \text{since } g(-x) = -g(x) => g\big(-f(x)\big) = -g\big(f(x)\big)$$

    Hence, statement III is not true.

    Hence, the correct answer is (D).

80. **Level of Difficulty:** Easy

    Topic: Functions

    The correct answer is 4.

    We have: $g(x) = x^2 + 3 - f(x) = x^2 + 3 - (|x - 2| + x^2 - 1) = x^2 + 3 - |x - 2| - x^2 + 1$

    $g(x) = 4 - |x - 2|$.

    $g(x)$ will be maximum when $|x - 2|$ is minimum. This would happen at $x = 2$ and the corresponding maximum value of $g(x)$ is 4.

This page is intentionally left blank

Chapter **5**

Additional Topics in Math

---

1 The use of calculator is **permitted.**

A solid cube is put in a sphere. What is the least percentage of the volume of the sphere not occupied by the cube?

(A) 44.44%

(B) 50%

(C) 57.66%

(D) 63.24%

A B C D
○ ○ ○ ○

2 The use of calculator is **not permitted**.

A circle intersects the X axis at $(1, 0)$ and $(7, 0)$. If the radius of the circle is 5, what is the sum of the coordinates of the center?

3   The use of calculator is **permitted.**

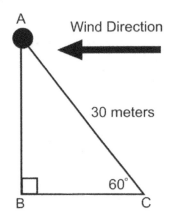

A hot air balloon was tied to a point on the ground using a rope 60m long. If the rope makes an angle of 60° with the ground, how high, in meters, is the balloon above the ground level?

(A) $\dfrac{30}{\sqrt{3}}$

(B) 30

(C) $\dfrac{60}{\sqrt{3}}$

(D) $30\sqrt{3}$

A   B   C   D
○ ○ ○ ○

4   The use of calculator is **permitted.**

How many points with integer coordinates lie on or inside a circle of radius three units centered at the origin?

(A) 16

(B) 28

(C) 29

(D) 30

A   B   C   D
○ ○ ○ ○

5 The use of calculator is **permitted.**

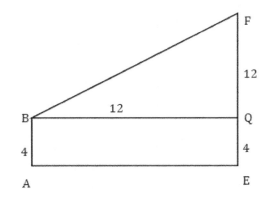

In the figure shown above, AB and EF are parallel and measure 4 and 24, respectively. If AB is perpendicular to AE and AE measures 12, what is the perimeter of the figure to the nearest integer?

6 The use of calculator is **not permitted**.

The imaginary number i is such that $i^2 = -1$. Which of the following statements is true about the complex number equivalent to $(4 - i) \times (1 + 2i) + (1 - i) \times (2 - 3i)$?

(A) It lies on the real axis

(B) It lies in the first quadrant

(C) It lies in the second quadrant

(D) It lies in the third quadrant

7 The use of calculator is **not permitted.**

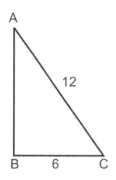

In the figure shown above, ABC is a triangle right angled at B. What is the value of angle A, in degrees?

8 The use of calculator is **permitted.**

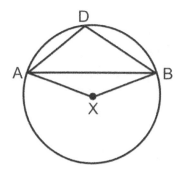

Angle ADB equals 110°. What is the value of angle BAX if X is the centre of the circle?

(A) 20°

(B) 35°

(C) 40°

(D) 70°

9 The use of calculator is **permitted**.

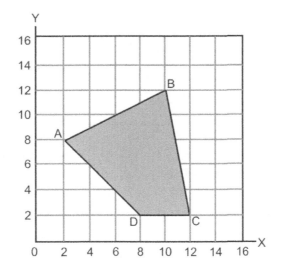

What is the area of the quadrilateral ABCD as shown in the figure above?

(A) 74

(B) 72

(C) 56

(D) 28

A   B   C   D
○ ○ ○ ○

10 The use of calculator is **not permitted**.

Which of the following statement(s) is/are correct about the angle $\dfrac{10\pi}{3}$ radians?

  I.   It is equivalent to 600^0.

 II.   The angle falls in the third quadrant.

III. $\operatorname{Cos}\dfrac{10\pi}{3}$ is positive.

(A) Only I

(B) Only II

(C) Both I and II

(D) Both I and III

A   B   C   D
○ ○ ○ ○

11 The use of calculator is **not permitted.**

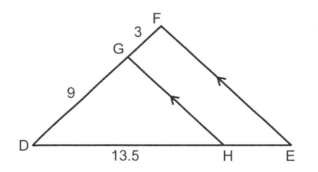

In the figure GH||EF. What is the length of HE?

11 grid answer box

12 The use of calculator is **not permitted.**

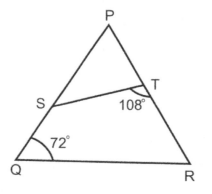

If $\dfrac{PS}{PR} = \dfrac{1}{2}$, PT = 6 and QS = 4, what is the length of PS?

(A) 12

(B) 10

(C) 9

(D) 8

A   B   C   D
O   O   O   O

13 The use of calculator is **not permitted**.

The imaginary number i is such that $i^2 = -1$. Which of the following options is equivalent to $\left(\frac{1-2i}{2+3i}\right)$?

(A) $-\frac{4}{7} - i$

(B) $\frac{4}{7} + i$

(C) $8 - 7i$

(D) $\frac{8}{7} + i$

A	B	C	D
○	○	○	○

14 The use of calculator is **not permitted.**

Matt has a garden in the shape of a right-angled triangle with one of the acute angles as 30°. If the longest side of the triangle is 4 m long, what is the perimeter, in meters, of the garden?

15 The use of calculator is **permitted.**

The angular elevation of a tower CD at a place A due south of it is 60°; and at a place B due west of A, the elevation is 30°. If AB = 300m, what is the height, in meters, of the tower?

(A) 30

(B) $30\sqrt{6}$

(C) $30\sqrt{10}$

(D) $30\sqrt{30}$

A	B	C	D
○	○	○	○

16   The use of calculator is **permitted.**

What is the perimeter, to the nearest integer, of an equilateral triangle inscribed in circle whose circumference is 6π units?

17   The use of calculator is **permitted**.

What is the area bounded by $x^2 + y^2 - 8x - 6y = 25$, $x \geq 4$ and $y \geq 3$?

(A) 39.3

(B) 78.6

(C) 123.4

(D) 157

A B C D
○ ○ ○ ○

18   The use of calculator is **permitted.**

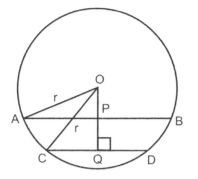

2 parallel chords 24 cm, and 18 cm, are on the same side of the centre of a circle. If the distance between the chords is 3 cm, calculate the radius of the circle.

(A) 15 cm

(B) 14 cm

(C) 13 cm

(D) 12 cm

A B C D
○ ○ ○ ○

19 The use of calculator is **permitted.**

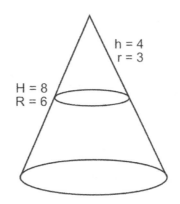

A right circular cone, with radius and height8 and 6 respectively, is cut parallel at the middle of the height to get a smaller cone and a frustum. By what percentage, to the nearest integer, is the combined total surface area of the smaller cone less than that of the frustum?

20 The use of calculator is **not permitted**.

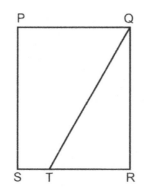

PQRS is a rectangle. T is a point on RS such that ST = 2. If the area of the triangle QRT is 24 and QR : RS = 2 : 1, what is the measure of QR?

(A) 12

(B) 14

(C) 15

(D) 16

A   B   C   D
○   ○   ○   ○

21 The use of calculator is **not permitted**.

What is the value of $\left(\frac{3\pi^c}{4} + \frac{11\pi^c}{5} + \frac{7\pi^c}{10}\right)$, when converted to degrees?

(A) 135°

(B) 245°

(C) 657°

(D) 810°

A   B   C   D
○   ○   ○   ○

22   The use of calculator is **permitted.**

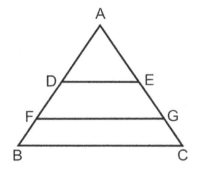

In ΔABC, D and E are the mid-points of AB and AC. Again, F and G are the mid-points of DB and EC. What is the ratio of areas of FDEG and BFGC?

(A) 2 : 3

(B) 3 : 5

(C) 5 : 7

(D) Data insufficient to answer

A   B   C   D
○ ○ ○ ○

23   The use of calculator is **permitted.**

A car is being driven, in a straight line and at a uniform speed, towards the base of a vertical tower of height 30 feet. The top of the tower is observed from the car and, in the process, the angle of elevation changes from 45° at B to 60° at A. What is the distance, in meters, to the nearest integer, between the points A and B?

24 The use of calculator is **permitted.**

The biggest possible cube is taken out of a right solid cylinder of radius 4 and height 5 respectively. What is the volume of the cube?

(A) 64

(B) 125

(C) $128\sqrt{2}$

(D) $256\sqrt{2}$

A   B   C   D
○   ○   ○   ○

25 The use of calculator is **permitted**.

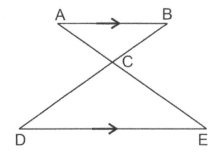

In the figure $AB \| DE$, $AC = 6$, $CE = 15$ and $DB = 28$. What is the length of CD?

26 The use of calculator is **not permitted.**

The imaginary number i is defined such that $i^2 = -1$. Which of the following options is equivalent to $\left(\frac{1}{i} + \frac{1}{i^2} + \frac{1}{i^3} + \frac{1}{i^4}\right)$?

(A) -1

(A) 0

(B) 1

(C) $-i$

A   B   C   D
○ ○ ○ ○

27 The use of calculator is **not permitted.**

The imaginary number i is such that $i^2 = -1$. Which of the following options is equivalent to $\sqrt{5 + 12i}$?

(A) $1 - i$

(B) $3 + i$

(C) $3 - 2i$

(D) $3 + 2i$

A   B   C   D
○ ○ ○ ○

28 The use of calculator is **permitted.**

A right-angled triangle ABC of sides AB = 6, BC = 8 and AC = 10 is spun once about AB and once about BC. What is the difference in volumes of the two solids formed?

(A) 24π

(B) 32π

(C) 64π

(D) 96π

A   B   C   D
○ ○ ○ ○

29 The use of calculator is **permitted.**

If $a + ib = \sqrt{5 + 12i}$, where $a > 0, b > 0$, which of the following is a possible value of $(a^2 b^2)$?

30 The use of calculator is **permitted.**

Two friends, Amy and Bob, are standing in line with a lamp post. The shadows of both friends meet at the same point on the ground. If the heights of the lamp post, Amy and Bob are 6 meters, 1.8 meters and 0.9 meters respectively, and Amy is standing 2 meters away from the post, then how far (in meters) is Bob standing from Amy?

(A) 0.43

(B) 0.90

(C) 1.80

(D) 2.00

31 The use of calculator is **not permitted.**

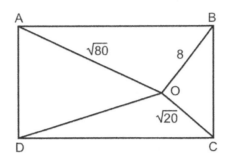

In the figure OA = √80, OB = 8, OC = √20.

What is the length of OD?

(A) 5

(B) 6

(C) 7

(D) 8

        A   B   C   D
        ○   ○   ○   ○

32 The use of calculator is **permitted.**

In a right-angled triangle ABC, right angled at B, an altitude BD is dropped on AC. If AB = 8 and BC = 6, what is the length of AD?

(A) 2.4

(B) 3.6

(C) 4.8

(D) 6.4

        A   B   C   D
        ○   ○   ○   ○

33 The use of calculator is **permitted.**

If the equation of the circle having the coordinates of the ends of its diameter as $(3, 5)$ and $(5, 11)$ is $(x - a)^2 + (y - b)^2 = r^2$, what is the value of $(a + b + r)$ to the nearest tenth?

34 The use of calculator is **permitted.**

If $a + ib = (5 + 3i)(6i + 1)$, what is the value of $a^2 + b^2$?

(A) 1258

(B) 1528

(C) 2158

(D) 3168

A   B   C   D
○   ○   ○   ○

35 The use of calculator is **not permitted.**

A well, 2m radius and 40m deep, is being dug. The excavated soil is transported using a truck of size 5m × 2m × πm. How many trips will the truck have to clear the excavated soil if it can be filled to 80% of its height?

(A) 10

(B) 12

(C) 20

(D) 24

A   B   C   D
○   ○   ○   ○

36 The use of calculator is **permitted.**

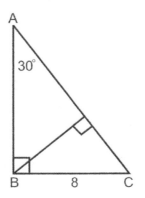

In the figure shown, ABC is a triangle, right angled at B. Through B, a line is drawn perpendicular to AC which meets AC in D. What is the length of BD?

(A) $\dfrac{4}{\sqrt{3}}$

(B) $\dfrac{8}{\sqrt{3}}$

(C) $2\sqrt{3}$

(D) $4\sqrt{3}$

A   B   C   D
O O O O

37 The use of calculator is **not permitted.**

From a cuboid of dimension 4 m × 6 m × 8 m, the largest possible cube is cut out. What is the minimum possible number of cubes, all of equal size, into which the remaining part of the solid can be cut, ensuring that no part of the solid remains?

38 The use of calculator is **permitted.**

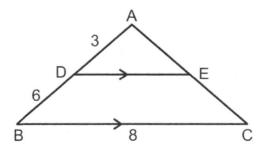

In the ΔABC, DE $\parallel$ BC, AD = 3, BD = 6, and BC = 6. What is the ratio of the areas of triangle ADE and trapezium BDEC?

(A) 1:3

(B) 1:4

(C) 1:8

(D) 1:9

A B C D
○ ○ ○ ○

39 The use of calculator is **not permitted**.

A vertical tower, OP stands at the center O of a square ABCD. Let h and b denote the length OP and AB respectively. If $\angle$APB = 60°, what is the relationship between h and b?

(A) $2b^2 = h^2$

(B) $2h^2 = b^2$

(C) $3b^2 = 2h^2$

(D) $3h^2 = 2b^2$

A B C D
○ ○ ○ ○

40 The use of calculator is **permitted.**

What is the shortest distance between the circle $x^2 + y^2 - 2x - 2y = 0$ and the line $x = 4$?

(A) 1.23

(B) 1.59

(C) 2.56

(D) 3.25

41 The use of calculator is **permitted.**

A balloon leaves the earth and rises at a uniform velocity. At the end of 2 min, an observer situated at 200m from the point the balloon was released, finds the angular elevation of the balloon to be 60°. What is the speed, in meters per minute, to the nearest integer, of the balloon?

42 The use of calculator is **permitted.**

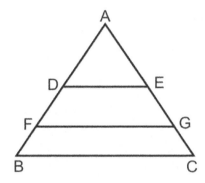

In $\triangle ABC$, D and E are the mid-points of AB and AC. Again, F and G are the mid-points of DB and EC. If BC = 12, what is the length of FG?

(A) 4

(B) 6

(C) 8

(D) 9

43 The use of calculator is **not permitted.**

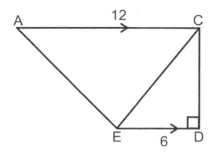

In the figure shown, area of triangle ACE is 48.If AC is parallel to DE, what is the length CE?

(A) 6

(B) 8

(C) 10

(D) 11

A   B   C   D
○   ○   ○   ○

44 The use of calculator is **permitted**.

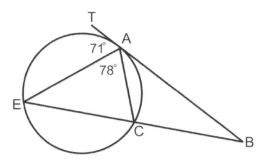

In the figure above, the line TAB is tangent to the given circle. If $\angle EAC = 78°$ and $\angle TAE = 71°$, what is the measure, in degrees, of $\angle ABC$?

(A) 21°

(B) 25°

(C) 31°

(D) 40°

A   B   C   D
○   ○   ○   ○

45 The use of calculator is **permitted.**

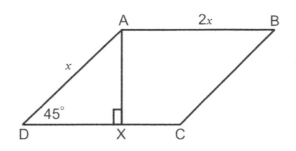

In a parallelogram, the ratio of the two adjacent sides is 1 : 2. If the area of the parallelogram is 20 square units and the angle between the two sides is 45°, what is the area, to the nearest integer, of the rectangle having the sides equal to that of the parallelogram?

Answers and Explanations

1. **Level of Difficulty:** Medium

    Topic: Volume word problems

    The correct answer is (D).

    The required percent would be the least if the largest cube is placed in the sphere.

    Let each side of the cube be s

    Thus, the body diagonal $= s\sqrt{3}$

    Also, volume of the sphere $= s^3$

    Thus, diameter of the sphere = The body diagonal $= s\sqrt{3}$

    Radius of the sphere $= \dfrac{s\sqrt{3}}{2}$

    Thus, volume of the sphere $= \dfrac{4\pi}{3}\left(\dfrac{s\sqrt{3}}{2}\right)^3 = \dfrac{\pi\sqrt{3}}{2}s^3 = 2.72s^3$

    Thus, volume of the sphere not occupied by the cube $= 2.72s^3 - s^3 = 1.72s^3$

    Thus, required percent $= \dfrac{1.72s^3}{2.72s^3} \times 100 = 63.24\%$

    The correct answer is option D.

2. **Level of Difficulty:** Difficult

    Topic: Circle equations

    The correct answer is 8.

    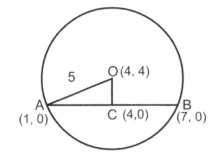

    Let the 2 points be A (1, 0) and B (7, 0)

    AB $= 7 - 1 = 6$

    Let the centre of the circle be O.

    A perpendicular from O on AB at C bisects AB => AC = BC = 3

    Thus, coordinates of D $= (1 + 3, 0) = (4, 0)$

    Thus, in right angled triangle OAD, AO = 5 (radius):

    $=> CO = \sqrt{AO^2 - AC^2} = \sqrt{5^2 - 3^2} = 4$

    Thus, the coordinates of the centre C $= (4, 4)$

    Thus, the sum of the coordinates $= 4 + 4 = 8$

    Hence, the correct answer is 8

3. **Level of Difficulty:** Easy

   Topic: Right triangle word problems

   The correct answer is (D).

   Let the balloon be at the point A and AC is the rope with which the balloon is tied to the ground.

   In triangle ABC, we have: $\text{Sin } 60° = \frac{AB}{AC} => \frac{\sqrt{3}}{2} = \frac{AB}{60} => AB = 30\sqrt{3}$ m

   The correct option is (D).

4. **Level of Difficulty:** Medium

   Topic: Circle equations

   The correct answer is (C).

   The equation of a circle of radius three units centered at the origin is given as: $x^2 + y^2 = 3^2$.

   Since we need points with integer coordinates lying on or inside the circle, we need to find all such values of x and y such that $x^2 + y^2 \leq 3^2 => x^2 + y^2 \leq 9$.

   Possible points which satisfy the above condition are shown in the table below:

x	y	$x^2 + y^2$	No. of points
0	0	0	1
±1	0	1	2
±2	0	4	2
±3	0	9	2
0	±1	1	2
0	±2	4	2
0	±3	9	2
±1	±1	2	4
±1	±2	5	4
±2	±1	5	4
±2	±2	8	4
Total number of points			29

   Alternative: We can count the number of points in each quadrant, multiply that by four and add the points on the axes as shown below:

   In the quadrant where both x and y are positive, there are four points: (1, 1), (1, 2), (2, 1), (2, 2).

   Thus, considering all four quadrants, we have $4 \times 4 = 16$ points.

   On the positive X-axis, we have the points (other than the origin): (1, 0), (2, 0), (3, 0).

   On the positive Y-axis, we have the points (other than the origin): (0, 1), (0, 2), (0, 3).

   Thus, considering positive and negative sides of the axes, we have: $(3 + 3) \times 2 = 12$ points.

   We also need to include the origin (0, 0) i.e. 1 point.

   Thus, total points $= 16 + 12 + 1 = 29$ points.

   Hence, the correct answer is (C).

5. **Level of Difficulty:** Easy

   Topic: Right triangle geometry

   The correct answer is 49.

   $AB = EQ = 4, AE = BQ = 12$ and $FQ = 12$

   From Pythagoras' theorem:

   $BF = \sqrt{BQ^2 + QF^2} = \sqrt{12^2 + 12^2} = 12\sqrt{2} = 16.97 \approx 17$

   Thus, perimeter of the figure

   $= 4 + 12 + 16 + 17 = 49$

   The correct answer is 49.

6. **Level of Difficulty:** Easy

   Topic: Complex numbers

   The correct answer is (B).

   We can simplify the given expression as follows:

   $(4 - i) \times (1 + 2i) + (1 - i) \times (2 - 3i)$

   $= (4 + 8i - i - 2i^2) + (2 - 3i - 2i + 3i^2) = (4 + 7i - 2 \times (-1)) + (2 - 5i + 3 \times (-1))$

   $= (4 + 7i + 2) + (2 - 5i - 3) = 5 + 2i.$

   Thus, the complex number has both positive real and imaginary parts.

   Thus, the complex number falls in the first quadrant.

   Hence, the correct option is (B).

7. **Level of Difficulty:** Easy

   Topic: Angles, arc lengths, and trig functions

   The correct answer is 30

   In the triangle, corresponding to angle A, we know the values of the opposite side and the hypotenuse. Hence, we work with Sin A.

   $\text{Sin A} = \dfrac{BC}{AC} = \dfrac{6}{12} = \dfrac{1}{2}.$

   We know that $\text{Sin } 30° = \dfrac{1}{2}.$

   Thus, $A = 30°$.

   Hence, the correct option is 30.

8. **Level of Difficulty:** Easy

   Topic: Circle theorems

   The correct answer is (A).

   Reflex $\angle AXB = 220°$ (Since angle at the centre = Twice the angle at circumference)

   $\Rightarrow \angle AXB = 360° - 220° = 140°$

   Thus, $\angle BAX = \angle ABX = \dfrac{180° - 140°}{2}$ (Since AX = XB = radius of circle) $= 20°$

   Hence, the correct answer is Option A.

9. **Level of Difficulty:** Difficult

   Topic: Right triangle geometry

   The correct answer is (D).

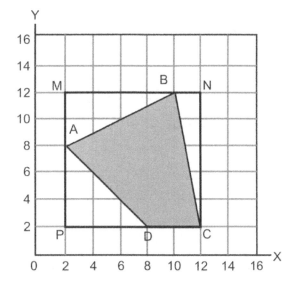

The required area ABCD = Area MNCP − (Area AMB + Area BNC + Area APD)

The coordinates of M, N, C and P are (2, 12), (12, 12), (12, 2) and (2, 2) respectively.

The coordinates of A, B and D are (2, 8), (10, 12), (12, 2) and (2, 2) respectively.

Thus, we have: AM = 4, MB = 8, BN = 2, NC = 10, CD = 4, PD = 6, PA = 6, MP = 10 and MN = 10.

Area MNCP = MP × MN = 10 × 10 = 100 sq units.

Area AMB $= \frac{1}{2}$ × AM × MB $= \frac{1}{2}$ × 4 × 8 = 16 sq units.

Area BNC $= \frac{1}{2}$ × BN × NC $= \frac{1}{2}$ × 2 × 10 = 10 sq units.

Area APD $= \frac{1}{2}$ × AP × PD $= \frac{1}{2}$ × 6 × 6 = 18 sq units.

Hence, area ABCD = 100 − (16 + 10 + 18) = 56 sq units.

Hence, the correct answer is (D).

10. **Level of Difficulty:** Medium

    Topic: Arc lengths, and trig functions

    The correct answer is (D).

    We know that π radians are equivalent to 180°

    Thus, $\frac{10\pi}{3}$ radians are equivalent to $180° \times \frac{10}{3} = 600°$

    Hence, the first statement is correct.

    Now, 600° = 360° × 1 + 240°.

    Thus, in order to trace the angle, we need to make one full revolution from 0° and then cover 240° extra.

    Thus, we finally end in the fourth quadrant.

Thus, the second statement is not correct.

We also know that in the fourth quadrant, the value of Cosθ is positive.

Thus, the third statement is correct.

Hence, the correct option is (D).

11. **Level of Difficulty:** Easy

    Topic: Congruence and similarity

    The correct answer is 4.5.

    Triangles DGH and DFE are similar since ∠DGH = ∠DFE and ∠DHG = ∠DEF (corresponding angles)

    Thus, we have: $\dfrac{DG}{DF} = \dfrac{DH}{DE} => \dfrac{9}{12} = \dfrac{13.5}{DE} => DE = 18$

    HE = 18 – 13.5 = 4.5

12. **Level of Difficulty:** Medium

    Topic: Congruence and similarity

    The correct answer is (D).

    Triangles PST and PRQ are similar since ∠P is common to both and ∠PTS = ∠PQR = 72°.

    Thus, $\dfrac{PS}{PR} = \dfrac{PT}{PQ} = \dfrac{1}{2} => PQ = 2PT = 12$

    Thus, PS = PQ – QS = 8

    Hence, the correct option is D

13. **Level of Difficulty:** Medium

    Topic: Complex numbers

    The correct answer is (A).

    We have a term $(2 + 3i)$ in the denominator of the expression. We need to rationalize it so that the denominator does not have any i present. To do that, we need to multiply the denominator with its conjugate. Thus, we have:

    $$\left(\dfrac{1-2i}{2+3i}\right) = \left(\dfrac{1-2i}{2+3i}\right) \times \left(\dfrac{2-3i}{2-3i}\right) = \dfrac{(1-2i)\times(2-3i)}{(2+3i)\times(2-3i)} = \dfrac{2-3i-4i+6i^2}{4-6i+6i-3i^2} = \dfrac{2-7i-6}{4+3} = -\dfrac{4+7i}{7} = -\dfrac{4}{7} - i.$$

    Hence, the correct option is (A).

14. **Level of Difficulty:** Difficult

    Topic: Angles, arc lengths, and trig functions

    The correct answer is 9.46.

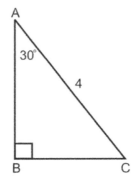

Let the garden be the triangle ABC as shown, right angled at B.

The longest side i.e. the hypotenuse is 4 m long.

We need to use Sinθ and Cosθ to find the other two sides of the triangle since only these two ratios relate the sides to the hypotenuse.

$\text{Sin } 30° = \frac{BC}{AC} => \frac{1}{2} = \frac{BC}{4} => BC = 2$ m.

$\text{Cos } 30° = \frac{AB}{AC} => \frac{\sqrt{3}}{2} = \frac{AB}{4} => AB = 2\sqrt{3}$ m.

Thus, perimeter of the triangle $= AB + BC + AC = 2\sqrt{3} + 2 + 4 = (6 + 2\sqrt{3})$ m

$= 6 + 2 \times 1.73 = 9.46$ m

Hence, the correct answer is 9.46

15. **Level of Difficulty:** Medium

Topic: Right triangle word problems

The correct answer is (D).

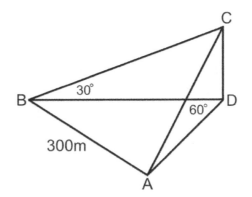

Let the tower height be h m

In triangle BCD: $BD = \frac{h}{tan30°} = h\sqrt{3}$

In triangle ACD: $AD = \frac{h}{tan60°} = \frac{h}{\sqrt{3}}$

Since A is to the south and B is to the west of D, $\angle BDA = 90°$

Thus, from Pythagoras' theorem:

$BD^2 + AD^2 = AB^2$

$$3h^2 + \frac{h^2}{3} = 300^2$$

$$h^2 = 300 \times 300 \times \frac{3}{10} = 30\sqrt{30} \text{ m}$$

The correct answer is option D.

16. **Level of Difficulty :**Medium

    Topic: Circle theorems

    The correct answer is 16.

    $$2\pi r = 6\pi => r = 3$$

    Let the side of equilateral triangle be s

    Thus, height of the triangle $= \dfrac{\sqrt{3}s}{2}$

    Thus, we have:

    $$r + \frac{r}{2} = \frac{\sqrt{3}s}{2}$$

    $$=> \frac{\sqrt{3}s}{2} = \frac{9}{2} => s = 3\sqrt{3}$$

    Thus, perimeter $= 3s = 9\sqrt{3} = 15.59 \approx 16$

    Hence, the correct answer is 16

17. **Level of Difficulty:** Difficult

    Topic: Circle equations

    The correct answer is (A).

    $$x^2 + y^2 - 8x - 6y = 25$$

    $$x^2 - 2(4)x + 4^2 + y^2 - 2(3)y + 3^2 = 25 + 3^2 + 4^2$$

    $$(x - 4)^2 + (y - 3)^2 = \left(5\sqrt{2}\right)^2$$

    Thus, the coordinates of the centre of the circle are $(4, 3)$ and the radius is $5\sqrt{2}$.

    Thus, the region of the circle satisfying $x \geq 4$ and $y \geq 3$ is the upper right quadrant of the circle.

    Thus, required area $= \dfrac{\pi\left(5\sqrt{2}\right)^2}{4} = 39.3$

    Hence, the correct answer is Option (A).

18. **Level of Difficulty:** Difficult

    Topic: Circle theorems

    The correct answer is (A).

    $$OQ^2 + QC^2 = r^2 = OP^2 + PA^2$$

    $$\left(\frac{18}{2}\right)^2 + (OP + PQ)^2 = OP^2 + \left(\frac{24}{2}\right)^2$$

    $$= 81 + OP^2 + 3^2 + 60P = OP^2 + 144 >$$

    $$60P = 54$$

    $$OP = 9$$

    $$r^2 = OP^2 + PA^2 = 81 + 144 = 225$$

$r = 15$

Hence, the correct answer is Option A.

19. **Level of Difficulty:** Medium

Topic: Volume word problems

The correct answer is 73.

Since the cone is cut at the middle of its height, its radius at that point will also be half.

For the upper small cone:

$r = 3, h = 4 =>$Slant height $= \sqrt{3^2 + 4^2} = 5$

Curved surface area $= \pi \times 3 \times 5 = 15\pi$

Base area $= \pi \times 3^2 = 9\pi$

Thus, total surface area $= 24\pi$

For the whole cone:

$R = 6, H = 8 =>$ Slant height $= \sqrt{6^2 + 8^2} = 10$

Curved surface area $= \pi \times 6 \times 10 = 60\pi$

Thus, curved surface area of the frustum $= 60\pi - 15\pi = 45\pi$

Base areas of the frustum $= \pi \times 3^2 + \pi \times 6^2 = 45\pi$

Thus, total surface area $= 90\pi$

Thus, required percent $= \dfrac{90\pi - 24\pi}{90\pi} \times 100 = 73.3\% = 73$ (to the nearest integer)

20. **Level of Difficulty:** Medium

Topic: Right triangle geometry

The correct answer is (A).

We have: $QR : RS = 2 : 1 => QR = 2x$ and $RS = x$

$RT = RS - ST = x - 2$

Thus, area of $\Delta QRT = \dfrac{1}{2} \times (2x) \times (x - 2) = 24$

$x(x - 2) = 6(6 - 2) => x = 6$

$QR = 2x = 12$

The correct answer is option A.

21. **Level of Difficulty:** Medium

Topic: Angles, arc lengths, and trig functions

The correct answer is (C).

We can simplify the above as follows:

$\dfrac{3\pi^c}{4} + \dfrac{11\pi^c}{5} + \dfrac{7\pi^c}{10} = \left(\dfrac{3\pi*5 + 11\pi*4 + 7\pi*2}{20}\right)^c = \left(\dfrac{15\pi + 44\pi + 14\pi}{20}\right)^c = \left(\dfrac{73\pi}{20}\right)^c.$

We know that π radians are equivalent to $180°$

Thus, $\dfrac{73\pi}{20}$ radians are equivalent to $180° \times \dfrac{73}{20} = 657°$.

Hence, the correct option is (C).

22. **Level of Difficulty:** Medium

    Topic: Congruence and similarity

    The correct answer is (C).

    Triangles ADE, AFG and ABC are similar

    Thus, we have:

    AD : AF : AB = DE : FG : BC

    Since AD = DB and DF = FB, we have: AD : DF : FB = 2 : 1 : 1

    AD : AF : AB = 2 : 3 : 4

    Area of triangle ADE : Area of triangle AFG : Area of triangle ABC = $2^2 : 3^2 : 4^2 = 4 : 9 : 16$

    Area of FDEG : Area of BFGC = (9 – 4) : (16 – 9) = 5 : 7

    The correct answer is option C.

23. **Level of Difficulty:** Difficult

    Topic: Triangle word problems

    The correct answer is 13.

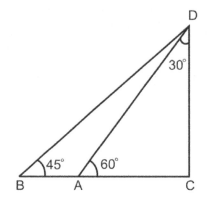

    The tower DC has height 30 m

    Since ∆BCD is isosceles right-angled ∆, BC = CD = 30 m

    In ∆ACD: $AC = \dfrac{30}{tan\,60^0} = \dfrac{30}{\sqrt{3}} = 10\sqrt{3} = 17.32$ m

    $BA = BC - AC = 30 - 17.32 = 12.68 = 13$ m (to the nearest integer)

    The correct answer is 13

24. **Level of Difficulty:** Medium

    Topic: Volume word problems

    The correct answer is (B).

    Let the side of the cube be s

    Assuming that the cube fits perfectly, we should have:

    Face diagonal of the top face = Diameter of the base circle of the cylinder

    $s\sqrt{2} = 8 => s = 4\sqrt{2} = 4 \times 1.4 = 5.6$

    Height of the cylinder = Height of the cube

$s = 5$

Thus, the required value of s must be the smaller of the two, i.e. $s = 5$

Thus, required volume $= 5^3 = 125$

The correct answer is option B.

25. **Level of Difficulty:** Easy

Topic: Congruence and similarity

The correct answer is 20.

Triangles DCE and BCA are similar since $\angle CDE = \angle CBA$ and $\angle CED = \angle CAB$ (alternate angles)

Thus, we have: $\dfrac{AC}{CE} = \dfrac{BC}{DC} => \dfrac{6}{15} = \dfrac{BC}{DC} => \dfrac{BC}{DC} = \dfrac{2}{5}$

Since BD = 28, we have:

$CD = \dfrac{5}{2+5} \times 28 = 20$

26. **Level of Difficulty:** Easy

Topic: Complex numbers

The correct answer is (B).

We have: $\dfrac{1}{i} + \dfrac{1}{i^2} + \dfrac{1}{i^3} + \dfrac{1}{i^4} = i^{-1} + i^{-2} + i^{-3} + i^{-4} = i^{-4} \times \left(i^3 + i^2 + i + 1\right) = \dfrac{(i^3+i^2+i+1)}{i^4}$.

$i = \sqrt{-1}$

$i^2 = \sqrt{-1} * \sqrt{-1} = -1$

$i^3 = i * i^2 = i * (-1) = -i$

$i^4 = i * i^3 = i * (-i) = -i^2 = -(-1) = 1$

Thus, $\dfrac{1}{i} + \dfrac{1}{i^2} + \dfrac{1}{i^3} + \dfrac{1}{i^4} = \dfrac{(i^3+i^2+i+1)}{i^4} = \dfrac{(-i)+(-1)+i+1}{1} = 0$.

Hence, the correct answer is (B).

27. **Level of Difficulty:** Medium

Topic: Complex numbers

We can simplify the given expression as follows:

$5 + 12i = 5 + 2 \times 3 \times i = 3^2 + 2 \times 3 \times i + (2i)^2$ since $(2i)^2 = -4$

$= \left(\pm(3 + 2i)\right)^2$ using $(a + b)^2 = a^2 + 2ab + b^2$

Thus, $\sqrt{5 + 12i} = \sqrt{\left(\pm(3 + 2i)\right)^2} = \pm(3 + 2i)$.

Hence, the correct option is (D).

28. **Level of Difficulty:** Medium

Topic: Volume word problems

The triangle is right angled at B since the sides satisfy Pythagoras' theorem ($6^2 + 8^2 = 10^2$)

If the triangle is rotated about AB = 6, we have a cone of height 6 and radius BC = 8;

$\text{Volume} = \dfrac{\pi}{3} 8^2 \times 6 = 128\pi$

If the triangle is rotated about BC = 8, we have a cone of height 8 and radius ABC = 6;

$\text{Volume} = \dfrac{\pi}{3} 6^2 \times 8 = 96\pi$

Thus, difference = $128\pi - 96\pi = 32\pi$

The correct answer is option B.

29. **Level of Difficulty:** Medium

    Topic: Complex numbers

    The correct answer is (A).

    Let us first simplify the value of $a + ib$

    It is given that $a + ib = \sqrt{5 + 12i}$

    $a + ib = \sqrt{5 + 2(3)(2i)}$

    $a + ib = \sqrt{(9 - 4) + 2(3)(2i)}$

    $a + ib = \sqrt{3^2 + (2i)^2 + 2(2)(3i)}$

    $a + ib = \sqrt{(3 + 2i)^2}$

    $a + ib = \pm(3 + 2i)$

    Now since it is given that $a > 0 \ and \ b > 0$, therefore we have $a + ib = 3 + 2i$

    $a^2 b^2 = 36$

    Hence, the correct answer is option (A).

30. **Level of Difficulty:** Difficult

    Topic: Right triangle word problems

    The correct answer is (A).

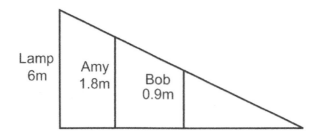

    From similar triangles, we have:

    $\dfrac{6}{2 + x + y} = \dfrac{1.8}{x + y} = \dfrac{0.9}{y}$

    $\dfrac{6 - 1.8}{(2 + x + y) - (x + y)} = \dfrac{1.8 - 0.9}{(x + y) - y}$

    $\dfrac{4.2}{2} = \dfrac{0.9}{x} => x = 0.43 \text{ m}$

31. **Level of Difficulty:** Medium

    Topic: Right triangle geometry

    The correct answer is (B).

    Let $OD = x$

    From O drop perpendiculars to AB, BC, CD, DA:

    $AO^2 + OC^2 = OD^2 + OB^2$

    $80 + 20 = 64 + X => X = 6$

    The correct answer is option B.

32. **Level of Difficulty:** Medium

    Topic: Congruence and similarity

    The correct answer is (D).

    From Pythagoras' theorem: $AC^2 = AB^2 + BC^2 = 64 + 36 = 100$

    $AC = 10$

    From the diagram, it is clear that triangle ABD is similar to triangle ACB

    $\dfrac{AB}{AC} = \dfrac{AD}{AB} => \dfrac{8}{10} = \dfrac{AD}{8}$

    $AD = 6.4$

    The correct answer is option D.

33. **Level of Difficulty:** Difficult

    Topic: Circle equations

    The correct answer is 15.2.

    Coordinates of the centre = Midpoint of the line joining the ends of the diameter

    $= \left(\dfrac{3+5}{2}, \dfrac{5+11}{2}\right) = (4, 8)$

    Radius = Distance between the centre and one end of the diameter

    $= \sqrt{(4-3)^2 + (8-5)^2} = \sqrt{10}$

    Thus, the required equation: $(x - 4)^2 + (y - 8)^2 = \left(\sqrt{10}\right)^2$

    $a + b + r = 4 + 8 + \sqrt{10} = 15.16 \approx= 15.2$

    Hence, the correct answer is 15.2

34. **Level of Difficulty:** Medium

    Topic: Complex numbers

    The correct answer is (A).

    Let us first simplify the given expression.

    $a + ib = (5 + 3i)(6i + 1)$

    $a + ib = 30i + 5 + 18i^2 + 3i$

    $a + ib = -13 + 33i$

    $a = -13, b = 33$

    $a^2 + b^2 = 169 + 1089 = 1258$

Hence, the correct answer is option(A)

35. **Level of Difficulty:** Medium

    Topic: Volume word problems

    The correct answer is (C).

    Volume of the well = $\pi \times 2^2 \times 40 = 160\pi$ cubic meters

    Volume of the truck = $5 \times 2 \times \pi = 10\pi$ cubic meters

    Volume of soil that can be filled in the truck = 80% of $10\pi = 8\pi$ cubic meters

    Thus, number of trips required = $\dfrac{160\pi}{8\pi} = 20$

36. **Level of Difficulty:** Medium

    Topic: Angles, arc lengths, and trig functions

    The correct answer is (D).

    We know that angle B is 90° and angle A is 30°.

    Thus, angle C = 180° − (90° + 30°) = 60°.

    In triangle BDC, with respect to angle C, BD is the opposite side and BC is the hypotenuse.

    Thus, in order to relate these two sides, we use Sinθ.

    Thus, Sin C = Sin 60° = $\dfrac{BD}{BC}$ => $\dfrac{\sqrt{3}}{2} = \dfrac{BD}{8}$ => BD = $4\sqrt{3}$.

37. **Level of Difficulty:** Difficult

    Topic: Volume word problems

    The correct answer is 16.

    The largest cube that can be cut out from a cuboid of dimensions 4 m × 6 m × 8 m is 4 m × 4 m × 4 m.

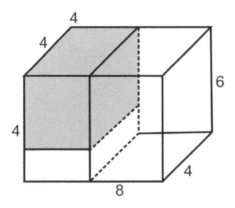

Thus, the remaining part can be broken down to 2 parts:

4 m × 2 m × 4 m => Volume = 32 cubic meters

4 m × 4 m × 6 m => Volume = 96 cubic meters

Total volume = 128 cubic meters

From these, the size of the largest identical cube would be the GCD of 2, 4 and 6, i.e. 2 m

Thus, volume of each cube $= 2^3 = 8$ cubic meters.

Thus, number of cubes $= \dfrac{128}{8} = 16$

38. **Level of Difficulty:** Medium

   Topic: Congruence and similarity

   The correct answer is (D).

   ΔADE and ΔABC are similar since $\angle$ADE $= \angle$ABC and $\angle$AED $= \angle$ACB (corresponding angles)

   $$\frac{AD}{AB} = \frac{AE}{EC} = \frac{3}{9} = \frac{1}{3}$$

   Also, we have:

   $$\frac{\text{Area of } \Delta ADE}{\text{Area of } \Delta ABC} = \left(\frac{AD}{AB}\right)^2 = \frac{1}{9}$$

   $$\frac{\text{Area of } \Delta ADE}{\text{Area of trapezium BDEC}} = \frac{1}{9-1} = \frac{1}{8}$$

   The correct answer is option D.

39. **Level of Difficulty:** Difficult

   Topic: Right triangle word problems

   The correct answer is (B).

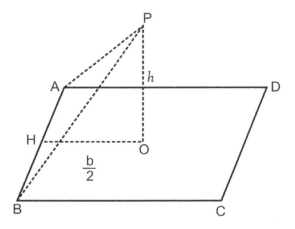

   Triangle APB is equilateral since $\angle$APB $= 60°$ and AP $=$ BP

   AP $=$ BP $=$ AB $= b$

   PH (where H is the midpoint of AB) $= \dfrac{\sqrt{3}}{2}b$

   Also, from right triangle PHD (using Pythagoras' theorem):

   $$\sqrt{h^2 + \left(\frac{b}{2}\right)^2} = \frac{\sqrt{3}}{2}b$$

   $$h^2 + \left(\frac{b}{2}\right)^2 = \frac{3}{4}b^2$$

   $$b^2 = 2h^2$$

The correct answer is option B.

40. **Level of Difficulty:** Difficult

    Topic: Circle equations

    The correct answer is (B).

    $x^2 + y^2 - 2x - 2y = 0$

    $(x - 1)^2 + (y - 1)^2 = 2$

    Thus, the center of the circle is at $(1, 1)$ and the radius is $\sqrt{2}$.

    Thus, the right-most point of the circle is $\left(1 + \sqrt{2}, 1\right) = (2.41, 1)$

    Thus, the line $x = 4$ doesn't intersect the circle.

    The distance between the right-most point of the circle and the vertical line $x = 4$ is $4 - 2.41 = 1.59$

    Hence, the correct answer is option (B)

41. **Level of Difficulty:** Easy

    Topic: Right triangle word problems

    The correct answer is 173.

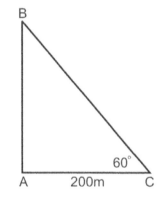

    The correct answer is 173.

    Let the balloon, released from point A, is at point B after 2 minutes.

    In triangle ABC: AB = AC × tan60° = $200\sqrt{3}$ meters

    Thus, speed (meters per minute) $= \dfrac{200\sqrt{3}}{2} = 100\sqrt{3} = 173.2$ m/min

    $= 173$ m/min (to the nearest integer)

    The correct answer is 173.

42. **Level of Difficulty:** Medium

    Topic: Congruence and similarity

    The correct answer is (D).

    Triangles ADE, AFG and ABC are similar

    Thus, we have:

AD : AF : AB = DE : FG : BC

Since AD = DB and DF = FB, we have: AD : DF : FB = 2 : 1 : 1

AD : AF : AB = 2 : 3 : 4

DE : FG : BC = 2 : 3 : 4

Since BC = 12, we have:

DE : FG : 12 = 2 : 3 : 4 = 6 : 9 : 12

FG = 9

The correct answer is option D.

43. **Level of Difficulty:** Medium

    Topic: Right triangle geometry

    The correct answer is (C).

    Area of $\triangle$ACE $= \dfrac{1}{2} \times$ AC $\times h = \dfrac{1}{2} \times$ AC $\times$ CD $= 48$

    CD $= 8$

    $CE^2 = ED^2 + CD^2 = 36 + 64 = 100$

    CE $= 10$

    The correct answer is option C.

44. **Level of Difficulty:** Medium

    Topic: Circle theorems

    The correct answer is (D).

    Since TAB is tangent to the circle at A, we have: $\angle$TAE $= \angle$ACE $= 71°$

    ($\angle$ACE is made on the alternate segment of $\angle$TAE made by chord AE with tangent AB)

    $\angle$BAC $= 180° - 71° - 78° = 31°$

    $\angle$ABC $= \angle$ACE $- \angle$CAB $= 71° - 31° = 40°$

    Hence, the correct answer is Option D.

45. **Level of Difficulty:** Medium

    Topic: Right triangle geometry

    The correct answer is 28.

    Let the parallelogram be ABCD, with AB : BC = 1 : 2

    $AB = CD = 2x$ and $AD = BC = x$

    AX is drawn perpendicular to CD.

    In triangle ADX: AX = DX

    $AD = \sqrt{AX^2 + DX^2} = AX\sqrt{2} => AX = \dfrac{AD}{\sqrt{2}} = \dfrac{x}{\sqrt{2}}$

    Area of the parallelogram = (AX)(CD)

    $20 = \dfrac{x}{\sqrt{2}} \times 2x => \sqrt{2}x^2 = 20$

    Thus, area of the required rectangle = (AD)(CD) = $(x)(2x) = 2x^2 = 20\sqrt{2} = 28$

This page is intentionally left blank

Chapter **6**

Math Practice Test

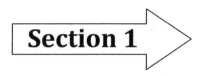

Section 1 – No Calculator

25 MINUTES, 20 QUESTIONS

Directions:

For questions 1-15, solve each problem, choose the best answer from the choices provided, and fill in the corresponding circle on your answer sheet.

For questions 16-20, solve the problem and enter your answer in the grid on the answer sheet. Please refer to the directions on page on how to enter your answers in the grid.

Notes:

1. The use of a calculator **is not permitted**.

2. All variables and expressions used represent real numbers unless otherwise indicated.

3. Figures provided in this test are drawn to scale unless otherwise indicated.

4. All figures lie in a plane unless otherwise indicated.

5. Unless otherwise indicated, the domain of a given function f is the set of all real numbers x for which $f(x)$ is a real number.

Reference:

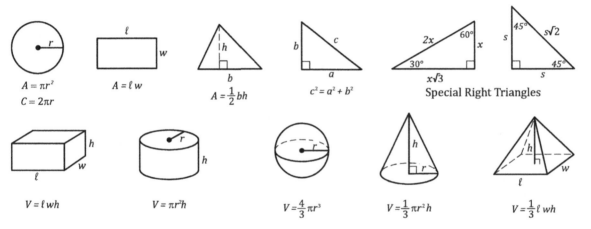

$A = \pi r^2$

$C = 2\pi r$

$A = \ell w$

$A = \frac{1}{2}bh$

$c^2 = a^2 + b^2$

Special Right Triangles

$V = \ell wh$

$V = \pi r^2 h$

$V = \frac{4}{3}\pi r^3$

$V = \frac{1}{3}\pi r^2 h$

$V = \frac{1}{3}\ell wh$

The number of degrees of arc in a circle is 360.

The number of radians of arc in a circle is 2π.

The sum of the measures in degrees of the angles of a triangle is 180.

1. If $a + 2b + 2c = 11, 2a + b + 2c = 10$ and $2a + 2b + c = 9$, what is the value of a?

    (A) 1

    (B) 2

    (C) 3

    (D) 4

2. The cost, in dollars, of producing tires by a manufacturing firm is determined by the following equation: $C = 120 + 90 \times W + 78 \times N$, where '$C$' represents the cost incurred, 'W' represents the number of workers, 'N' represents the number of units produced. If 10 units have to be produced, what is the maximum number of workers that can be employed so that the total cost doesn't exceed $2700?

    (A) 18

    (B) 19

    (C) 20

    (D) 21

3. If the quadratic $x^2 - (2a - 3)x + (a^2 + 5) = 0$ has roots whose sum is five, what is the product of the roots of the above quadratic equation?

    (A) 6

    (B) 7

    (C) 8

    (D) 9

4. Which of the following are the coordinates of the left-most point on the circle represented by the equation $x^2 + y^2 - 8x + 6y = 0$?

    (A) $(9, -3)$

    (B) $(1, 3)$

    (C) $(-1, -3)$

    (D) $(-9, 3)$

5. x and y are positive integers with $x > y$. The numbers $(x + 2y)$ and $(2x + y)$ leave remainders 6 and 1 respectively when divided by 7. What is the remainder when $(x - y)$ is divided by 7?

    (A) 1

    (B) 2

    (C) 3

    (D) 4

6. Adam bought 23 pencils, 15 erasers and 20 sharpeners from a stationery shop and spent a total of $111. Bob bought 19 erasers, 12 pencils and 40 sharpeners from the same stationery shop and spent $10 more than Adam. Which of the two equations satisfy the above two conditions, if the price of a pencil is a, price of an eraser is b and price of a sharpener is c?

    (A) $23a + 15b + 20c = 111, 19a + 12b + 40c = 101$

    (B) $23a + 15b + 20c = 111, 19a + 12b + 40c = 121$

    (C) $23a + 15b + 20c = 111, 12a + 19b + 40c = 101$

    (D) $23a + 15b + 20c = 111, 12a + 19b + 40c = 121$

7. $f(x) = x^2 - 6x + 8$ and $g(x) = x - 2$. At how many points do the graphs of the two functions intersect?

    (A) 0

    (B) 1

    (C) 2

    (D) 3

8.

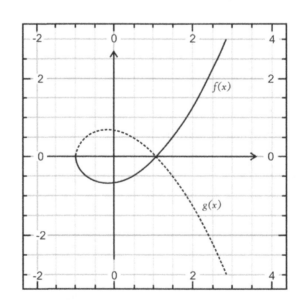

The graphs of $f(x)$ and $g(x)$ are shown above. Which option is true?

    (A) $f(x) = g(-x)$

    (B) $f(x) = g(x) - x$

    (C) $f(x) = -g(x)$

    (D) $f(x) = -g(-x)$

9.

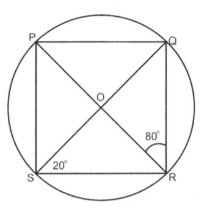

PQRS is a cyclic quadrilateral, its diagonals intersect at O. If∠PRQ = 80°, and∠QSR = 20°,what is the measure, in degrees, of∠PSR?

(A) 45°

(B) 50°

(C) 80°

(D) 100°

10. Refer to the number line below where the numbers a, b, c, d have been marked. All tick-marks are equally spaced. Choose the correct option based on the values of a, b, c and d.

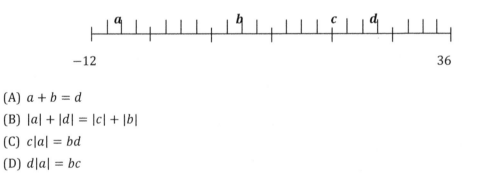

(A) $a + b = d$

(B) $|a| + |d| = |c| + |b|$

(C) $c|a| = bd$

(D) $d|a| = bc$

11. For all numbers x, let $f(x) = x^2 - 6x + 8$, and $g(x) = x - 2$. For how many integer values of x is $g(x) \geq f(x)$?

(A) 1

(B) 2

(C) 3

(D) 4

12. $N = 4^{61} + 4^{61} + 4^{61} + 4^{62} + 4^{62} + 4^{62}$. Choose the correct statement(s):

    I. N is divisible by 3.

    II. N is divisible by 5.

    III. N is a perfect square.

    (A) Only I

    (B) Only II

    (C) Only III

    (D) Only I and II

13. Abe reads a book every day, some pages in the morning and some in the evening. He reads 23 pages every morning and 31 pages every evening. The number of pages completed by Abe after some number of days can be written as a function of the number of pages read in the morning and number of pages read in the evening. If the number of days is represented by 'N', the number of pages read in the mornings be 'M' and the number of pages read in the evenings be 'E', which of the following represents the number of days for which Abe read the book? It is known that if Abe read in the morning, he did not read in the evening and vice versa.

    (A) $N = 23M + 31E$

    (B) $N = 31M + 23E$

    (C) $N = \dfrac{M}{23} + \dfrac{E}{31}$

    (D) $N = \dfrac{M}{31} + \dfrac{E}{23}$

14. If $a^3 b^4 c^7 d^2$ is negative, where a, b, c, d are integers, all of the following statements are incorrect EXCEPT

    (A) $ab^2 cd^2$ is positive

    (B) $b^2 d$ is positive

    (C) $bc^2 d$ is positive

    (D) $a^3 b^2 c$ is negative

15. If the roots of the equation $x^2 - (a - b)x + c = 0$ are integers which are equal in magnitude and opposite in sign, which of the following statements are true?

    I. $a = -b$

    II. $a = b$

    III. $c + a^2 = 0$

    (A) Only I

    (B) Only II

    (C) Only III

    (D) Both I and II

16.

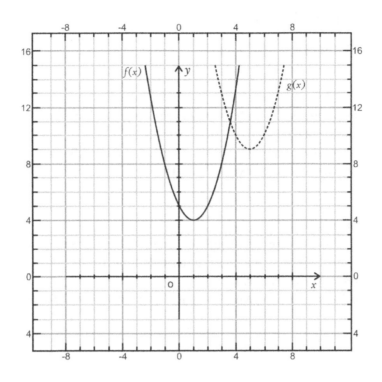

The graphs of $f(x)$ and $g(x)$ are shown below. If $g(x) = f(x + k) - m$, what is the value of $|k + m|$?

17. Some friends decided to buy a Nikon camera priced at $300 by contributing equal amount of money. At the time of purchase, one more friend decided to contribute along with the others, thus reducing the contribution of each friend by $10. How many friends were there originally?

18. The relation between the numbers of pieces p Amy has learnt to sing at the end of n weeks of singing lessons is given as: $p = 2n + 3$

After how many weeks would Amy be able to sing 17 pieces?

19. If p, q, r are positive integers, find the maximum possible value of $(p + q + r)$ if $px - q(x + r) = 23x - 15$.

20. If the correct form of $2i^4 + 4i^3 - i^2 + 3i$ is a + ib, where the imaginary number i is such that $i^2 = -1$, what is the value of $(a + b)$?

Section 2 – No Calculator
55 MINUTES, 38 QUESTIONS

Directions:

For questions 1-30, solve each problem, choose the best answer from the choices provided, and fill in the corresponding circle on your answer sheet.

For questions 31-38, solve the problem and enter your answer in the grid on the answer sheet. Please refer to the directions on page on how to enter your answers in the grid.

Notes:

1. The use of a calculator **is permitted**.
2. All variables and expressions used represent real numbers unless otherwise indicated.
3. Figures provided in this test are drawn to scale unless otherwise indicated.
4. All figures lie in a plane unless otherwise indicated.
5. Unless otherwise indicated, the domain of a given function f is the set of all real numbers x for which $f(x)$ is a real number.

Reference:

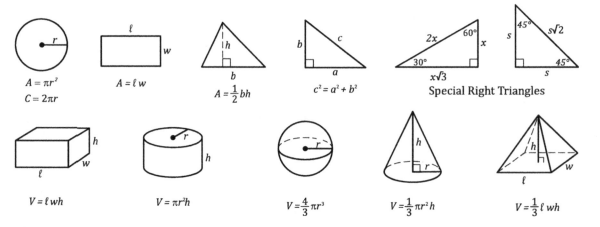

$A = \pi r^2$
$C = 2\pi r$

$A = \ell w$

$A = \frac{1}{2} bh$

$c^2 = a^2 + b^2$

Special Right Triangles

$V = \ell w h$

$V = \pi r^2 h$

$V = \frac{4}{3} \pi r^3$

$V = \frac{1}{3} \pi r^2 h$

$V = \frac{1}{3} \ell w h$

The number of degrees of arc in a circle is 360.

The number of radians of arc in a circle is 2π.

The sum of the measures in degrees of the angles of a triangle is 180.

1. When 1189 and 643 are divided by a positive integer N, the remainder obtained in each case is the same. What is the sum of digits of the largest two-digit value of N?

   (A) 10

   (B) 15

   (C) 37

   (D) 78

2. Among 40 employees in an office, 60% are men. Out of them, 33.33% play rugby. If 30% of the total employees play rugby, how many of the total employees are women who do not play rugby?

   (A) 4

   (B) 12

   (C) 16

   (D) 20

3. A model of a planned city is made where an actual distance of 10 miles is represented as 5 meters. If the area of the city is 60 square miles, and 1 mile = 1600 meters, what is the area of the model in square miles?

   (A) 5.9×10^{-4} square miles

   (B) 5.9×10^{-5} square miles

   (C) 5.9×10^{-6} square miles

   (D) 5.9×10^{-7} square miles

4. A man earns \$40 for a period of 5 hours that he works per day. Thereafter, for every additional hour, he earns \$5 per hour. If the man earns \$$P$ in a day by working for t hours, where $t > 5$ and is an integer, and $P \leq 60$, which of the following sets of values of P and t satisfy the above conditions?

   (A) $P = 60, t = 10$

   (B) $P = 55, t = 10$

   (C) $P = 50, t = 9$

   (D) $P = 50, t = 7$

5. $z = \dfrac{7-5i}{11+4i}$. Which of the following options is equivalent to z where the imaginary number i is such that $i^2 = -1$?

   (A) $0.42 - 0.61i$

   (B) $0.38 - 0.69i$

   (C) $0.32 - 0.21i$

   (D) $0.61 - 0.42i$

6. If $3x + 2y + 4z = 20, 5x + 7y - 9z = -10$, which of the following can be a set of values of x, y and z?

    (A) $x = 2, y = -1, z = 4$

    (B) $x = 4, y = 2, z = 1$

    (C) $x = 1, y = 3, z = 2$

    (D) $x = 2, y = 1, z = 3$

7. Three friends, Joe, Matt and Bruce decided to have a beer party. Joe and Matt brought along three and five bottles of beers respectively. Bruce did not bring along any beer for the party. The friends shared the beer equally and at the end of the party, Bruce paid Joe and Matt a total of $16 for his share. How much out of the $16 did Matt get (assume that each beer bottle was priced the same)?

    (A) $2

    (B) $6

    (C) $10

    (D) $14

8. If n is an even number which leaves a remainder of two when divided by five, what is the remainder if $(3n + 7)(2n + 5)$ is divided by 10?

    (A) 1

    (B) 3

    (C) 5

    (D) 7

9. Which of the following is the correct value of $\left(\frac{7\pi^c}{4} + \frac{4\pi^c}{3} - \frac{5\pi^c}{12} \right)$?

    (A) $\dfrac{5\pi^c}{4}$

    (B) $\dfrac{5\pi^c}{3}$

    (C) $300°$

    (D) $480°$

10. Two marbles are picked simultaneously from a box containing three red and five blue marbles. What is the probability that the marbles are of the same color?

    (A) 0.11

    (B) 0.36

    (C) 0.46

    (D) 0.53

11. The average of five distinct integers is 60. If the largest integer is 70, what is the minimum possible value of the smallest integer?

    (A) 0

    (B) 1

    (C) 20

    (D) 26

12.

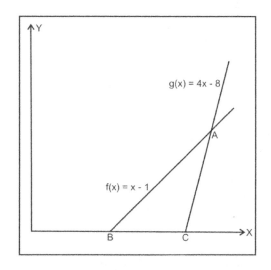

What is the area of the triangle ABC bounded by the graphs of $f(x) = x - 1$ and $g(x) = 4x - 8$ and the X-axis as shown in the graph below?

    (A) $\dfrac{2}{3}$

    (B) 1

    (C) $\dfrac{4}{3}$

    (D) 2

13. If the equation $3 - x = \sqrt{x^2 - 15}$ has an extraneous solution, what is the extraneous solution?

    (A) -7

    (B) 0

    (C) 2

    (D) 4

14.

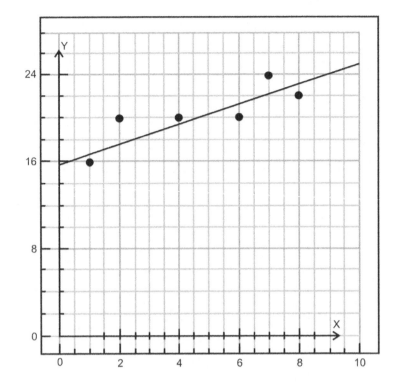

In an experiment, a set of points denoted by the (x, y) coordinates are shown in the graph above along with the line of best fit. Which of the following is the best equation for the above line?

(A) $y = 0.7x - 3.7$

(B) $y = 0.9x + 15.8$

(C) $y = 1.2x - 6.8$

(D) $y = 1.2x + 12.3$

15. In the formula $\dfrac{3y}{2x-y} - 2 = 5x$, what is the correct expression of y in terms of x?

(A) $\dfrac{2x(5x+2)}{5(x+1)}$

(B) $\dfrac{x(5x+2)}{(x+5)}$

(C) $\dfrac{5x(5x+1)}{2(x+1)}$

(D) $\dfrac{5x(x+5)}{2(5x+2)}$

16. Acer.com recently purchased 30 printers, each at $120. The store then sold the printers, to a dealer, all at the same price. Had the store sold each printer for $10 more than what it actually did, the total profit made would have been $1800. What was the selling price of each printer?

    (A) $50

    (B) $120

    (C) $150

    (D) $170

17. Amy, Joe and Ron contributed a total of $255 for a trip to an amusement park. Had each friend managed $5 more, the ratio of their contributions would have been $2 : 3 : 4$ respectively. What was the actual ratio in which they had contributed $255?

    (A) $11 : 17 : 23$

    (B) $13 : 19 : 25$

    (C) $5 : 6 : 9$

    (D) $3 : 5 : 7$

18. The population of a town increases by 20% in each year starting 2010. If the total population of the town in 2013 is 77940, what was the population of the town in 2010?

    (A) 60000

    (B) 45000

    (C) 40000

    (D) 35000

19. $f(x) = (5 - x^p)^{\frac{1}{2}}$. *If* the value of $f(f(2)) = 2$, what is the value of p?

    (A) 1

    (B) 2

    (C) 3

    (D) 4

20. Joe, a fruit vendor, sold 3 apples, 4 oranges and 6 bananas to a customer for $25. He sold 5 apples, 3 oranges and 11 bananas to another customer for $36. If a third customer wants to buy one apple, 5 oranges and one banana, how much would he have to pay?

    (E) $9

    (F) $14

    (G) $18

    (H) $22

21. The profit, in dollars, of a company is determined by the following equation: $P = 50.5 \times N - 210.5$, where '$P$' represents the profit of the company and 'N' represents number of units manufactured by the company. When can the company expect a profit of \$92.50?

    (A) When the number of units manufactured is 2

    (B) When the number of units manufactured is 3

    (C) When the number of units manufactured is 4

    (D) When the number of units manufactured is 6

22. In a field trip organized by a school for the 6th grade students, it was decided that there should be at least one teacher for every 8 students. A total of 48 teachers and students combined participated in the trip. How many students were there in the trip?

    (A) 40

    (B) 41

    (C) 42

    (D) 43

23. $f(x) = 2^x + 1$ and $g(x) = x^3 - \frac{x}{2} + 2$. At which of the points given by the options below do the graphs of the two functions intersect?

    I. $(x, y) = (-1, 2)$

    II. $(x, y) = (0, 2)$

    III. $(x, y) = (1, 3)$

    (A) Only I

    (B) Only II

    (C) Only III

    (D) Both I and II

24. Amazon.com offers successive discounts of 30% and 20% on laptops. Its rival, Wal-Mart, offers successive discounts of 10% and 40% on the same laptops. If a laptop is listed at \$600 in both the stores, how much does a customer stand to save by choosing one store over the other?

    (A) No difference

    (B) \$6

    (C) \$12

    (D) \$15

25. If $\frac{1}{x} + \frac{1}{y} = 2$ and $\frac{3}{x} + \frac{4}{y} = 7$, what is the value of $(x + y)$?

    (A) 1

    (B) 2

    (C) 3

    (D) $\frac{7}{2}$

Questions 26 and 27 are based on the following graph.

The following graph shows the breakup of the type of employees of company Z from 1997-2000: Managerial, Staff, Unskilled and Temporary.

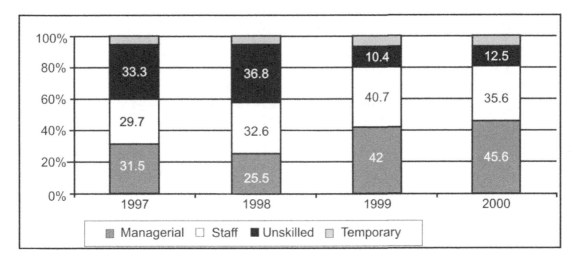

26. If the total number of employees remained the same throughout, what is the approximate percent increase in the number of staff employees between 1997 and 1998?

    (A) 16.4%

    (B) 9.8%

    (C) 8.9%

    (D) 2.9%

27. If the total strength of all employees in 1997 was 5000, and there was a 20% increase in total strength for every year from 1997, what is the number of managerial employees in 1999?

    (A) 3080

    (B) 3024

    (C) 2908

    (D) 2806

28. A man buys a apples and g oranges, each costing 80 cents and 60 cents respectively. If the man buys less than 18 fruits and spends less than $12, which of the following values of a and g satisfy the above conditions?

    (A) $a = 12, g = 5$

    (B) $a = 9, g = 8$

    (C) $a = 11, g = 6$

    (D) $a = 8, g = 9$

29.

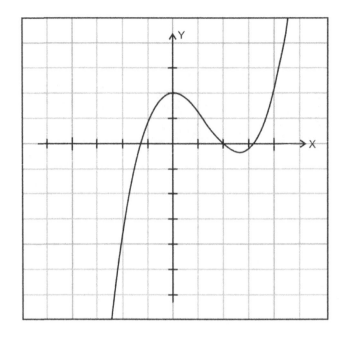

Which of the following could be the equation of the graph shown above?

(A) $y = -(x - 4)(x - 6)(x + 2)$

(B) $y = (x - 4)(x - 6)(x + 2)$

(C) $y = (x + 4)(x - 6)(x + 2)$

(D) $y = -(x - 4)(x - 6)(x - 2)$

30. What is the value of $\left\{ \dfrac{(a+b)^2 - (a^2 + b^2)}{(a+b)^2 - (a-b)^2} \right\}$?

(A) 0.3

(B) 0.4

(C) 0.5

(D) 2.0

31. The first term of a sequence is $\dfrac{1}{2}$ and the second term is $\dfrac{1}{4}$. Each term thereafter is the sum of the all the terms before it. If the nth term is the first term of the sequence that is an integer, what is the value of n?

32. Given that the equation $(3x + 2)k + 5 = 12x + 7m$ has infinite solutions, what is the value of $(k + m)$?

33. A line makes a positive X-intercept and a negative Y-intercept and has a slope equal to $\frac{4}{3}$. If the coordinates of the points where the line intersects the X and Y axes are integers, what is the area of the triangle formed by the line with the X and Y axes?

34. The average of x and 3y is 12, the average of $2x$ and $3z$ is 21. What is the average of x, y and z?

35. The equations $(a - 3)x + 3y = 12$ and $4x + (a - 2)y = k$ have infinitely many solutions. What is the sum of all the possible values of k?

36. Two tangents are drawn from a point P, 40 units from the center of the circle and inclined to each other at 60°. What is the area, to the nearest integer, of the region AXBP?

37. A vendor has two containers containing milk and water solutions of volume 10 liters and 20 liters. What would be the minimum concentration (%) of milk in any of the containers so that he could mix them to get an 80% milk solution?

38. The heights of the 10th grade students of Manhattan Public School are measured. It is found that in section A, the minimum height is $(x^2 + 1)$ feet while the maximum is $(4x - 1)$ feet. In section B, the minimum height is $(x^2 + 1.5)$ feet while the maximum is $(4x - 0.5)$ feet. If all the students are considered, their range (i.e. difference between the maximum and minimum height) comes to 2.5 feet. What is the height of the tallest student (in feet) in the 10th grade, if both sections taken together?

ANSWER SHEET
Section 1

	A B C D		A B C D		A B C D		A B C D		A B C D
1	○ ○ ○ ○	4	○ ○ ○ ○	7	○ ○ ○ ○	10	○ ○ ○ ○	13	○ ○ ○ ○
2	○ ○ ○ ○	5	○ ○ ○ ○	8	○ ○ ○ ○	11	○ ○ ○ ○	14	○ ○ ○ ○
3	○ ○ ○ ○	6	○ ○ ○ ○	9	○ ○ ○ ○	12	○ ○ ○ ○	15	○ ○ ○ ○

Only answers that are gridded will be scored. You will not receive credit for anything written in the boxes.

16	17	18	19	20

ANSWER SHEET
Section 2

	A B C D		A B C D		A B C D		A B C D		A B C D
1	○○○○	7	○○○○	13	○○○○	19	○○○○	25	○○○○
2	○○○○	8	○○○○	14	○○○○	20	○○○○	26	○○○○
3	○○○○	9	○○○○	15	○○○○	21	○○○○	27	○○○○
4	○○○○	10	○○○○	16	○○○○	22	○○○○	28	○○○○
5	○○○○	11	○○○○	17	○○○○	23	○○○○	29	○○○○
6	○○○○	12	○○○○	18	○○○○	24	○○○○	30	○○○○

ANSWER SHEET
Section 2 (Continued)

Only answers that are gridded will be scored. You will not receive credit for anything written in the boxes.

31	32	33	34	35

Grid-in bubbles for questions 31–35, each with fraction bar (/), decimal point (.), and digits 0–9.

Only answers that are gridded will be scored. You will not receive credit for anything written in the boxes.

36	37	38

Grid-in bubbles for questions 36–38, each with fraction bar (/), decimal point (.), and digits 0–9.

Answers and Explanations

Section 1

1. **Level of Difficulty:** Medium | **Category:** Heart of Algebra | **Topic:** Solving systems of linear equations

   The correct answer is (A).

   Adding the 3 equations:

   $a + 2b + 2c = 11$ ... (i)

   $2a + b + 2c = 10$ ... (ii)

   $2a + 2b + c = 9$ ... (iii)

   $5a + 5b + 5c = 30$

   $a + b + c = 6$

   $2a + 2b + 2c = 12$

   Subtracting (i): $a = 1$

2. **Level of Difficulty:** Medium | **Category:** Heart of Algebra | **Topic**: Interpreting linear functions

   The correct answer is (A).

   $C = 120 + 90 \times W + 78 \times N$

   For 10 units, total cost $= 120 + 90W + 780 = 900 + 90W$

   Thus: $900 + 90W \leq 2700$

   $W \leq 20$

   The correct answer is option C.

3. **Level of Difficulty:** Easy | **Category:** Advanced Math | **Topic:** Solving quadratic equations

   The correct answer is (A).

   We know that in a quadratic equation $ax^2 + bx + c = 0$, the sum of the roots is given by $\left(-\frac{b}{a}\right)$ and the product of the roots is given by $\left(\frac{c}{a}\right)$.

   Thus, in the above equation, we have sum of the roots $= -\frac{-(2a-3)}{1} = 2a + 3$.

   Thus, since sum of the roots is five, we have: $2a + 3 = 5 => a = 1$.

   The product of the roots in the above equation is given by $\frac{a^2+5}{1} = a^2 + 5 = 1^2 + 5 = 6$.

   Hence, the correct answer is (A).

4. **Level of Difficulty:** Difficult | **Category:** Additional Math | **Topic:** Circle equations

   The correct answer is (C).

   $x^2 + y^2 - 8x + 6y = 0$

$$x^2 - 2(4)x + 4^2 + y^2 + 2(3)y + 3^2 = 3^2 + 4^2$$

$$(x - 4)^2 + (y + 3)^2 = 5^2$$

Thus, the coordinates of the center of the circle are $(4, -3)$ and the radius is 5.

Thus, the left-most point has the coordinates: $(4 - 5, -3) = (-1, -3)$

Hence, the correct answer is Option (C).

5. **Level of Difficulty:** Easy | **Category:** Heart of Algebra | **Topic:** Solving linear equations and inequalities

    The correct answer is (B).

    Since $(x + 2y)$ leaves a remainder 6 when divided by 7, we have: $x + 2y = 7k + 6$ ... (i) (where k is the quotient).

    Similarly, since $(2x + y)$ leaves a remainder 1 when divided by 7, we have: $2x + y = 7m + 1$ ... (ii) (where m is the quotient).

    Subtracting the above two equations: (ii) – (i):

    $$x - y = 7(m - k) - 5.$$

    Thus, when we divide $(x - y)$ by 7, the first term, i.e. $7(m - k)$ will be divisible by 7. Only the second term will leave a remainder.

    Thus, the remainder will be -5.

    A negative remainder of -5 signifies that the dividend is 5 less than the next multiple of 7, or, in other words, the dividend is 2 more than the previous multiple of 7 (say, for example, 16 when divided by 7, leaves a remainder of 2, i.e. 16 is 2 more than twice of 7 or, it can be thought of as 16 being 5 less than thrice of 7).

    Thus, the actual remainder is 2 (remainder of $-5 \equiv -5 + 7 = 2$).

    Hence, the answer is (B).

6. **Level of Difficulty:** Easy | **Category:** Heart of Algebra | **Topic:** Linear function (word problems)

    The correct answer is (D).

    As the cost of a pencil is '$\$a$', the cost an eraser is '$\$b$', the cost of a sharpener is '$\$c$', then Adam should have spent $23a + 15b + 20c$, which must be equal to $70

    $$23a + 15b + 20c = 111 \text{ ... (i)}$$

    Also, Bob must have spent $19b + 12a + 40c$ and as he spent $10 more than Adam, this spending must be equal to $\$(70 + 2) = \$121$.

    $$19b + 12a + 40c = 121 \text{ ... (ii)}$$

    The answer is option (D).

7. **Level of Difficulty:** Medium | **Category:** Advanced Math | **Topic:** Functions

    The correct answer is (C).

    At the points where $f(x)$ and $g(x)$ intersect, the values of the functions will be equal.

    Thus: $f(x) = g(x) => x^2 - 6x + 8 = x - 2 => x^2 - 7x + 10 = 0 => (x - 2)(x - 5) = 0$

$=> x = 2$ or 5.

Thus, the two graphs intersect at two points, $x = 2$ and $x = 5$.

Hence, the correct answer is (C).

8. **Level of Difficulty:** Easy | **Category:** Advanced Math | **Topic:** Nonlinear equation graphs

The correct answer is (C).

It appears that the graph of $g(x)$ has been reflected about the X-axis to get the graph of $f(x)$. Thus, $fx = -g(x)$.

Say, $x = \frac{1}{2}$: $g\left(\frac{1}{2}\right) = \frac{1}{2}$ and $f\left(\frac{1}{2}\right) = -\frac{1}{2} => f\left(\frac{1}{2}\right) = -g\left(\frac{1}{2}\right)$.

Similarly, we can check for all other points.

Thus, $f(x) = -g(x)$.

Hence, the correct answer is (C).

9. **Level of Difficulty:** Easy | **Category:** Additional Math | **Topic:** Circle theorems

The correct answer is (D).

$\angle QPR = \angle QSR = 20°$ [angle made by the chord QR]

$\therefore \angle PQR = 180° - (80° + 20°) = 80°$

$\therefore \angle PSR = 180° - 80° = 100°$

Hence, the correct answer is Option D.

10. **Level of Difficulty:** Easy | **Category:** Heart of Algebra | **Topic:** Solving linear equations and inequalities

The correct answer is (D).

The first mark is at -12 and the last is 36. Thus, the gap is $36 - (-12) = 48$.

There is a total of 24 gaps. Hence, each gap $= \dfrac{48}{24} = 2$.

We can identify the values at the major points as shown below:

Hence, $a = -12 + 4 = -8, b = 12 - 2 = 10, c = 20 + 4 = 24, d = 28 + 2 = 30$.

Let us verify the options:

(A): $a + b = -8 + 10 = 2 \neq d$. Hence, the statement is incorrect.

(B): $|a| + |d| = |-8| + |30| = 8 + 30 = 38$.

$|c| + |b| = |24| + |10| = 24 + 10 = 34$.

Hence, $|a| + |d| \neq |c| + |d|$. Hence, the statement is incorrect.

(C): $c|a| = 24 \times |-8| = 24 \times 8 = 192$.

bd $= 10 \times 30 = 300$.

Hence, $c|a| \neq$ bd. Hence, the statement is incorrect.

(D): $d|a| = 30 \times |-8| = 30 \times 8 = 240$.

bc $= 10 \times 24 = 240$.

Hence, $d|a| = bc$. Hence, the statement is correct and is our answer.

Hence, the answer is (D).

11. **Level of Difficulty:** Easy | **Category:** Advanced Math | **Topic:** Linear and quadratic systems

The correct answer is (D).

Solving $g(x) \geq f(x)$:

$x - 2 \geq x^2 - 6x + 8$

$x^2 - 7x + 10 \leq 0$

$(x - 2)(x - 5) \leq 0$

$2 \leq x \leq 5$

Thus, the integer values of x are: 2, 3, 4 and 5.

Thus, there are 4 possible values of x.

The correct answer is option D.

12. **Level of Difficulty:** Medium | **Category:** Advanced Math | **Topic:** Radicals and rational exponents

The correct answer is (D).

We have: N $= 4^{61} + 4^{61} + 4^{61} + 4^{62} + 4^{62} + 4^{62} = 4^{61}(1 + 1 + 1 + 4 + 4 + 4) = 4^{61} \times 15$.

Hence, we can see that N is divisible by both 3 and 5.

Hence, both the first and second statements are correct.

Now, we can also write N $= 4^{61} \times 15 = 4^{61} \times 3 \times 5 = 2^{122} \times 3 \times 5$.

Since all the exponents of the prime factors are not even numbers, N is not a perfect square.

Hence, the third statement is not correct.

Hence, the answer is (D).

13. **Level of Difficulty:** Medium | **Category:** Heart of Algebra | **Topic:** Linear function (word problems)

The correct answer is (C).

As Abe reads 23 pages every morning, number of mornings he read $= \dfrac{M}{23}$

Also, as Abe reads 31 pages every evening, number of evenings he read $= \dfrac{E}{31}$

Since Abe did not read in morning and evening of the same day, the number of days he read

$$N = \frac{M}{23} + \frac{E}{31}$$

The correct answer is option C.

14. **Level of Difficulty:** Easy | **Category:** Advanced Math. | **Topic:** Radicals and rational exponents

The correct answer is (D).

We know that an even exponent of any number is always positive irrespective of whether the original number is positive or negative.

We have: $a^3 b^4 c^7 d^2 = a^2 b^4 c^6 d^2 \times ac$.

We can say that $a^2 b^4 c^6 d^2$ has all even exponents. Hence, it is positive.

However, since the given expression is negative, we can conclude that ac must be negative.

Working with options:

(A): $ab^2 cd^2 = b^2 d^2 \times ac$.

$b^2 d^2$ is positive (even exponents) and ac is negative. Hence, the product is negative.

Thus, this option is incorrect.

(B): In $b^2 d$, we can say that b^2 is positive. But we do not know whether d is positive or negative. Hence, $b^2 d$ can be either positive or negative depending on d.

Thus, this option is incorrect.

(C): In $bc^2 d$, we can say that c^2 is positive. However, we do not know the nature of b and d. Hence, $bc^2 d$ can be either positive or negative depending on b and d.

Thus, this option is incorrect.

Hence, (D) must be our answer. Let us verify (D):

(D): $a^3 b^2 c = a^2 b^2 \times ac$. We can say that $a^2 b^2$ is positive. Also, we know that ac is negative. Hence, $a^3 b^2 c$ must be negative.

Thus, this option is correct.

Hence, the answer is (D).

15. **Level of Difficulty:** Difficult | **Category:** Advanced Math | **Topic:** Solving quadratic equations

The correct answer is (B).

We know that in a quadratic equation $ax^2 + bx + c = 0$, the sum of the roots is given by $\left(-\frac{b}{a}\right)$ and the product of the roots is given by $\left(\frac{c}{a}\right)$.

Let the roots of $x^2 - (a - b)x + c = 0$ be p and $-p$ where p is an integer.

Thus, sum of roots $= -\frac{-(a-b)}{1} = a - b$.

However, sum of the roots $= p + (-p) = 0$.

Thus, we have $a - b = 0 \Rightarrow a = b$.

Hence, statement I is false and statement II is true.

Again, product of the roots $= \dfrac{c}{1} = c$.

Also, product of the roots $= p \times (-p) = -p^2$.

Thus, we have $c = -p^2 \Rightarrow c + p^2 = 0$.

However, since p and a are not related, statement III is not necessarily true.

Thus, only statement II is true.

Hence, the correct answer is (B).

16. **Level of Difficulty:** Medium | **Category:** Advanced Math | **Topic:** Nonlinear equation graphs

The correct answer is 9

We can see from the graph that the graph of $f(x)$ has shifted right and up.

In order to find the amount of the shift, let us pick a reference point on the graphs.

The easiest point to check is the lowest point on the graphs.

The lowest point on $f(x)$ is at $(1, 4)$ and the corresponding point on $g(x)$ is $(5, 9)$.

Thus, $f(x)$ has shifted 4 units right and 5 units up.

We know that if the function $f(x)$ is modified to $f(x + a)$, then the graph shifts a units left and if the function is modified to $f(x - a)$, then the graph shifts a units right where a is positive.

Again, if the function $f(x)$ is modified to $f(x) + b$, then the graph shifts b units up and if the function is modified to $f(x) - b$, then the graph shifts b units down where b is positive.

Since $f(x)$ has shifted 4 units right and 5 units up, the modified function $(x) = f(x - 4) + 5$.

Comparing with the given form: $g(x) = f(x + k) - m$, we get $k = -4, m = -5$.

Thus, $|k + m| = |-4 - 5| = 9$.

Thus, the correct answer is 9.

17. **Level of Difficulty:** Difficult | **Category:** Advanced Math | **Topic:** Quadratic and exponential (word problems)

Let the number of friends be x.
Price of the camera $= \$300$.

Thus, contribution from each friend $= \$\dfrac{300}{x}$.

Contribution from each friend after one more friend joined $= \$\dfrac{300}{x+1}$.

Th/0000000000**.363s, we have: $\left(\dfrac{300}{x} - \dfrac{300}{x+1}\right) = 10 \Rightarrow \dfrac{30}{x} - \dfrac{30}{x+1} = 1 \Rightarrow \dfrac{30}{x^2+x} = 1 \Rightarrow x^2 + x - 30 = 0$

$(x + 6)(x - 5) = 0 \Rightarrow x = -6$ or 5.

Thus, the numbers of friends originally were 5.

Hence, the correct answer is 5.

18. **Level of Difficulty:** Easy | **Category:** Heart of Algebra | **Topic:** Interpreting linear functions

The correct answer is 7.

$p = 2n + 3$

Thus, for $p = 17$: $17 = 2n + 3 => n = 7$

19. **Level of Difficulty:** Difficult | **Category:** Heart of Algebra | **Topic:** Solving linear equations and inequalities

The correct answer is 54.

We have: $px - q(x + r) = 23x - 15 => x(p - q) - qr = 23x - 15$.

Comparing the coefficient of x and the constant term, we get: $p - q = 23$ and $qr = 15$.

Since $qr = 15$, we have the possible values of q and r as shown below:

q	r
1	15
3	5
5	3
15	1

Using $p - q = 23$ and the above values of q, we get the following values of p as shown below:

q	r
1	24
3	26
5	28
15	38

Hence, the possible values of p, q, r and $p + q + r$ are shown below:

p	q	r	p + q + r
24	1	15	40
26	3	5	34
28	5	3	36
38	15	1	54

Hence, the maximum possible value of $(p + q + r)$ is 54.

Hence, the correct answer is 54.

20. **Level of Difficulty:** Easy | **Category:** Additional Math | **Topic:** Complex numbers

The correct answer is 2.

We know that the imaginary number i is such that $i^2 = -1$.

Therefore, $i^4 = (i^2)^2 = (-1)^2 = 1$.

Similarly, $i^3 = i * i^2 = i * (-1) = -i$.

Therefore, we can write the given expression as

$2i^4 + 4i^3 - i^2 + 3i$

$= 2 \times 1 + 4(-i) - (-1) + 3i$

$= 2 - 4i + 1 + 3i$

$= 3 - i$.

$=> a = 3, b = -1 => a + b = 2$

Hence, the correct answer is 2.

Answers and Explanations

Section 2

1. **Level of Difficulty:** Difficult | **Category:** Heart of Algebra | **Topic:** Linear inequality and equation (word problems)

    The correct answer is (A).

    Let the remainder in each case be r. Let the quotients in the two cases be m and p respectively.

    Thus, we have:

    $1189 = Nm + r$ and $643 = Np + r$.

    Subtracting the above two equations, we get: $1189 - 643 = N(m - p) => N(m - p) = 546$.

    Thus, we can say that N is a factor of 546 and we need to find the largest two digit factor of 546.

    On breaking 546 into its factors, we get: $546 = 2 \times 3 \times 7 \times 13$.

    We need to combine the factors above to get the largest two digit number.

    We can see that among all combinations, $7 \times 13 = 91$ is the largest (the other combinations would be: $2 \times 3 = 6; 3 \times 7 = 21; 13 \times 3 = 39; 2 \times 3 \times 13 = 78$; etc).

    Thus, $N = 91$ and the sum of digits of N is $1 + 9 = 10$.

    Hence, the answer is (A).

2. **Level of Difficulty:** Easy | **Category:** Problem Solving and Data Analysis | **Topic:** Data inferences

    The correct answer is (B).

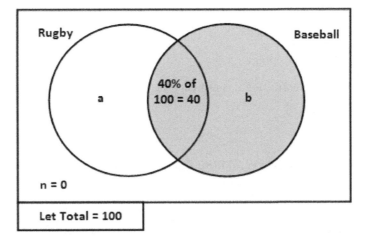

    Number of men $= 60\%$ of $40 = 24$.

    Number of women $= 40 - 24 = 16$.

    Number of men who play rugby $= 33.33\%$ of $24 = 8$.

    Number of employees who play rugby $= 30\%$ of $40 = 12$.

    Thus, number of women who play rugby $= 12 - 8 = 4$.

Thus, the number of women who do not play rugby = 16 − 4 = 12.

Hence, the correct answer is (B).

3. **Level of Difficulty:** Medium | **Category:** Problem Solving and Data Analysis | **Topic:** Units

   The correct answer is (C).

   10 miles is represented as 5 meters.

   Thus, $10 \times 10 = 100$ square miles would be represented as $5 \times 5 = 25$ square meters

   60 square miles would be represented as $\dfrac{25}{100} \times 60 = 15$ square meters

   Since 1 mile = 1600 meters, we have: 1 square mile = (1600×1600) square meters

   Thus, 15 square meters $= \dfrac{15}{1600 \times 1600} = 0.059 \times 10^{-4} = 5.9 \times 10^{-6}$ square miles

   The correct answer is option (C).

4. **Level of Difficulty:** Easy | **Category:** Heart of Algebra | **Topic:** Systems of linear inequalities (word problems)

   The correct answer is (D).

   Earnings for the first 5 hours = \$40

   Earnings for the remaining $(t − 5)$ hours = $\${5(t − 5)\} = \$(5t − 25)$

   Since he earns \$P: $P = 40 + (5t − 25)$

   $P = 5t + 15$

   Since $P \leq 60$: $5t + 15 \leq 60$

   $t \leq 9$

   Thus, only options C and D are possible.

   If $t = 9, P = 5t + 15 = 60$ - Thus, option C is not correct.

   The correct answer is option D.

5. **Level of Difficulty:** Difficult | **Category:** Additional Math | **Topic:** Complex numbers

   $$z = \dfrac{7 − 5i}{11 + 4i}$$

   We need to rationalize it so that the denominator does not have any i present. To do that, we need to multiply the denominator with its conjugate.

   Thus, we have: $\dfrac{7−5i}{11+4i}$

   $= \dfrac{7−5i}{11+4i} \times \left(\dfrac{11−4i}{11−4i}\right)$

   $= \dfrac{77−55i−28i+20i^2}{121−16i^2}$

$$= \frac{57 - 83i}{137}$$

$$= \frac{57}{137} - \frac{83}{137}i$$

$$= 0.42 - 0.61i$$

Hence, the correct option is (A).

6. **Level of Difficulty:** Easy | **Category:** Heart of Algebra | **Topic:** Solving systems of linear equations

$3x + 2y + 4z = 20 \dots$ (i)

$5x + 7y - 9z = -10 \dots$ (ii)

Working with the options:

Option A: $x = 2, y = -1$ and $z = 4$ satisfies only (i), not (ii)

Option B: $x = 4, y = 2$ and $z = 1$ satisfies only (i), not (ii)

Option C: $x = 1, y = 3$ and $z = 2$ satisfies neither (i), nor (ii)

Option D: $x = 2, y = 1$ and $z = 3$ satisfies both (i) and (ii)

The correct answer is option D.

7. **Level of Difficulty:** Easy | **Category:** Heart of Algebra | **Topic:** Linear inequality and equation (word problems)

The correct answer is (D).

Let the price of each beer bottle was $\$x$.

Total bottles purchased = 8.

Thus, total cost = $\$8x$.

Since the friends shared the beer equally, share of each friend = $\$\frac{8x}{3}$.

Since Bruce paid $16 for his share, we can say that $\frac{8x}{3} = 16 => x = 6$.

Thus, total amount spent by Matt for his five bottles = $5x = \$30$.

Since each friend shared the beer equally, we can say that Matt consumed the same amount as Bruce i.e. Matt consumed $16 worth of beer.

Thus, Matt must have given Bruce the remaining $30 – $16 = $14 worth of beer.

Hence, Bruce must return back $14.

(Note: Total amount spent by Joe for his three bottles = $3x = \$18$.

Since each friend shared the beer equally, we can say that Joe also consumed the same amount as Bruce i.e. Joe consumed $16 worth of beer.

Thus, Matt must have given Bruce the remaining $18 – $16 = $2 worth of beer.

Hence, Bruce must return back $2).

Thus, out of the $16 given by Bruce, Matt got $14 (and Joe got $2).

Hence, the correct answer is (D).

8. **Level of Difficulty:** Difficult | **Category:** Advanced Math | **Topic:** Interpreting nonlinear expressions

The correct answer is (D).

We have: $n = 5m + 2$, where m is some non-negative integer (since n leaves a remainder of 2 when divided by 5).

However, we know that n, i.e. the left-hand-side is even. Thus, m should also be even as only then the right-hand-side will be even as well.

Thus, let us assume $m = 2k$, where k is some other non-negative integer.

Hence, we have: $n = 10k + 2$.

Thus, $(3n + 7)(2n + 5) = (3(10k + 2) + 7)(2(10k + 2) + 5) = (30k + 13)(20k + 9)$

$= (600k^2 + 530k) + 117.$

We can see that $(600k^2 + 530k)$ is divisible by 10 and hence would not leave any remainder. The remainder would come from 117, which when divided by 10 leaves a remainder 7.

Thus, the remainder is 7.

Hence, the answer is (D).

9. **Level of Difficulty:** Medium | **Category:** Additional Math | **Topic:** Angles, arc lengths, and trig functions

The correct answer is (D).

We can simplify the above as follows: $\dfrac{7\pi^c}{4} + \dfrac{4\pi^c}{3} - \dfrac{5\pi^c}{12} = \left(\dfrac{7\pi*3+4\pi*4-5\pi*1}{12}\right)^c$

$= \left(\dfrac{21\pi+16\pi-5\pi}{12}\right)^c = \left(\dfrac{32\pi}{12}\right)^c = \dfrac{8\pi^c}{3}.$

We know that π radians are equivalent to 180°

Thus, $\dfrac{8\pi}{3}$ radians are equivalent to $180° \times \dfrac{8}{3} = 480°$

Hence, the correct option is (D).

10. **Level of Difficulty:** Easy | **Category:** Problem Solving and Data Analysis | **Topic:** Data inferences

The correct answer is (C).

The marbles would be of the same color if either both are red, or both are blue.

The number of ways of getting both red or both blue $= C_2^3 + C_2^5 = \dfrac{3!}{2!1!} + \dfrac{5!}{3!2!} = 13.$

Thus, there are 13 favorable cases.

Total ways of drawing 2 marbles from $3 + 5 = 8$ marbles is $C_2^8 = \dfrac{8!}{2!6!} = 28.$

Thus, required probability $= \dfrac{13}{28} = 0.46.$

Hence, the correct answer is (C).

11. **Level of Difficulty:** Medium | **Category:** Problem Solving and Data Analysis | **Topic:** Center, spread and shape of distributions

The correct answer is (D).

The total of the five integers $= 60 \times 5 = 300$.

The largest integer is 70.

Since we need to minimize the smallest integer, we need to assign the largest possible values of the remaining three integers (leaving out the largest and the smallest from the set of five integers).

Thus, the other three integers are 69, 68 and 67 which add up to 204.

Thus, the minimum possible value of the smallest integer $= 300 - (70 + 204) = 300 - 274 = 26$.

Hence, the correct answer is (D).

12. **Level of Difficulty:** Medium | **Category:** Heart of Algebra | **Topic:** Graphing linear equations

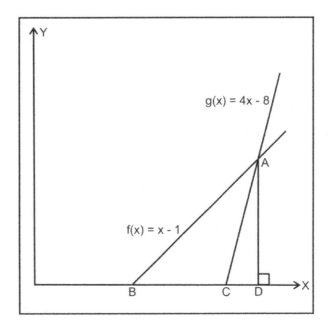

The correct answer is (A).

We need to find the coordinates of A, B and C. Solving $f(x) = g(x)$:

$x - 1 = 4x - 8 => x = \frac{7}{3} => f\left(\frac{7}{3}\right) = \frac{7}{3} - 1 = \frac{4}{3}$.

Thus, $f\left(\frac{7}{3}\right) = g\left(\frac{7}{3}\right) = \frac{4}{3}$. Thus, coordinates of A are $\left(\frac{7}{3}, \frac{4}{3}\right)$.

Again, $f(x)$ intersects X-axis at B.

Thus, $f(x) = 0 => x - 1 = 0 => x = 1$.

So, coordinates of B are $(1, 0)$.

Again, $g(x)$ intersects X-axis at C.

Thus, $g(x) = 0 => 4x - 8 = 0 => x = 2$.

So, coordinates of C are $(2, 0)$.

Thus, length of BC $= 2 - 1 = 1$ unit.

Height of triangle ABC i.e. AD $= \dfrac{4}{3}$ units.

Hence, area of triangle ABC $= \dfrac{1}{2} \times$ bas $\times$ height $= \dfrac{1}{2} \times$ BC $\times$ AD $= \dfrac{1}{2} \times 1 \times \dfrac{4}{3} = \dfrac{2}{3}$ square units.

Hence, the correct answer is (A).

13. **Level of Difficulty:** Medium | **Category:** Advanced Math | **Topic:** Rational expressions and polynomials

The correct answer is (D).

An extraneous solution is a solution that emerges from the process of solving the problem but is not a valid solution to the original problem.

We have:

$3 - x = \sqrt{x^2 - 15}$

Squaring both sides: $x^2 - 6x + 9 = x^2 - 15$

$\Rightarrow \quad x = 4$

We observe that there is only one solution for x.

Substituting $x = 4$ in the given equation, we have:

LHS $= 3 - 4 = -1$

RHS $= \sqrt{16 - 15} = 1$ (Note: By definition, the '$\sqrt{\ }$' symbol returns only the positive square root).

Thus, for $x = 4$, LHS $\neq$ RHS. Since there is no other solution, the above equation has no solutions at all. Thus, the extraneous solution is $x = 4$.

The correct answer is option D.

14. **Level of Difficulty:** Difficult | **Category:** Problem Solving and Data Analysis | **Topic:** Scatter plots

The correct answer is (B).

From the graph, we can clearly observe that:

When x changes from $x = 2.5$ to $x = 9$, the value of y changes approximately from $y = 18$ to $y = 24$

Thus, the slope of the line $= \dfrac{24 - 18}{9 - 2.5} = \dfrac{6}{6.5} = 0.92$, i.e. less than 1.

Also, the Y – intercept is positive, approximately 16.

Thus, the only equation which satisfies is option B.

The correct answer is option B.

15. **Level of Difficulty:** Medium | **Category:** Advanced Math | **Topic:** Isolating quantities

The correct answer is (A).

$$\frac{3y}{2x - y} - 2 = 5x$$

$$\frac{3y}{2x - y} = 5x + 2$$

$$\frac{2x - y}{3y} = \frac{1}{5x + 2}$$

$$\frac{2x}{3y} - \frac{1}{3} = \frac{1}{5x + 2}$$

$$\frac{2x}{3y} = \frac{1}{5x + 2} + \frac{1}{3} = \frac{5x + 5}{3(5x + 2)}$$

$$\frac{3y}{2x} = \frac{3(5x + 2)}{5(x + 1)}$$

$$y = \frac{2x(5x + 2)}{5(x + 1)}$$

Alternative: Plug in $x = 1$ in the given expression:

The value of $y = 1.4$

Plugging in $x = 1$ in each option, only option A gives $y = 1.4$

The correct answer is option A.

16. **Level of Difficulty:** Easy | **Category:** Problem Solving and Data Analysis | **Topic:** Percents

The correct answer is (D).

If the price of each printer was increased by $10, additional profit generated = $10 × 30 = $300.

Thus, initially, the total profit generated on selling 30 printers = $(1800 − 300) = $1500.

Thus, profit made on each printer = $$\$ \frac{1500}{30} = \$50.$$

Cost of each printer = $120.

Hence, the selling price of each printer = $(120 + 50) = $170.

Hence, the answer is (D).

17. **Level of Difficulty:** Easy | **Category:** Problem Solving and Data Analysis | **Topic:** Ratios, rates, and proportions

The correct answer is (A).

If each friend had contributed $5 more than what they did, they would have managed to have $5 × 3 = $15 more than $255 i.e. $270.

The ratio in which they would have contributed $270 is 2 : 3 : 4.

Hence, contribution of Amy $= \$ \left(\frac{2}{2+3+4} \times 270\right) = \$60$.

Contribution of Joe $= \$ \left(\frac{3}{2+3+4} \times 270\right) = \$90$.

Contribution of Ron $= \$ \left(\frac{4}{2+3+4} \times 270\right) = \$120$.

Thus, before contributing \$5 extra, their respective contributions were

$= (60-5) : (90-5) : (120-5) = 55 : 85 : 115 = 11 : 17 : 23$.

Hence, the answer is (A).

18. **Level of Difficulty:** Medium | **Category:** Problem Solving and Data Analysis | **Topic:** Linear and exponential growth

The correct answer is (B).

If the population of the town increases by 20%, the new population becomes $\frac{120}{100}$ times the original population.

Therefore, population in every year becomes $\left(\frac{120}{100}\right) = \frac{6}{5}$ times the population of previous year.

Let us consider the population of 2010 as x.

Therefore, with 20% increase, the population in 2014 will become $\left(\frac{6}{5}\right)x$.

The population in 2015 will be again $\frac{6}{5}$ *times* the population of 2014 and so on. Hence, we get

$$\left(\frac{6}{5}\right)^3 \times x = 77940$$

$$\frac{216}{125} \times x = 77940$$

$$x = 77940 \times \frac{125}{216}$$

$$x = 45000$$

The correct answer is option (B).

19. **Level of Difficulty:** Difficult | **Category:** Advanced Math | **Topic:** Functions

The correct answer is (B).

$f(2) = (5 - 2^p)^{\frac{1}{2}}$.

Thus, $f(f(2)) = \left(5 - (f(2))^p\right)^{\frac{1}{2}} = \left(5 - \left((5 - 2^p)^{\frac{1}{2}}\right)^p\right)^{\frac{1}{2}}$ replacing $f(2) = (5 - 2^p)^{\frac{1}{2}}$

Hence, we have: $\left(5 - \left((5 - 2^p)^{\frac{1}{2}}\right)^p\right)^{\frac{1}{2}} = 2 \implies 5 - \left((5 - 2^p)^{\frac{1}{2}}\right)^p = 2^2 = 4$

$$\left((5 - 2^p)^{\frac{1}{2}}\right)^p = 5 - 4 = 1$$

$$(5 - 2^p)^{\frac{1}{2}} = 1^{\frac{1}{p}} = 1$$

$$5 - 2^p = 1^2 = 1$$

$$2^p = 5 - 1 = 4$$

$$2^p = 2^2 => p = 2.$$

Hence, the correct answer is (B).

20. **Level of Difficulty:** Difficult | **Category:** Heart of Algebra | **Topic:** Linear inequality and equation

The correct answer is (B).

Let the price of one apple, one orange and one banana be a, r and b respectively.

Thus, we have: 3a + 4r + 6b = 25 ... (i)

Also, 5a + 3r + 11b = 36 ... (ii)

Using the above, we need to calculate the value of r.

Since there are only two equations with three variables, we cannot solve for all the variables.

Thus, we need to manipulate the above equations such that we can determine the value of r.

Let us multiply (i) with k and (ii) with l and add those to get the value of r. Thus, we have:

$$3ka + 4kr + 6kb = 25k$$

$$5la + 3lr + 11lb = 36l$$

On adding, we get: $(3k + 5l)a + (4k + 3l)r + (6k + 11l)b = 25k + 36l$.

Since we need one apple, 5 oranges and one banana, i.e. $a + 5r + b$, we have:

$3k + 5l = 1$ ... (iii)

$4k + 3l = 5$ ... (iv)

$6k + 11l = 1$ ... (v)

We need to solve the above to get the values of k and l. Let us solve (iii) and (v).

Thus: (iii)x 2 $-$(v): $(6k + 10l) - (6k + 11l) = 2 - 1 => l = -1$.

Substituting the value of l in (v): $6k = 1 - 11l = 1 - (-11) = 1 + 11 = 12 => k = 2$.

Thus, we have $k = 2, l = -1$.

We need to substitute these values in the final equation (iv) to verify whether they satisfy:

Thus, in (iv): $4k + 3l = 8 - 3 = 5$. Hence, it satisfies.

Thus, what we have basically done is multiply (i) with 2 and subtract (ii) to get the required value. This could have also been done by observation or by hit and trial.

Thus, the required price is given by 25k + 36l = 25 $\times$ 2 $-$ 36 $\times$ 1 = 50 $-$ 36 = 14.

Hence, the answer is (B).

21. **Level of Difficulty:** Easy | **Category:** Heart of Algebra | **Topic:** Interpreting linear functions

The correct answer is (D).

If we put $P = 92.50$, we get

$$92.5 = 50.5 \times N - 210.5$$

$$50.5N = 303 => N = \frac{303}{50.5} = 6$$

$$N = 6$$

The correct answer is option D.

22. **Level of Difficulty:** Difficult | **Category:** Problem Solving and Data Analysis | **Topic:** Ratios, rates, and proportions

The correct answer is (C).

We know that the ratio of teachers to students should be $1 : 8$ or more (i.e. there can be more than one teacher per 8 students).

Let the number of teachers be x, so the number of students = 8x.

Thus, total participants in the field trip $= x + 8x = 9x$.

Thus, we have: $9x = 48 => x = \frac{48}{9} = 5.33$.

However, the number of teachers cannot be a fractional number. So, the value of x will be either 5 or 6.

But, with 5 teachers and $48 - 5 = 43$ students, the required ratio of one teacher per 8 students won't be satisfied.

Thus, the number of teachers should be more than 5.33 i.e. 6.

Thus, number of students $= 48 - 6 = 42$ (observe that teacher to student ratio $= 6 : 42 = 1 : 7$ is more than the required ratio of $1 : 8$).

Hence, the answer is (C).

23. **Level of Difficulty:** Difficult | **Category**: Advanced Math | **Topic:** Functions

The correct answer is (B).

At the points where $f(x)$ and $g(x)$ intersect, the values of the functions will be equal.

However, one cannot solve the two equations. So, it is best to use the options.

Statement I: $f(-1) = 2^{-1} + 1 = \frac{1}{2} + 1 = 1.5$.

$g(-1) = (-1)^3 - \frac{-1}{2} + 2 = -1 + 0.5 + 2 = 1.5$.

Since $f(-1) = g(-1)$, the graphs intersect at $x = -1$. However, the values of the functions at $x = -1$ are 1.5 and not 2. Hence, Statement I is not true.

Statement II: $f(0) = 2^0 + 1 = 1 + 1 = 2$.

$g(0) = 0 - 0 + 2 = 2$.

Since $f(0) = g(0) = 2$, the graphs intersect at $x = 1, y = 2$. Hence, Statement II is true.

Statement III: $f(1) = 2^1 + 1 = 3$.

$g(1) = (1)^3 - \frac{1}{2} + 2 = 1 - 0.5 + 2 = 2.5.$

Since $f(1) \neq g(1)$, the graphs do not intersect at $x = 1$. Hence, Statement III is not true.

Hence, the correct answer is (B).

24. **Level of Difficulty:** Medium | **Category:** Problem Solving and Data Analysis | **Topic:** Percents

The correct answer is (B).

We can calculate the net discount offered by each store using the formula for successive percentage change:

Successive percentage changes of x% and y% result in a net percentage change of $\left(x + y + \frac{xy}{100}\right)$%.

For Amazon, $x = -30, y = -20 =>$ net percentage change $= -20 - 30 + \frac{(-20)(-30)}{100} = -44\%.$

Thus, Amazon offers a net discount of 44%.

For Wal-Mart, $x = -10, y = -40 =>$ net percentage change $= -10 - 40 + \frac{(-10)(-40)}{100} = -46\%.$

Thus, Wal-Mart offers a net discount of 46%.

Thus, if a customer chooses Wal-Mart over Amazon, he stands to save

$= 46 - 44 = 2\%$ of the listed price $= \$(2\%$ of $600) = \$12.$

Hence, the answer is (B).

25. **Level of Difficulty:** Medium | **Category:** Problem Solving and Data Analysis | **Topic:** Solving systems of linear equations

The correct answer is (B).

Let $\frac{1}{x} = a$ and $\frac{1}{y} = b$

$a + b = 2 \dots$ (i)

$3a + 4b = 7 \dots$ (ii)

From (ii) – (i) x 3: $b = 1 => a = 1$

$\frac{1}{x} = \frac{1}{y} = 1 => x = y = 1$

$x + y = 2$

The correct answer is option B.

26. **Level of Difficulty:** Easy| **Category** | Problem Solving and Data Analysis | **Topic:** Data collection and conclusions

The correct answer is (B).

Since the number of employees remains the same throughout, the above percent values are equivalent to the actual number of people under each category.

Thus, the required percent change $= \dfrac{32.6 - 29.7}{29.7} \times 100 = 9.76\% \approx 9.8\%$

27. **Level of Difficulty:** Medium | **Category:** Problem Solving and Data Analysis | **Topic:** Data collection and conclusions

The correct answer is (B).

The total number of employees in 1997 = 5000.

Thus, the number of employees in 1999, at a 20% growth rate

$$= 5000 \times \left(1 + \dfrac{20}{100}\right)^2 = 7200$$

Thus, the number of managerial employees in 1999

$$= \dfrac{42}{100} \times 7200 = 3024$$

28. **Level of Difficulty:** Medium | **Category:** Heart of Algebra | **Topic:** Systems of linear inequalities (word problems)

The correct answer is (D).

Since total number of fruits is less than 15, we have: $a + g < 18$

Since total amount spent is less than \$12, we have: $80a + 60r < 1200 => 4a + 3r < 60$

Each of the options satisfies the first condition.

We need to verify the second condition regarding the amount spent.

Only Option D satisfies that condition since $4a + 3g = 32 + 27 = 59 < 60$.

The correct answer is option D.

29. **Level of Difficulty:** Medium | **Category:** Problem Solving and Data Analysis | **Topic:** Key features of graphs

The correct answer is (B).

The above graph has 3 roots since it intersects the X-axis at 3 points.

Also, 2 roots are positive, and 1 root is negative. This is satisfied only by options A and B.

Also, the graph has a positive Y-intercept. The Y-intercept is obtained by the coefficient of the constant term (with sign) in the expansion.

In option A, the constant term $= (-)(-4)(-6)(+2) = -48 < 0$

In option B, the constant term $= (+)(-4)(-6)(+2) = +48 > 0$

The correct answer is option B.

30. **Level of Difficulty:** Easy | **Category:** Advanced Math | **Topic:** Structure in expressions

The correct answer is (C).

$$\frac{(a+b)^2-(a^2+b^2)}{(a+b)^2-(a-b)^2}$$

$$=\frac{a^2+2ab+b^2-(a^2+b^2)}{(a^2+2ab+b^2)-(a^2-2ab+b^2)}$$

$$=\frac{2ab}{4ab}=0.5$$

The correct answer is option C.

31. **Level of Difficulty:** Difficult | **Category:** Problem Solving and Data Analysis | **Topic:** Data inferences

The correct answer is 5.

In order that a term of the sequence is an integer, we need to have added $\frac{1}{2}$ an 'even' number of times (so as to cancel the 2 in the denominator) and $\frac{1}{4}$ a 'multiple of four' number of times (so as to cancel the 4 in the denominator).

The terms of the sequence are shown below (without calculating their values):

$t_1 = \frac{1}{2};\ t_2 = \frac{1}{4};\ t_3 = t_1 + t_2 = \left(\frac{1}{2}\right) + \left(\frac{1}{4}\right);\ t_4 = t_1 + t_2 + t_3 = \left(\frac{1}{2}\right) + \left(\frac{1}{4}\right) + \left(\frac{1}{2} + \frac{1}{4}\right) = 2\left(\frac{1}{2} + \frac{1}{4}\right);$

$t_5 = t_1 + t_2 + t_3 + t_4 = \left(\frac{1}{2}\right) + \left(\frac{1}{4}\right) + \left(\frac{1}{2} + \frac{1}{4}\right) + 2\left(\frac{1}{2} + \frac{1}{4}\right) = 4\left(\frac{1}{2} + \frac{1}{4}\right).$

We can see that in every term after the first two terms, $\frac{1}{2}$ and $\frac{1}{4}$ are present an equal number of times:

In the third term, each is present once;

In the fourth term, each is present twice;

In the fifth term, each is present four times; and so on; i.e. the number of times each is present doubles in the successive term from the third term onwards.

Alternatively:

$t_3 = (t_1 + t_2);$

$t_4 = t_1 + t_2 + t_3 = 2(t_1 + t_2);$

$t_5 = t_1 + t_2 + t_3 + t_4 = 4(t_1 + t_2);$ and so on.

Since we need $\frac{1}{2}$ an even number of times and $\frac{1}{4}$ a 'multiple of four' number of times, the fifth term i.e. t_5 satisfies the condition (since each term is present four times).

Hence, the 5th term is the first term that will be an integer (we have $t_5 = 4\left(\frac{1}{2} + \frac{1}{4}\right) = 3$, an integer).

Hence, $n = 5$.

Hence, the correct answer is 5.

32. **Level of Difficulty:** Medium | **Category:** Heart of Algebra | **Topic:** Solving systems of linear equations

The correct answer is 5.86

$$Ax + B = Cx + D$$

The above has infinite solutions if: $A = C$ and $B = D$

$$(3x + 2)k + 5 = 12x + 7m$$

$$3kx + (2k + 5) = 12x + 7m$$

$$3k = 12 \text{ and } 2k + 5 = 7m$$

$$k = 4 \text{ and } m = \frac{13}{7} = 1.86$$

$$k + m = 5.86$$

33. **Level of Difficulty:** Difficult | **Category:** Heart of Algebra | **Topic:** Graphing linear equations

The correct answer is 0.67.

The line having a positive X-intercept and a negative Y-intercept is shown below.

The X and Y intercepts are at $(-b, 0)$ and $(0, a)$, where a and b are positive integers.

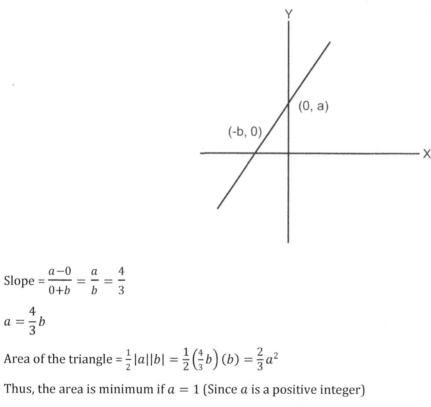

Slope $= \dfrac{a-0}{0+b} = \dfrac{a}{b} = \dfrac{4}{3}$

$$a = \frac{4}{3}b$$

Area of the triangle $= \frac{1}{2}|a||b| = \frac{1}{2}\left(\frac{4}{3}b\right)(b) = \frac{2}{3}a^2$

Thus, the area is minimum if $a = 1$ (Since a is a positive integer)

Thus, the minimum area $= \dfrac{2}{3} = 0.67$

34. **Level of Difficulty:** Easy | **Category:** Problem Solving and Data Analysis | **Topic:** Center, spread and shape of distributions

Since the average of x and 3y is 12, we have: $\dfrac{x+3y}{2} = 12 \Rightarrow x + 3y = 24$.

Since the average of $2x$ and $3z$ is 21, we have: $\frac{2x+3z}{2} = 21 \Rightarrow 2x + 3z = 42$.

Adding the above two equations: $(x + 3y) + (2x + 3z) = 24 + 42 \Rightarrow 3(x + y + z) = 66$

$x + y + z = \frac{66}{3} = 22$.

Thus, the average of $x, y,$ and $z = \frac{22}{3}$.

Hence, the correct answer is $\frac{22}{3} \sim 7.33$.

35. **Level of Difficulty:** Medium | **Category:** Advanced Math | **Topic:** Interpreting nonlinear expressions

The correct answer is 4.

We know that if two equations $px + qy = r$ and $mx + ny = s$ have infinite solutions, then: $\frac{p}{m} = \frac{q}{n} = \frac{r}{s}$.

The given equations having infinite solutions are:

$(a - 3)x + 3y = 12$ and $4x + (a - 2)y = k$.

Thus: $\frac{a-3}{4} = \frac{3}{a-2} = \frac{12}{k}$.

Taking the first two terms:

$\frac{a-3}{4} = \frac{3}{a-2} \Rightarrow (a - 3)(a - 2) = 12 \Rightarrow a^2 - 5a + 6 = 12$

$a^2 - 5a - 6 = 0 \Rightarrow (a - 6)(a + 1) = 0 \Rightarrow a = 6 \text{ or } -1$.

Using $a = 6$: $\frac{6-3}{4} = \frac{12}{k} \Rightarrow \frac{3}{4} = \frac{12}{k} \Rightarrow k = 16$.

Using $a = -1$: $\frac{-1-3}{4} = \frac{12}{k} \Rightarrow k = -12$.

Thus, k can have two values: $k = 16$ or -12.

Thus, sum of all possible values of $k = 16 + (-12) = 4$.

Hence, the correct answer is 4.

36. **Level of Difficulty:** Medium | **Category:** Additional Math | **Topic:** Circle theorems

The correct answer is 72

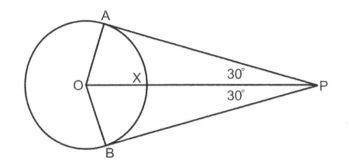

In triangle OAP:

$OA = \dfrac{40}{2} = 20$ (using 30, 60, 90 property)

$AP = 20\sqrt{3}$

Area of triangle $OAP = \left(\dfrac{1}{2}\right) x\, (20) x\, \left(20\sqrt{3}\right) = 200\sqrt{3} = 346.41$

Area of sector $OAXB = \pi \times 20^2 \times \left(\dfrac{120}{360}\right) = 418.67$

Thus, required area $= 346.41 - 418.67 = 72.26 \approx 72$

Hence, the correct answer is 72

37. **Level of Difficulty:** Difficult | **Category:** Problem Solving and Data Analysis | **Topic:** Percents

The correct answer is 40.

One of the containers could have the minimum possible milk concentration if the other container had the maximum possible milk concentration, i.e. 100%.

The container with a higher volume (i.e. 20 liters) should be assigned the 100% milk solution as that would allow the other container to have an even lower concentration of milk.

Thus, the 20 liter solution should be of 100% milk concentration and let us assume that the 10 liter solution have x% milk solution. The resultant mixture of these solutions would have 80% milk concentration.

Thus, using weighted average, we have: $\dfrac{20 \times 100 + 10 \times x}{20 + 10} = 80 \Rightarrow 2000 + 10x = 2400 \Rightarrow x = 40$.

Thus, the minimum concentration of milk in any of the containers is 40%.

(Note: One can see the effect if we assume that the 10 liter solution is of 100% concentration and the 20 liter solution has the minimum concentration of x%. In this case, x comes out to be 70%.)

Hence, the answer is 40.

38. **Level of Difficulty:** Difficult | **Category:** Problem Solving and Data Analysis | **Topic:** Center, spread and shape of distributions

The correct answer is 7.5.

We can see that the minimum height of the students in section A is $(x^2 + 1)$ feet and that in section B is $(x^2 + 1.5)$ feet.

Thus, the minimum height of the students in section A is less than that in section B.

Again, the maximum height of the students in section A is $(4x - 1)$ feet and that in section B is $(4x - 0.5)$ feet.

Thus, the maximum height of the students in section A is less than that in section B.

Thus, when all students of sections A and B are considered, the minimum height would be the lower one of A and B i.e. $(x^2 + 1)$ feet while the maximum height would be the higher one of A and B i.e. $(4x - 0.5)$ feet.

Thus: range=maximum height $-$ minimum height= $(4x - 0.5) - (x^2 + 1) = (4x - x^2 - 1.5)$.

Thus, we have: $4x - x^2 - 1.5 = 2.5 => x^2 - 4x + 4 = 0 => (x - 2)^2 = 0 => x - 2 = 0 => x = 2$.

Thus, height of the tallest student when both sections are considered together $= (4x - 0.5) = 7.5$ feet.

Hence, the correct answer is 7.5.

NOTES

Made in the USA
Middletown, DE
13 June 2020